For my mother

Mary

Charlie Carroll is a *nom de plume*, and the names, descriptions and locations of every school, teacher and student I worked with during the year of this book have also been changed. Some events have been switched from one location or time-period to another, while others have been collapsed together or telescoped, so that the privacy of every institution and individual mentioned may remain private. However, everything documented herein is true and devoid of exaggeration.

Introduction

HIS FACE WAS just a few inches from mine.

I could make out the blood vessels in the whites of his unblinking eyes, his tight jaw muscles, the smattering of acne across his forehead.

'Who the *fuck* are you talking to?' he spat, his head bobbing and flicking with each splenetic syllable, so close that it filled my field of vision.

I returned his stare, my head tilted back to compensate for the few inches he had on me. Peripherally, I could see that a small crowd had begun to form around us. But I kept my focus on Ben.

Five minutes earlier, I had been at my desk marking the books of the Year 9 class who had just left. It was the end of the school day, and although the air was cold I had a window open to dissipate the collective aroma of 33 14-year-olds. I could hear the playground directly outside as it began to fill with loud and liberated teenagers. Then the window creaked, and I looked up from my work to see the grinning face of a student as he popped his head in, cast a quick look about the room, and then disappeared. Moments later, a hand appeared, launching a large water-bomb into my classroom before vanishing quickly. The missile exploded messily across a table, and I ran to the door and out into the playground. I caught a brief glimpse of the back of the culprit's head as he sprinted off behind the maths block, and even as I called out to him to stop I already knew how fruitless the action was, how pitiful my command sounded.

It was then that I noticed Ben Street heading towards me. Ben was a notorious Year 11 boy, a tall and thickly-built 16-year-old whose aura at Taylor College was so famed that, even on my second day at the school, I already knew exactly who he was. I had seen the boy who had thrown the water-bomb by Ben's side before; perhaps Ben was providing a cover for his escape. Or perhaps it was just an excuse to do what he loved.

Ben stormed up to me with the urgency of a pit-bull, squared his shoulders, pointed his face down at mine, and barked his question at me: *'Who the fuck are you talking to?'*

I kept myself calm, searched for words, for a response, unsure whether to assert myself or back down.

'Go on, then,' he shouted. 'Try it.'

We held each other's stares. The crowd around us grew with every passing moment, a pulsating but silent audience to this stand-off between the new teacher and the school bully. I found what I hoped would be the correct approach and took a step forward. I knew that I could not let Ben dominate this confrontation, that to do so would be to invite trouble for the rest of my time at this school. I needed to stand up to him, to take a step forward and let him know that I would not be spoken to like that, that I would be talking with his Tutor and Head of Year and informing them of his atrocious behaviour this afternoon, that I would...

Ben interrupted my stream of consciousness with a mocking chuckle aimed directly and openly at me, and then turned and walked off in the same direction as his friend. About me, the crowd quickly lost interest, shouldering their bags and pulling their coats around them, immediately absorbed in indifference or each other. I returned to the classroom. As I removed my jacket, I felt two large sweat stains under my armpits. I looked at the stack of unmarked books, realised there was no motivation left within me, and picked up my bag.

Leaving the school, I drove my rusting blue VW camper van out through Birmingham's suburbs. It was already dark by the time I reached the city's grimy outskirts and pulled up into the lay-by in which

Introduction

I had been sleeping for the last two weeks. Turning off the engine, I began the familiar routine: drawing the curtains before switching on the light, pulling out the bed and covering it with a multitude of thick duvets and blankets, lighting the gas hobs to boil two kettles, decanting them into my hot water bottles, and then crawling under the covers to wait for the warmth to spread.

A light rain began to fall, and I peered out of the window. My view was a stretch of dual-carriageway, and it was filled with the glinting headlights of the late rush hour traffic as it coursed slowly through the freezing November night. A dim orange glow hung low over the fields behind the road, flecked with drizzle and hiding beneath the dark, shifting sky. I pulled the curtains back in place and looked at my watch. It was six o'clock, Thursday, somewhere near the end of the year.

*****

The really sickening thing, I suppose, was that I was working at Taylor College by choice. I had not fallen on hard times, nor been the victim of any series of unfortunate events, nor the hapless recipient of the swinging caprices of fate. I was living in that van, and I was teaching at that challenging school, because I had decided to.

Seven months earlier, I had been living in Somerset, forging a successful career for myself as an English teacher in a good secondary school. It was my third year of teaching: I had taken my Postgraduate Certificate of Education (PGCE) at the University of Nottingham, spent my Induction year as a Newly Qualified Teacher (NQT) at a difficult school in Cornwall, and then moved to Somerset. By April of that year I was doing well, had established myself as an effective teacher of the subject with both staff and students alike, and was already starting my slow climb up the promotional hierarchy of the secondary system.

But something was wrong.

In part, it was the teaching itself. Despite my idealistic love of education, despite my acknowledgement of it as one of the benchmarks of civilisation, I found that the vocation I had chosen was far more challenging than I had ever anticipated. Beset by a consistent deluge of paperwork and implausible targets, cerebrally strait-jacketed by the rigorous government standards dictating what should occur in every single lesson I taught, and working late into each night after school (and through much of the Easter and Christmas holidays) so that I could ensure that my students received the learning they deserved, I began to fade. My twenties, it seemed, were being stolen from me in an astonishing combination of confrontation and bureaucracy. I loved the idea of being a teacher, loved the nobility and humility of the profession, but the reality of it was far different from my romantic imaginings.

I had also developed a desire to travel unlike any I had experienced before. Until then, I had been able to satisfy the nagging ache of my wanderlust during the long summer holidays teaching affords, and I had spent each August stumbling gleefully through the backwaters of Europe and Asia. But that was no longer enough. I was tired of being just a backpacker, and tired of the absolute meaninglessness it entailed. To backpack is merely to brush the surface of a culture, to travel at such speed that understanding is fleeting and experience blurred. I wanted my travel to have meaning, a purpose, to be something more than just following the trail a popular guidebook had laid out for me and thousands before. I was after a different kind of journey.

The idea for just such a journey came to me one afternoon whilst reading the educational supplement of a national broadsheet newspaper. Nearly half of all England's Newly Qualified Teachers, it said, were leaving the profession within their first five years. Such a statistic was no surprise, I had heard it in many a staff room and after-school meeting since I had started in the job. The fact was undeniable.

By the end of the 1970s, the number of state teachers in the UK was at an all-time high. The various governments of that particular decade had placed a massive emphasis on education; by 1979, an extra 100,000 people had taken up teaching. Class sizes were low; staff room morale was high. Britain was investing in its future in the most sustainable way it could, through the country's schools.

But in the 1980s, Margaret Thatcher's government noticed that pupil numbers were on the decrease with demography, and immediately saw the opportunity to save money. Approximately 50,000 of all those teachers who had been employed throughout the seventies lost their jobs as schools were squeezed in every department. Local Education Authorities (LEAs) had their budgets cut and council-funded services which gave support to schools were frozen. Between 1980 and 1996, over 900 mainstream secondary schools were closed across the country, and teacher numbers were at an all-time low – with, at the end of the Thatcher-Major Conservative government's rule, only 454,000 teachers to support the 9.8 million children in state education.

When Tony Blair came to power in 1997, he recognised the looming crisis and vowed to do something about it. His government began pumping heady amounts of money into the profession, launching a sentimental but successful advertising campaign to attract new entrants and focusing on education in many of its public statements and speeches. And, for a short while, these efforts met with success. As the 20th century drew to a close, teacher numbers were indeed on the rise once again. Perhaps things, as that campaign song had suggested, really could only get better.

But it didn't last. Recent figures show that there were only 441,000 full-time teachers in the UK for the academic year 2004-2005, fewer than there had been in 1997 at the changeover of government, and a full ten percent fall since 1981, while the size of the pupil population had remained roughly the same. Two years later, in 2006-2007, it was revealed that most secondary subjects had struggled to recruit teachers and had fallen well below target, even though those targets had actually been lowered. Under Tony Blair and then under Gordon Brown, things didn't get better, and they didn't even plateau. They actually got worse.

And suddenly, I wanted to know why. Why were so many teachers leaving the profession? Why were they mostly those who had only just started? Was there a single reason, or myriad? In light of these questions, an idea began to form. I did not need to launch myself halfway across the world to travel; I could explore in depth my own country, and I could do so with meaning. By wending my way across England and working in its secondary schools, I would be initiating exactly the kind of adventure I craved, and I might also find some answers to the problems facing my profession. I could observe. I could experience. And I could write a book about it.

I was resolved, and handed in a letter of resignation to my Headteacher the following week. Contractually obliged to serve the rest of the year, I had three months left to wait, three months of preparation. First, I needed to decide on duration. To see an adequate number of schools and enough of England to satisfy my intentions, I had to spend at least a year on the road. Such a span fitted nicely: I was after more than the month-long excursions my previous travelling had been confined to, and with a whole academic year I could fully immerse myself in my task, visiting ten areas with just over a month in each.

Next, I needed transport and accommodation – or, better still, both combined. Given that my life for the next 12 months was to be fundamentally peripatetic, the most viable way to live and travel would be by van. Since childhood, I had dreamed of owning a VW Campervan, so now I bought one – old, rusting and dirty-blue – and set about kitting it out with dented saucepans and chipped plates; thick duvets and thicker hats; a toolkit; engine-oil; scouring pads and washing-up liquid; a pack of journals and a cupboardful of books; and more soap than I was ever going to need.

Finally, I came to the hardest part of all: where to go. As much as I wanted to see the beautiful parts of England – the National Parks, the historic cities, the coastlines and the countrysides – I would find no answers there. If I truly wanted to discover why teachers were leaving, I needed to find the most challenging schools there were, and these would not be in idyllic rural locations. To unearth the answers I sought, I had to find out what teaching was like at its most difficult. To discover where this was, I needed to do some research.

Melding together statistics and figures, I searched for the ten most challenging areas in England for a secondary school teacher. I looked primarily at the LEAs and the individual schools which had come at the bottom of the League Tables, and then followed that by examining anything else which might affect today's teenagers and their capacity for learning. I looked into infant mortality rates, unemployment levels and teacher turnover. I scrutinised population and crime figures, percentages of free school meals within schools, and student truancy rates. From these lists, I began to compile a Top Ten of target areas.

The summer holidays arrived. I filled my hours with planning and reading, and the weeks slipped past without incident. I grew increasingly nervous. I was fascinated by the journey ahead of me, and thought of it every day with obsessive excitement. I was about to experience England's state secondary system in a way that perhaps no-one else ever had, was about to experience England itself in a similarly unique fashion. But I could not ignore the creeping doubts which built as the summer days got slowly shorter, the brief moments of terror which occasionally ripped me from sleep, or the engulfing day dreams which left me silent for minutes in the middle of conversations and made my friends suspicious. The year I had ahead of me would be fascinating, I knew, but I also understood it would not be without horror.

September 1st came, my departure-date. I loaded my clothes and some food into the van and set off north. It was time to begin.

NOTTINGHAM

THE SUMMER HAD been wet and English, but, as September began, the weather took a sudden turn for the better. I arrived in Nottingham in the early afternoon of my first day, clothed in a travelling wardrobe of sunglasses, shorts and sandals, the van's windows wound down low. It was a far cry from the first time I had entered the city almost seven years earlier.

I had been 20 years old, and driving up to begin my first year at university. Back then, a light drizzle, vintage Midlands weather, had been falling as I joined the M1 just south of the city, the eight domineering towers of the Ratcliffe-on-Soar power station rising up to greet me with their thick plumes of steam. I had tuned the car radio to Trent FM, just catching the tail end of the local news: the previous night, a university student had been gunned down outside a pub in the city. My introduction to Nottingham was apt.

One of the worst places in the UK for gun crime (which earned it the nickname 'Shottingham' in some quarters), it was said while I was at university that, of the five areas in England where the police carried guns, three were in this city. Whether or not that was true, I did not doubt it at the time. Urban myths bounced about the student hall corridors with apocryphal distortion: stories about men on motorbikes taking pot shots at pedestrians with sawn-off shotguns; stories featuring gang shootings and druglord assassinations; stories which would often have less melodramatic, but still worryingly similar, interpretations each day in the local newspaper.

Yet, despite all of this, Nottingham was the safest place I could think of to begin my new journey – or, at least, the safest of the ten places I was to visit. I had spent four years living there, I knew the area well, and I had even taught in some of its schools. Friends of mine from that period were still dotted here and there about the city. Nottingham was familiar, and I found this a comfort.

I aimed the van directly for the city centre, dipping into and then out of it once quickly; my gratitude for each familiar landmark underscored by a childlike fear of the unknown that awaited me here and throughout the rest of England over the following year. The journey I had planned, fretted over, yearned for and frequently almost turned my back on for so long was finally actualised. I was now part of it.

I had booked into a campsite I remembered on the outskirts of the city for two weeks, and it was with some relief that I rumbled down on to the large field to set up my first temporary home. I had been driving non-stop for four hours, and both the van and I needed a rest.

With the VW parked up beneath a line of spindly trees, I tied my hammock between two of them and erected my awning on the other side. There were only a smattering of other campers around – four canoeists with impeccably symmetrical tents; three young couples who clustered around an ever-burning barbecue; a large multi-generational family of southern England males who liked to dance with their tops off to loud ska music; the silent old man who never moved from the chair in front of his caravan – and so I was left alone to an enviable privacy. Opening a can of cheap lager, I rolled clumsily into the hammock, opened a book, and sipped until sunset. Night crept in slowly and lazily, and the dim lights of the campfires, torches and electric bulbs grew stronger. I wanted to wander about the campsite and talk of my grand adventure to everyone. I wanted them all to know what I was doing. I wanted to get very drunk.

But I had too much to do the following day. While planning my expedition, I had decided that the only way I could viably experience an adequate number of schools throughout England would be if I demoted myself and entered them as a supply teacher. Accordingly, I had contacted one of the country's largest supply agencies to arrange an interview. The agency was perfect for my intentions: it had offices all over England which dealt with every LEA, and daily sent teachers out to the majority of the country's schools. My interview was to be conducted in the reception area of a chain hotel just outside the city.

'I want to work in the most challenging schools,' I told my interviewer the next morning, once we had got past the formalities.

She tried to disguise her delight, but it was written clearly across her face. She scribbled something on to her form and said, 'Then I'm sure you'll be very popular.'

'Do you think I'll get much work?'

'That depends. Are you willing to teach any subject?'

'I'm willing to, yes, but I'm only qualified to teach English.'

'That doesn't matter. A lot of our staff aren't even qualified teachers.'

This came as a surprise to me. 'Isn't that illegal?' I said. 'To have an unqualified teacher in sole responsibility of a class?'

'I don't know. As a parent, I'd say it should be. But I'd be out of a job if it was enforced.'

She ticked and jotted, her biro scratching across the form.

'Can we consider you for any long-term positions that may arise?' she asked.

'I'd like to focus more on the day-to-day vacancies,' I said. 'Ideally, I want to spend this year working in a number of cities throughout England. That way, I can really extend my professional development as a teacher within a variety of cultures and locations.'

'Where exactly are you hoping to go?'

'I'm not too sure just yet. But it'll probably be the usual big names: Manchester, London, Birmingham, that kind of thing.'

'And you want to work at the most challenging schools?'

'Absolutely.'

For the first time, the interviewer put down her pen. 'May I ask why?' She looked at me quizzically, and then laughed. 'Not that we're complaining or anything, but our new supply teachers often request *not* to be sent to the difficult schools. And haven't you just told me that your last school – which you left voluntarily, right? – was really successful?'

I smiled. 'I got bored.'

The interview passed. I agreed to teach any subject that came up, and agreed to work with all the year groups a secondary school has (students begin secondary school at the age of 11 in Year 7, and then leave at the age of 16 in Year 11. Those who go on to sixth form or college spend Years 12 and 13 there, leaving at the age of 18).

'We'll assign you a liaison from head office,' she said. 'That's just someone who will consult with the local office wherever you happen to be and contact you whenever there's work.'

That seemed to draw things to their natural conclusion, so we stood and shook hands. I thanked the interviewer for her time. She thanked me for joining the agency. I had not, of course, told her the real motive behind my plans: such an admission would do me no favours.

As I turned to leave, she stopped me. 'By the way, you'll be lucky if anything comes in for the first couple of weeks.'

I had expected this: with teachers invigorated and refreshed from the long summer holidays, the beginning of the academic year is always the quietest time for the supply teacher. I knew I had a fortnight to kill, so I made the most of it.

The sun those two weeks was boastful, and I spent many lazy hours in my hammock, drinking cheap red wine and reading novels.

I enjoyed Nottingham itself. I walked along the canals into the city, fantasising about living on a barge, popping up in the shadow of the castle. I met old friends, joining them to drink ale by the water, eat fresh baguettes in the square, explore bohemian Hockley or the old Lace Market, and trip through afternoons of white sunlight which bounced up from the paving stones. Whatever was going to happen to me over the next year, I was going to begin it joyfully.

It was during the third week of September that I could feel the summer ending and the real journey beginning. The weather began to cool. With little left of my final pay cheque from the Somerset school, I initiated my new frugal life and checked out of the campsite, returning only under the cover of darkness to top up my fresh water supply and use the site's shower facilities while no-one was around.

To sleep, I moved to the lay-bys: some poking off from quiet and eerie country lanes; others slapped on the side of A-road dual carriageways and lined with motionless lorries, where cars hurtled past and made the van rock in their wake. During the day, I stayed close to the city and waited for the call to work.

It refused to come. Monday passed, and then Tuesday. Wednesday vanished in turn, and by Thursday I had still heard nothing. I felt like Conrad's Marlow, waiting desperately: silently urging and wishing for that summons to the jungle, into my own personal heart of darkness. I wanted to work, was already growing jittery from inactivity, and so I almost burst with relief when, early on the Friday morning, I picked up my ringing phone, and took my first booking.

'Charlie?'

'Hello?'

'Is this Charlie Carroll? Currently living in Beeston, Nottingham?'

I had given the agency interviewer a false address – a student house I had once lived in – when she had demanded one.

'It is. Who's this?'

'My name's Emma and I'm your supply liaison,' said the voice. 'Blonde, blue eyes, GSOH. I'll be the one who sorts you out with work until you get a real job.'

'Isn't this a real job?' I said.

'No,' she said. 'Not really.'

'Oh.'

'I'm obliged to tell you,' she continued, 'that you are free to turn down anything I might offer. I am not obliged to tell you that if you're nice to me and occasionally ask how I've been, then we'll get on wonderfully.'

'Okay. How have you been?'

'Fantastic. Last Friday, I still managed to pull despite this cast on my leg. But that's not important right now. Are you available to work today?'

I never met Emma, but I grew to look forward to our occasional telephone conversations. With a thick Lancashire accent punctuated by sudden bursts of rapid laughter, she was always keen to move on from business to the details of her adventurous private life. Often, after I had accepted whatever school had been offered, she would give me a brief run-down on the dalliances she had been party to that weekend. On one occasion, I asked how her Saturday night had been, and she replied with a brief and nonchalant, 'Threesome'. Throughout the year, Emma became a good friend, a voice in the dark, who never once questioned why I seemed so hell-bent on experiencing the worst the English educational system had to offer, and who never once asked why I could not sit still for long.

'I'm available, yes,' I said. 'Definitely.'

'Good. I've got a booking for a school fairly close to you. They need an English teacher for today and all of next week. Can you do it?'

'Sure. What's the school like?'

'It says here on your profile that you have a preference for the more challenging schools,' said Emma. 'This one should be perfect for you. It's called Tompkins Technology College.'

She rattled through the directions, and then I put down the phone and took a deep breath. Though I had been officially travelling now for nearly three weeks, I had felt like I was shadow-boxing. The crux of my journey, the fruit of it, was finally here.

I lit a gas-hob to boil the kettle and opened the wardrobe, taking out my single, cheap suit. I should have practised dressing in formal clothing in the van before, for doing so whilst lying flat on the bed was far more difficult than I had anticipated; anyone standing outside would have heard the sporadic bangs and clangs of my elbows hitting the walls and my head smacking the ceiling. The kettle whistled and I made tea, drinking it in short bursts between opening the curtains, folding the bed away, stashing some crisps in my rucksack, and finally climbing into the driver's seat and putting the keys in the ignition.

The van started first time, and I coasted out into Nottingham's rush hour traffic. The long line of slow-moving cars gave me some time to think. I had been out of the classroom for nearly two months now – how was I feeling about going back in? Sweat patches were beginning to form under my arms; the tea I had just drunk was casually being churned around inside my stomach; my feet were icy but my face was on fire. I had no idea what to expect for the day ahead, and such uncertainty left me more nervous than I could remember ever being at the start of a school day.

I pulled the van off the ring road and on to the residential street which would lead me to Tompkins. Swarms of students filled the pavements on either side of the road as they filed noisily along to school, their uniforms covered by thick jackets, their heads bobbing around inside hoods or melon-sized hats. Bicycles weaved between the cars, pogo-ing off kerbsides and dipping in and out of the thronging pedestrians. A boy took a gentle tumble from his bike on to the pavement and was engulfed in a clamour of teenagers laughing and shouting, 'Rayyyyy!'

Swinging the van into the staff car park, I navigated slowly through the stationary packs: 12-year-old girls giggled and pointed at the rust; surly 15-year-old boys stared through the windscreen.

After parking, I walked through to the reception area, steeling myself against the bodies which shoved and pushed against me as we all spilt through the front door.

'Hello, I'm Mr...'

'Supply?' the receptionist barked before I could finish.

'Yes, I wondered if...'

'Good,' she interrupted again. 'Here's your pack.' She dumped a plastic wallet bursting with paper on to the desk before me. 'Timetable. Map of the school. Lesson plans. Resources. Welcome to Tompkins.'

I was about to ask her how to get to my first lesson, but she had already picked up the phone and introduced herself and the school to whoever was on the line. I checked my timetable and map. My first ever lesson as a supply teacher was with a group of 16 Year 10s in a block behind this building. I made my way to it, children buzzing at me from all directions; and, as I arrived outside, I looked through the small window in the door. The classroom was flooded with students sprawled across the tables, leaning from the open windows, and throwing missiles at each other. I took another deep breath, and walked in.

* * * * *

Tompkins Technology College sits on the outskirts of Nottingham, a few miles from one of the city's most deprived and violent areas, known for its gang crime. There are nearly three and a half thousand secondary schools in England, and Tompkins had spent years as one of the country's worst-performing schools according to the League Tables. It had only just avoided closure after a series of visits from OFSTED (the Office for Standards in Education, a government watchdog which sends inspectors out to assess each school in England, usually once every three to five years). I remembered its name and reputation from my PGCE year, when it was one of those places we prayed we would not be sent to on placement. During my time there, though I never saw either of them, I was told more than once that the school had not only a full-time policeman on site but also a resident glazier.

One indicator – general, but prescient – of a school's performance is its rate of staff turnover. If a school is particularly difficult to work at, teachers will leave it. The year before I arrived, 24 members of staff left Tompkins College – out of 100. In one department alone, four out of the eight teachers quit. This remarkably high number speaks volumes. There are few other organisations where you will find very nearly a quarter of the staff body resigning at the same time. Perhaps you might find this sort of turnover in fast-food outlets or student nightclubs, where the staff are largely composed of temporary, part-time workers; but in a vocational profession, peopled by qualified, full-time members of staff, a rate of 24 per cent is both ludicrous and unsettling.

Granted, Tompkins' exodus is not quite the norm, but it is not exceptional. Many schools are finding it difficult to replace the numbers of staff who are leaving: between 2004 and 2007, recruitment figures for initial teacher training courses dropped from 42,000 to 31,000 entrants – a fall of over a quarter. (The year of my journey saw a 7 per cent drop on applications for initial teacher training courses for secondary subjects compared to the previous year's figures.) The system, it seems, is revealing a remarkable lack of longevity: not only are nearly half of all NQTs leaving within five years, fewer and fewer people have been signing up to replace them. (As the recession bit, these recruitment numbers began to rise again: the country will always need teachers, and this sense of stability has lent the profession an advantage in post-credit crunch Britain. Nevertheless, many believe that once the economy re-establishes and rights itself it will only be a matter of time before these figures fall once more.)

All this has the biggest impact on England's more challenging schools, like Tompkins. When students begin to find that they have been at the school longer than the majority of those who are teaching them, ownership of the school passes to the pupils, and teacher authority is undermined. A student who has endured a succession of teachers appearing and then quitting soon finds himself becoming cynical of those above him, and his respect for them is lost in the convolution of the turnover.

This is the source of many of the problems at Tompkins College: it seemed to me that the students had very little respect for a large number of the staff, and I felt it immediately that morning. Though there were only 16 kids in the class, I had never before felt so lacking in control, and so out of my depth.

I walked in and made my way to the front. My presence was barely acknowledged, aside from a few sideways, uninterested glances. Children were running around, yelling and tussling wherever I looked.

'Morning, Year 10,' I hollered over the din. 'Time to sit down, please.'

Chairs were being flung over, snatches of insults occasionally broke free of the general hubbub, and it appeared that no-one had heard me.

'Year 10!' I shouted again, this time louder. 'Seats, please!'

The children, high and red-faced after their short registration periods, ignored me again, and it was only after I began approaching them individually, to grab their attention, that they began, grudgingly, to do as I asked. I looked at my watch; by the time I had all 16 seated and looking in my general direction, seven minutes of the lesson had been wasted.

I started to introduce myself. 'All right,' I said. 'My name is Mr Carroll, and I'm here for the next week or so. Today, we're going to be working on…'

There were four heavily-made up girls in the front row; out of the corner of my eye, I saw one of them lean over and snatch something from her neighbour's desk. The neighbour immediately exploded.

'For fuck's sake, Michaela!' she yelled. 'Give it back, you bitch!'

More yelling, more chairs falling over as they fought over the stolen object. I tried to make the girls return to their seats, but they knew as well as I did that I could not force them to obey me, and the next three minutes passed before they got tired of fighting and sat back down of their own accord. I had now been in that classroom for 10 full minutes and not even taken the register. I picked it up from the desk and began.

'Stephen? Stephen Bamber? Is Stephen here?' No-one answered.

I ran through half a dozen names, with the same result.

I looked up from the register at the class. Some stared back at me with contempt, others with indifference. Most ignored me completely and started talking amongst themselves. I turned and wrote on the board: 'For every minute you waste of mine, I'll take two off your break-time'. Underneath that, in red pen, I wrote a large number '2'.

Behind me, the noise grew.

'Look,' I said. 'We need to …'

'No-one's listening to you,' one lad politely told me.

Discarding the register for the time being, I grabbed a pile of A4 paper and strode past the desks, handing one out per person, before returning to the front of the room and writing the task on the board: *Write a letter to your Headteacher, persuading him to get rid of school uniform.* I decided the best approach would be to talk to the students individually, urging them to begin one by one. I started at the front row. 'Right, girls,' I said. 'What I need you to do is...'

'I'm *doing* it!' erupted one of them, Tracey. '*God*! Just *fuck off*, will you?'

'I can't have you talking to me like that,' I said, calmly. 'Please go and stand outside, and I'll be out in a minute to discuss this with you.'

She clapped her hands, hoorayed and rushed out of the door. When I checked a moment or two later, she had vanished, taking the opportunity to go for a 20-minute walk around the school.

Over the next five minutes, I gradually managed to get a few students to quieten down somewhat and begin the first sentence of their letters, when suddenly a boy burst into the room. Ignoring me, he reached into his bag and produced a large box of fizzy sweets.

'Who wants some?' he shouted.

'No!' I protested, but I was ignored by all as they swamped the newcomer and shoved his bright green sweets down their throats.

I had just about got them seated again, when a fight between two 16-year-olds erupted outside my room, and the entire class rushed out to stand around them and chant and holler. Another five minutes wasted.

Once they were all back inside again, a dark-haired lad suddenly leapt across his table and began stabbing another boy in the back of the hand with a straightened paperclip, drawing blood.

Tracey came back, and her return sparked a loud argument among her front-row friends.

'Fuck off, ya white bitch!'

'That's racist!'

'No, if you called her a nigger, that'd be racist'

'I ain't a fucking nigger, it's a birthmark!'

Five minutes before the end of the lesson, the class unanimously decided to pack up and walk out, despite my protestations, leaving me drained and exhausted, reduced, less than zero.

The class now empty and still, I checked my timetable for the day. The teacher I was covering had a free period next, which meant – to my relief – that I could recuperate. Dazed, I drifted towards the empty English department office and fell into the nearest chair, the horrific lesson replaying in my head on a continual loop.

I had three lessons left that day: a double-period with a Year 8 group, and then last thing with a class of Year 7s, the youngest in the school. I was dreading it all, but I reminded myself that this was the kind of school I had come to see. I could not renounce the whole project after just one lesson. As the bell for break-time went, I returned to the classroom to set up for the Year 8s and ready myself.

The second bell sounded, and they arrived.

There followed two hours of noise – of frantic, urgent, unstoppable noise – which echoed about the room with deafening resonance. With only a few paltry, old-fashioned exercise books which dictated the rudiments of grammar to keep them occupied, the students saw the lesson for the joke it was, and saw me for a flustered fool. They made the most of it.

Omar had a penchant for sneaking up to the board whenever I had my back turned to draw large and often spurting penises. Zoe had to be moved five or six times after starting loud and vulgar arguments with anybody she happened to be close to. Raymond made his best friend cry when he graffitied the words 'Mr Carroll swallows' on to the cover of his book, held it up for me and the rest of the class to see, and then exclaimed, 'Sir! Look what Dimitri wrote!' Sharn, after ceaseless taunting from Zoe, unloaded her tormentor's bag all over the floor, kicked aside her chair, and then stormed out, never to return. And just when I thought it could get no worse, Luke calmly walked over to Habib, and spat on his head.

With a shrill scream of disgust, Habib grabbed his coat from the back of his chair, wrapped it around his head to wipe off the saliva, and then stayed beneath it, hidden and cowering.

'*Luke*!' I shouted, my temper close to ripping. 'Go and stand outside of the room *now*!'

Luke looked up at me with hurt disbelief. 'But I didn't do anything!'

The lie enraged me. 'Get out now. I'll talk to you outside.'

The boy's face suddenly filled with anger. 'You can't send me out,' he spat. 'I didn't do anything! If you send me out, I'll break your nose.'

I was stunned. For the first time in almost two hours, the room was suddenly silent. I looked at this small, freckly child and knew immediately he would not carry through his threat; but the very fact that the threat had been made was itself a shock.

'It's a very serious thing,' I began, 'to threaten a teacher, Luke. Do you know that?'

He stared back at me, and I saw that his eyes were growing moist. 'I don't care!' he suddenly yelled. 'I didn't do anything!'

With that, he ran from the classroom. I followed, but by the time I reached the door he had disappeared.

I came back in. The class had returned to normal, the noise levels with it. A paper aeroplane sailed over and bounced lightly off the top of my head. 'Oi, sir!' Terry called out. 'Chuck it back?'

* * * * *

I got up early on Saturday. I had barely slept, the insistent thrum of passing cars breaking into my semi-dreams each time my eyelids flickered shut. It was my fault: I'd chosen a bad lay-by to bed down in. I wouldn't repeat that mistake – or, if I did, I would be armed with alcohol.

After a slight breakfast, I drove the van into the city and parked. In a drowsy state, I aimlessly climbed the hill up to the castle. I found an isolated bank of grass and sat cross-legged, wrapping my coat around my torso in the cold morning wind. The weather was typically autumnal, warm when the sun slipped out from behind the clouds, freezing when it stayed coy. I reached into my backpack for a book, but reading was useless. My mind was focused elsewhere. Instead, I contented myself with gazing out over the view before me: the hilly, tumultuous city backed by fields, canals and the looming power station. I stood and walked around the perimeter of the castle grounds, trying to pinpoint places familiar from student days, spotting tower blocks and parks and structures and the avenues which cut through them, and recalling memories of street signs and night clubs and bus routes. My spirits began to lift. Over there was a house I had lived in for the best part of a year; there, the building in which I had weathered and loved and loathed so many lectures and seminars; there, the canal I had once walked at four in the morning to get home, credit cards tucked safely in my socks, because no taxi would take me.

I started to remember the city, to remember it as the home it had been for four important years of my life. I started to walk. Down from the castle and then into town, following the undulations of the sandstone which Nottingham is built upon, skirting the dips and rises of the karst-like bulges which pockmark the city. I wandered through old haunts and dives, the skanky late night bars and kebab takeaways, the outcroppings of my own intimate heritage, the pathways of any generic Nottingham student. As I retraced these old footsteps, thumbing through the city's streets like the pages of a favourite book, I soon remembered what it was that I had loved so about this place while I was at university.

It would have been good to go out that night, to drink away the tension with old friends, but no-one I knew in Nottingham was around. So I made my way alone to the Ye Olde Trip to Jerusalem pub near the castle, under it in fact; there I ate dinner and drank a good pint of Doom Bar ale. It had been a fine day – a reminder that I wasn't just here to teach, I was also here to travel.

* * * * *

I arrived back at Tompkins on Monday morning just as the bell was going for registration. Members of the school's Senior Management Team (the SMT – this corporate title is used in all schools to collectively describe the Headteacher, Deputy Headteacher and Assistant Headteachers) patrolled the premises with whistles, barking, 'You're late, get to your form room!'

Straggling students pushed away from them, shouting, 'Yeah, what*evaaah*!'

As I walked up to reception to sign in for the day, I took in the buildings. Tompkins has a deceptive appearance, in much the same way as many schools I was to see throughout the year. Stretching across the front of the grounds, the only part visible to the road is the one-storey tall new block, only a few years old, all polished chrome and sparkling glass, sweeping and modern. Inside the new block is the reception, manned by smiling women and washed over by elevator music piped in through hidden speakers. A long and twisting corridor curves out from the reception, snaking between classrooms installed with abundant computers, digital projectors and interactive whiteboards. This building is, clearly, the flagship of the school. It is what passers-by see from the road. It is where prospective parents are shown, where new teachers are given their interviews. Any photographs for the local papers are taken here.

Behind this building, though, the 'old' school hides away, decaying and flaky. This is where most school life goes on. The dining hall; the exam and assembly rooms; the playgrounds and tennis courts; the administration offices; most of the departments – all are situated here. This is the reality behind the facelift, the truth behind the architectural botox. It is the area the visitor is kept from, but it is the area where Tompkins exists in genuine. All is concrete, and the only hint of greenery is the huge mural of Robin Hood and his band dotted about a lush Sherwood Forest which is plastered across one wall of the maths block, and which feels deeply incongruous in this stony environment.

The English block sits here, right at the back of the compound, tacked on to the end of the dining hall, and looking like an abandoned, bright pink fire station. At break times and lunch times it is bolted – from the inside. All the staff, apart from those poor unfortunates on yard duty, lock themselves in and try to ignore the students banging on the windows and screaming obscenities at each other.

I made my way to this block, the surrounding area now quiet as the last of the students were mopped up into their form rooms. Inside, I was met by Mr Johns, the Head of English.

'How did Friday go?' he asked amiably.

'It was a struggle, but I got through it.'

'You can't have found it that bad – you came back.'

I laughed, and then noticed that he didn't.

'Have you just qualified?'

'No, I've taught for three years,' I said. 'But I fancied a bit of a break from permanent work.'

'Where did you teach before?'

'I've just come up from Somerset.'

'Somerset?' He looked at me, almost pityingly. 'Yeah. You might find things a little different here.'

My classroom at Tompkins was a small box, crowded with tables and chairs, and surrounded by windows whose curtains would not open. With the door shut it felt air tight, and within minutes of the arrival of a class the room began to swelter, the oozing smells of 30 children – of varying standards of hygiene – becoming trapped and amplified. The room's ceiling was composed of three layers: the first, six thin wooden beams; the second, a mesh of chicken-wire; the third, resting on the wire, sheets of sugar paper. Where the paper had frayed or torn, holes revealed gaping darkness above, reminding me of the ceiling of a barn.

It was here that I passed my final five days in Nottingham, here that I endured the insults and continuous disobedience, here that I found myself having to make any request at least six times before it was even acknowledged.

The Year 10s forced their loathing on to me with increasing vehemence each day, and the Year 8s did their best to follow suit. I faced each class with shrinking optimism, increasingly and visibly weathered by each wave of students. The work became a slog, but it was work nevertheless, and I was thankful not just for the much-needed money it brought in, but that it was coming to an end. Every day was one step closer to my emancipation. I pushed on with a grim fortitude. Friday would come; with it, release.

And it did. The four preceding days went slowly, but they went, and that was all that mattered. I woke on the Friday morning with a blithe disposition. I knew the day was not going to be easy, but I resolved to keep my head down, detach all sensibilities, and just get the whole thing over without any major problems.

Period 1 with my Year 8s began clumsily. I had booked the class into an ICT (Information Communication Technology) Suite in the new block and planned a computer-based lesson. It involved substantial work and was sure to keep the children occupied, particularly since it allowed them to utilise the internet, which I had supposed would keep them quiet. Arriving at my classroom to collect them, I stated my expectations for the lesson.

'Any inappropriate behaviour,' I told them, 'will result in us leaving the ICT Suite immediately and returning back here. This lesson is a privilege, not a right, and can be revoked whenever I see fit...'

I stopped speaking. The class had already stampeded past me.

I followed the sound of their disappearing footsteps through the corridors of the English building and outside. As I entered the new block I was presented with the sight of freckly Luke skidding out of a science classroom, the door slamming behind him, the raucous laughter from within audible and clear.

'What are you doing, Luke?'

'Who are you?' he shouted, and then turned and raced down the corridor.

By the time I reached the ICT Suite, the students were already sitting down at their terminals. 'Okay,' I began. 'What I...'

I was interrupted by a sudden chorus. 'These computers are *shit*, sir. They won't work!'

I walked around, peering at screens, trying to work out the problem. It seemed to be password-related – none had been recognised. I called the school technician, enduring 10 minutes of unbounded chaos while we waited. He arrived, walked from computer to computer, logged each student on without difficulty, and then came over to me.

'They all spelt their usernames wrong on purpose so it wouldn't work,' he said. 'It's the oldest trick in the book, mate. Didn't you realise?'

He slapped me on the back, laughed, and walked out. I looked at the students, who were quietly sniggering at their screens.

The rest of the day continued in this fashion. I had to remove a Year 7 lad for obnoxiously shouting at his classmate, an orphaned Somali refugee, 'At least I've got a family to go home to! At least I've got a family to go home to!'

A Year 9 boy later went the same way for loudly describing the imagined sexual habits of a timid girl's mother.

By lunch time, I was exhausted already. I shut myself in the English office with the faculty, feeling increasingly tense as the wind whistled through the playground, whipping the kids into a frenzy. Twice we were forced outside to present a united front as enormous groups of children threatened to explode into each other, their shouted insults and taunts only seconds away from turning violent. We surrounded them like a poorly-equipped riot police team, using words for protection instead of body armour. As the bell went to signal the end of lunch, the confrontations evaporated and the students streamed into the warmth of the building, noses red and hair Einsteinian, cheeks glowing and puffing.

The Year 11s I took for Period 4 were wired and fearless, bobbing about the classroom like animatronic puppets, senseless to any kind of command or entreaty, fuelled by volume and movement. I did my best to contain them, feeling all the while like I was holding together a disintegrating bag of coins. Finally, the bell went, and they burst out into the corridor.

I had but one lesson left, and then freedom. I was shattered and drained after one of the hardest days of my teaching career; and this class was the notorious Year 10s. I readied myself.

The first student to arrive was Tracey. She marched down the corridor with a group of friends and, as she spotted me through the window, began to sing (to the tune of 'If You're Happy And You Know It, Clap Your Hands'):

If you think Sir's a waste,
Clap your hands.
If you think Sir's a waste,
Slap him round the face.
If you think Sir's a waste,
Clap your hands.

I stopped her at the door.

'Tracey,' I said, 'there is no way I can let you into this classroom now.'

'What the fuck are you talking about?' she hollered, spinning in circles and addressing the gang of youths surrounding her. 'I haven't done nothing!'

'Tracey, I heard full well what you were singing,' I said. 'I cannot let you into this classroom after that.'

'Are you fucking mad? I wasn't even singing! What the *fuck* is wrong with you?'

The 15 other members of the class slowly began to filter in as her invective went on: I noticed that they were cautious as they passed Tracey, but that they made no similar effort to avoid jostling me.

'All I want to do is go in and learn some fucking *English*, and my fucking *English teacher* won't even let me,' she continued, verbally poking me in the chest with each splenetic *fuck*.

I kept calm; in fact, I don't really get angry at work. Partly, I suspect, it's because I am desensitised; partly it is because a good teacher keeps his or her temper – losing it is one of the least effective things you can do in a school.

Mr Johns – the head of department – came around the corner, shooing off those who had gathered, and commanding the remainder of my class to get to their seats. Tracey continued shouting, oblivious to his presence.

'Can you take Tracey away for the lesson?" I said. 'She can't come in when she's behaving like this.'

He sized up the situation and agreed, but Tracey was having none of it.

'This is a fucking piss-take. I never said *nothing*! I don't even know what he's going on about!'

I left the issue in Mr Johns' hands, entered the classroom and tried to start the lesson. But it was difficult. Tracey, refusing to leave with Mr Johns, hopped angrily about outside the window, screaming so loudly that she drowned out my instructions. The rest of the class, seeing that she could not be tamed, decided that they would not be either, and there followed an hour of chaos, fuelled by the obstinate Tracey. Eventually, Mr Johns gave up and went to enlist the help of the 'On-Call Team' – members of the SMT who are used to remove unruly pupils who refuse to remove themselves.

They never came.

Tracey continued her biting insults outside the classroom, and the rest of the students continued their disobedience inside. Abdul threw a chair at Peter. Vicky began playing loud dance music on her phone. Alan stole Tyrone's left shoe, and ran about the room with it, ululating like a tribesman. Charmaine produced a lighter, and tried to set fire to Tyrone's exposed sock. And, all the while, Tracey stood outside, calmly repeating that I was a twat, a prick, a wanker.

Kris, a quiet lad, came up to me and, with a wry smile, said: 'You know, the Head would probably have come and got her by now if you was a normal teacher. But you're just a supply teacher.'

Finally, the hour came to its close. Tracey had walked off to go home, and I was standing before the shut door, blockading the surging teenagers from leaving before they were supposed to. I had succeeded in creating one iota of orderliness in the conclusion, encouraging students to put the desks back in place and tuck their chairs under, and was all ready to let them loose on the world and free myself of Tompkins Technology College forever, when, out of the corner of my eye, I saw Will advance ominously towards Ashley.

'What did you just say?' Will hissed, squaring up to Ashley.

'You heard,' Ashley replied, jutting his chin out at the other boy.

Will pushed Ashley hard. Ashley fell back a few steps and then flung a wild swing at Will's head. It was all Will, the larger of the two, needed. Grabbing Ashley by the jumper, he struck him twice in the face.

'Stop that!' I shouted, but Will ignored me. As Ashley careered backwards, he advanced, smashing him in the face with another resounding punch which spun the smaller boy around. Will kicked him hard in the back, sending Ashley flying out over a chair and on to the floor. As he lay there, Will stamped on his stomach.

My natural instinct was to get between them, to pull the two boys apart, to do whatever I could to stop this fight. But this is a risky thing to do inside a school. The teaching unions explicitly advise against it; Senior Management Teams do the same; teacher training courses will devote whole sessions to the fact that you should, at all costs, avoid getting involved. Why? Because if a teacher so much as lays a hand on a student, that teacher can be reported for assault, or sued. And once that happens, the outcome is – unfortunately – a lottery. So whilst Will quite seriously assaulted Ashley before my eyes, there was little I could do except shout at him to stop, and be ignored. It was only when some space opened up between them that I was able to use my body as a blockade.

As Will stood backwards, I stepped into the gap. Heady with adrenalin myself, both arms splayed outwards to prevent him moving any closer to the floored Ashley, I said, 'Get out!'

He looked at me, and then at Ashley.

'Get out *now*!' I said.

Will turned and left. I crouched down next to Ashley, checking him for injury. There was no blood, and no obvious welts or bruises, but tears were streaming down his face. The class, for the first time that day, were completely silent: clustered around the two of us and staring in shock.

'Please,' I said to them as I helped Ashley to his feet, 'go home'. As they pushed their way from the room, a passing member of staff poked his head in, and, to my eternal gratitude, took over. Ashley was led by the arm from the room, bent double. I took in the emptiness now around me, and collapsed into a nearby chair.

Violence is an everyday occurrence for England's secondary school teachers, but what is most frightening about it is the absolute powerlessness the teacher has in dealing with such situations. I felt it then: it coursed through my body as I slumped, deep-breathing, on my chair. I was massively distressed by the fight between Will and Ashley, not least because I knew that I could quite easily have stopped it. But I had dared not. A teacher has the right to use 'reasonable force' if it means preventing one student harming another. A student, on the other hand, has the right not to have his 'privacy, dignity and physical integrity compromised'. There is a plain conflict between these rights, not least because the former is vague and hazy ('reasonable force' can be interpreted in a number of ways) while the latter is clear-cut and well-defined. All it takes is for a student to report that he was harmed by a teacher as he tried to break up the fight, and that teacher can face grave consequences. Where the two competing 'rights' conflict, the law often supports the child over the adult, regardless of the facts. This protection of children is important, but it can lead to unjust outcomes, as many media stories will confirm. One London teacher was recently suspended after being accused of hitting a student as he pulled him off another. The allegation was wholly false, and the teacher was eventually reinstated – but not before an entire year had passed.

I knew full well what the possible consequences of any physical intervention could be, and so I had held myself back. Though I hated myself for it, I had to be selfish.

Far worse than violence between pupils is violence enacted upon teachers. Albeit rarer, it is still prevalent, and is a reality every teacher must be prepared for. In 2006, 740 children were permanently excluded and 8,240 temporarily excluded for assaulting members of staff. Those are the *official* figures, but a much larger number of assaults on teachers go unreported. I know this from my own experience. One former colleague of mine was 'held hostage' in front of his class by two Year 11 boys brandishing a very real-looking (though, as it turned out, fake) gun. Another had a door slammed shut in her face so violently that the glass window shattered over her. When you consider that pushing is, technically, an assault – though not something any teacher should have to endure – the numbers must be enormous; I have been pushed or shoved out of the way by a student more times than I can count.

The fact is, many teachers themselves choose to ignore these happenings: if it has caused nothing save a brief flurry of emotional distress, it is usually best just to put it down to experience and not blow things out of proportion. Nevertheless, when teachers *do* decide to report such incidents they are often ignored by the Senior Management Teams and governors, who do not want to damage the reputations of their schools.

This system becomes most trying for teachers when they find themselves not only unsupported but blamed for the incident. One young teacher in an inner-city London school found himself getting punched by a student after barring her unauthorised exit from the classroom. While no sanction was issued to the student for the incident, the victim was reprimanded because he had acted 'provocatively'.

Therein lies the problem. It is not so much that we have to face violence in our workplaces; it is that, when we do, in many cases nothing is done about it. It is extremely rare that a teacher who has just been assaulted will be relieved of any immediate duties and allowed to go home to recover, or given counselling or compensation. Instead, in so many cases, that teacher will be told to just get on with things, perhaps even with the added insult that, actually, they only have themselves to blame.

About 10 years ago, a colleague of mine taught at a school which had a 'stalker'. A man wearing a white mask and carrying a machete was seen prowling around the lower field. All the students were brought into the sports hall, and the PE staff stood around the building with hockey-sticks and rounders bats. After a long wait, the police finally arrived: one rather short individual officer.

'But the point is,' my colleague said, 'that the police had sent *someone*, and that someone represented an authority which was not to be challenged. The consequences of attacking a police officer are serious, and the stalker must have realised this, because he disappeared.'

He was right. Society is hierarchical, and schools – microcosms of the wider world – also rely upon a system which places teachers and the SMT at its pinnacle. If that hierarchy is not supported from the outside then it will crumble. This is not an argument for the return of corporal punishment: its absence within schools today is a welcome change from 40 years ago. A good teacher does not need the cane. It is, instead, an argument to allow us a very simple thing: the power to stop children hurting each other. For, by refusing to support teachers in the face of such incidents as discussed, the authorities who have the power to do so are, through their apathy or ideology, instead sending out the message to our nation's children that, in England's educational system, violence is largely inconsequential.

* * * * *

On my last night in Nottingham, I went out into the city for a few drinks with an old university friend. She had once begun a PGCE course, only to give it up three months later when she discovered teaching to be far from what she had expected. It was a Friday night, and it seemed right to revisit our old local pub. We were playing pool upstairs when we heard loud noises coming from the outdoor smoking area directly below us. Looking down, we witnessed a group of 15 young men, all in their early 20s, all drunk and getting out of hand. They began by growing unnecessarily loud, shouting obscenities and chanting tribal songs. They were intimidating, and those not belonging to their group quickly began to head back into the pub. One lad, an 18-year-old with dreadlocks, bravely stayed.

Until someone threw a glass at him.

It smashed on the wall a foot away from his face. It was enough. He stubbed his half-smoked cigarette out on the door and hurried inside. The tribe, however, had only just begun. They picked each of the empty pint glasses from the benches and began hurling them around the courtyard, the sound of the shattering glass punctuating their bellowed songs. There was no security at the pub, and the bar staff, too frightened to intervene, let them get on with it.

Anyone who has lived in England will recognise this scene. It is what happens on Friday and Saturday nights in cities throughout the country. It is achingly familiar. And, in being so, it becomes a template for children. When violence is a norm, is routine, is to be expected, it becomes self-perpetuating. When children see this stuff weekly in the streets, and hear about it daily in the news, it becomes a norm for them, too, and it permeates *their* culture and *their* lives, especially in schools.

As I watched these men liberating their primitive pack-mentality, I was reminded of the classroom, where – on a smaller, snack-size scale – violence happens every day.

On The Edge

I thought ahead to Manchester, said to have some of the most dangerous schools in England. And I felt terrified.

MANCHESTER

I KNOW MANCHESTER well. I know its inescapable cultural vibrancy, its easy blend of the old and new. I know it has a musical history unlike any other, know the chipper but homely accent, and know the way Mancunians can hold up two fingers with more feeling and expression than anyone else in the world (they somehow seem to put their whole body behind the gesture). I know Manchester because I was born there.

When I was three, my parents moved to Cornwall. Though I think of myself as Cornish, I cannot ignore Manchester's part in my history. It is my heritage. My entire extended family comes from the city and, as far as I know, always has. Apart from my mother and father, my two brothers and myself, the rest of them still live there.

When I was a boy, there was always at least one annual trip up north to visit the clan. I can clearly recall the excitement I felt – the early morning wake-up while it was still dark; a sunrise over the Tamar; the stops at motorway service stations which I always associated with the opportunity to buy a *Bumper Wordsearch Book* and, more importantly, chocolate; the crazy maze of flyovers and kangarooing traffic at Birmingham; and then Manchester, always entered when it was growing dark, always splashed with rain, a network of streets and houses which never failed to strike me as so immaculately orange.

Most of the time we would sit in the houses of my ancestors, saturated with endless cups of tea, occasionally tearing our gazes from the ever-present television to engage in conversations which I didn't really understand. But sometimes we would venture out into the city. As a timid West Country boy, Manchester both scared and enthralled me. It was huge − huge and *dirty* − a gigantic urban sprawl where I marvelled at the towering structures around me whilst my mother struck up easy conversations with shopkeepers she had never met. I would return to my Cornish village each time with a whole list of wonders to report to my little friends: there's at least *three* McDonalds up there; there's a place called a Virgin Megastore (that always evoked a titter from the girls) with *two floors* of records and tapes; I think I even saw a *prostitute*!

But, beneath the wonder, I always felt uneasy in the city. My grandparents lived on a rough estate where, to my country eyes, the other children were terrifying. My cousins were confident and much, much harder versions of me, and Manchester itself, with its dilapidated buildings and industrial character, made me yearn for my Cornish cosiness, where it was always safe after dark, and where I never saw a teenager brazenly strolling the streets with a hammer in his fist.

As I grew older, Manchester remained in my mind as I remembered it from those early years − low and squalid − so even as I was finishing my time at Tompkins and preparing for the weekend move over the Peak District and into the house of my grandmother, my stomach was churning. Manchester was among England's toughest areas: in one edition of the local newspaper alone, I read about a 16-year-old boy on trial for accidentally shooting his 13-year-old sister dead in their family home; a 36-year-old man who was beaten close to death by five teenagers in Rochdale; a 30-year-old Asda security guard in Longsight who was assaulted by robbers who were trying to use a steamroller to break into the supermarket and who hit him over the head with a pick axe handle; and a 20-year-old man who stabbed an acquaintance twice in the stomach in Sale. In Moss Side, two gangs had a gunfight, between them firing over a dozen shots. In Ashton-Under-Lyne, a man broke into a woman's house and raped her in her own bed. And in Newton Heath, the area I was moving to, in one single day someone fired a pistol through a house's letter-box, a 30-year-old was in hospital after two men broke into his home and fractured his skull by beating him about the head with a wooden chair leg, and a 68-year-old had his jaw broken as he walked down Culcheth Lane.

As I arrived in the city via the A6 and skirted my way round to Grandma's house, I felt justifiably anxious.

My grandma is a doddering yet stalwart old woman who has survived most of the hideous happenings of the 20th century. She has seen and experienced more than I ever hope or would care to, and has, in the process, assumed an air of indefatigable authority. She is our family's matriarch, a staunch and hopping bird who I suspect sometimes feigns senility just so she can catch the rest of us out with her moments of lucidity.

She has lived all her life in Newton Heath, an estate built in the 1930s on the edge of Collyhurst, one of the oldest parts of Manchester. When I was young, she used to tell me stories about the Second World War, when her husband – my late grandfather – helped build the wings of planes, and when the two of them would run through the streets together as the bombs fell. In fact, Grandma was just down the road from the first bomb to hit the city: she saw the maimed and the dead right before her eyes, and ran blindly to find her husband and force him home to hide beneath the false safety of their kitchen table.

Today, she is 93 (though she refuses to admit it), yet she still retains a single-minded logic which is impossible to argue against. When I told her that I was coming to Manchester to work for a month and asked if I might visit, she replied, 'Visit? You'll bloody stay with us, that's what you'll do!'

I did as I was told.

My Auntie Sylvia – who had recently moved in with Grandma to look after her – welcomed me at the door and showed me to my new room. I had always felt a special connection with Sylvia, perhaps because, like me, she was the youngest of three. During my stay, the two of us often stayed up late into the night drinking Bacardi until our words were slurred, me constantly goading her into telling me story after magnificent story of the family I had never really known. Among them were tales of my grandfather's variegated connections – some glamorous (his cousin was Gracie Fields), some funny (as a child, he used to push Les Dawson about in a pram), and some best forgotten (he knew Bernard Manning). In the morning, after Sylvia had somehow managed to pull herself from her bed at half six in the morning to go to her job as an office-worker down at the newly-regenerated Salford Quays, Grandma would take over with tea, a couple of biscuits and a seat in front of whatever daytime TV chat-show she had on.

I happened to be in Manchester during a particularly dry patch. Work was scarce, and so I spent a lot of time watching telly with my grandma, being bested in arguments, eating orange-flavoured Kit Kats and taxiing her all over Newton Heath so she could buy her daily newspapers or egg sandwiches for her adult daughters. She loved riding up front in the van – my grandfather had owned a VW split-screen back in the '60s – but struggled to clamber in to the passenger seat. Instead, I would open up the side door and she would commando-roll in, brush off her coat, and demand to be taken to Netto.

Grandma hadn't left Manchester in 30 years, and had only ever done so grudgingly. She had flown once and then never again – it 'wasn't bloody natural' – and seemed to imagine Cornwall as it had been during her last visit in the 1970s. She would often smugly say to me, 'I bet you don't get these down there, do you', pointing at such things as takeaways, phone books and, once, a row of terraced houses.

I soon grew to love living with my granny, and secretly took delight in her idiosyncrasies and the way she would fuss over me until she was satisfied that I was warm enough, fed enough and caffeinated enough. And I believe she loved having me living there, too. Of the school that families should be as close together as possible, she was at her most contented when her house was filled with my aunties, cousins and their children. And, for the record, so was I.

*****

After a week in Manchester with no work, I decided to take a few bookings that I otherwise would not have. These were not teaching jobs, but supporting roles. For two days, I was to be a Learning Support Assistant (LSA – replacing the outdated but better known Teaching Assistant, or 'TA') in Coggan Specialist School on the edge of the city.

It was all rather humiliating to begin with: my status was even lower than that of a supply teacher; members of staff were condescending to me and I had to patrol the cold playgrounds for break and lunch duties while the teachers stayed inside and drank tea by radiators. But I began to develop an appreciation for the LSAs I worked with; they are heroic, but receive far less thanks for the valuable work they do in our nation's schools than do teachers. I looked back on my own experience with LSAs, realised I had been as condescending to them as these teachers were being to me, and felt slightly ashamed.

In no place do LSAs work harder than in specialist schools for students with learning difficulties. These schools are filled with extremes, and I spent my time at Coggan in a perpetual state of vacillation. Some students would hug me tightly, lead me into the classroom and then beg that I sit next to them; others would panic at my presence and throw ferocious barrages of punches at me. All learning difficulties were catered for – dyspraxia, ADHD, autism, Asperger's Syndrome, cerebral palsy, extreme dyslexia, paralysis – and the LSAs guided and helped these children with the patience of saints, like a cross between teachers and nurses, yet paid far less than either (some earn as little as £8,000 a year).

I shadowed one LSA, a maternal and no-nonsense lady called Linda. In the space of one morning, she taught the two students she worked with in the lessons, accompanied them in the playground at break, spoon-fed them at lunch, and changed their nappies (and sometimes whole uniforms) when they had an accident. In the afternoon, she took them both swimming in the school's hydro-pool. The rigmarole she had to go through to get them in the water was intensive: pushing their wheelchairs into the changing room; strapping them into an elaborate harness and lifting them on to a bed with a small crane; removing the clothes from their inert and unyielding bodies and dressing them in swimming outfits; and then repeating the whole process in reverse afterward. For those two days, I was there to help her, but usually she had to do it all single-handed.

I felt privileged to have seen classrooms from the other side of the coin, and when we got our 15 minutes to wolf down some sandwiches at lunchtime, I asked Linda how she felt about teachers.

'Don't get me wrong,' she said, 'I know how hard their job is. My husband's a science teacher. But, sometimes, it'd be nice to be asked my opinion.'

'Be nice to be paid a little more, too,' I said. 'Considering all the things you have to do.'

She gave me an odd look. 'You think I do this for the *money*?' she said. And then she laughed, spraying out a few tiny pieces of processed chicken.

I took her point.

On my last day there, the two of us were given an unexpected free period, and I asked Linda if she might show me around. It was my first time in a specialist school, and I wanted to see how it differed from the mainstream. Much of it was similar, but it did have two strikingly unique features.

The first was the hydro-pool – a small, over-heated swimming pool where those students with the most severe physical disabilities were taken for hydrotherapy. They certainly couldn't swim – they couldn't even walk – but, as the LSAs donned their own swimsuits and guided them up and down the pool, it was immediately clear how effective this therapy was. One young boy, Oliver, had not made a sound all day, but as soon as he entered the pool with Linda, he gurgled with pleasure and smiled for the first time.

The second was 'The Soft Room', a place where misbehaving students were sent. Linda mentioned it in passing as we made our way down the corridor, but it did not really interest me: all schools have rooms like this, and SMTs love dressing them up with various pet names – from the calming ('The Green Room', or 'The Time-Out Zone') to the sophisticated ('The Behaviour Suite', or 'The Referral Unit') to the clinical ('The Centre'). I guessed The Soft Room was just another of these. I was wrong.

The school did have a standard 'Support Suite', but they also needed an area where students who were in serious danger of harming themselves or others were sent as a last resort. We stopped outside, and Linda opened the door. It was literally a *soft room* – all the surfaces were padded with a light green foam, and the only object inside was a single, spongy mattress. I thought of horror-film asylums, and shuddered.

'Pupils come here if they can't control themselves physically,' Linda said, adding extra weight to the adverb. 'We have a young lad called Dylan who's often in here when he loses it. Once we get him in, he'll generally hurl himself against the walls for a bit, and we'll just have to wait until he calms down.'

I looked through the tiny window in the door which the staff used to check on the interred student.

'I hate having to put them in here,' Linda said, sadly. 'It's demeaning. But we have to protect ourselves and the other kids.'

'I know what you mean,' I said, and we continued our tour.

* * * * *

I was offered a day covering an ICT teacher at Burns Technology College. Though I am not an ICT specialist myself, I accepted, thinking that at least any behavioural issues might be tempered by allowing the students to use the internet. It is a common tactic for teachers who are struggling with a class, and many of us have booked an ICT suite for a group who we know are not going to do any work that lesson (perhaps it is the last lesson on a Friday; perhaps the kids have just had an exam; perhaps they are simply such a challenging group of teenagers that sticking them in front of a computer screen for an hour every now and then is a temporary relief from the normal chaos and lurking danger). There is at least the solace that every school will have a filter on its system, so that – usually – the most offensive things they will Google are the latest online games.

Sometimes, however, they will find loopholes. During Period 1, I had to send Max Darby out of the classroom for finding and then playing a game which involved gunning down naked, large-breasted women. Later, another went the same way for pulling up his homepage on a social networking website, locating a picture from his photo album which featured a waist-down shot of himself distressingly naked, and then inviting the entire class over to have a look for themselves.

Generally, however, the lessons followed a similar pattern. As I walked around the classroom each period, students would frantically click back to the Microsoft Word or PowerPoint document they were working on while I passed, and then resume their illicit activities again once I had gone. There were some who were too slow for my random perambulations, and made guilty excuses when I confronted them. I returned to my desk each time and made notes on the various activities I had witnessed: two boys playing online pool with each other; three girls looking at tattoos; one lad playing Pac-Man and another playing The Sims. (The old versus the new; I felt a weird pride in the fact that, on my next tour, the latter had capitulated and started playing Pac-Man, as well. The Classics, it seemed, had won.) Two girls spent quite some time looking through the thousand different mobile phones on the Vodafone website.

There was one boy – Elijah – who had done no work all lesson, barely even making the pretence to try whenever I strolled past. At the end of the lesson, he approached me and handed over the report card which had to be filled in by each of his teachers to document how well he had done that day. I wrote the truth in my allotted space: that he had done nothing.

'Why did you give me a shit report, sir?' he protested when he saw what I had written.

'Because you deserve it,' I replied. 'You've done nothing all lesson.'

'Oh, but please, sir,' he said. 'I really need a good report this week.'

'Elijah, if you had actually worked, I would have given you a good report.'

'If I do detention with you now and get the work done, will you change it?' It was now lunchtime. 'I'll get all the work done, I promise.'

I felt it was right to give him the opportunity to make up for his lack of work, especially since he had offered.

'All right,' I said. 'Complete everything you were supposed to do in the lesson, and I'll give you a glowing report.'

Elijah sat down at his computer and laboured away, completing and printing off the work his teacher had assumed it would take him an hour to do in the space of 20 minutes.

'Elijah,' I said when he presented his work to me. 'Why bother to put yourself through this when you easily could have done it during the lesson?'

'I dunno, sir. I'm lazy. But I really need a good report this week.'

'Why?'

'My mum said that, if I did well this week, she'd pay for my haircut at this really expensive place down town. And if I don't, she said she'd cut it herself.'

I laughed.

'Don't laugh, sir, she means it. Last time, she came into my room at night and cut it while I was sleeping. I had to come into school looking a right twat for three weeks before she gave me the money to have it done proper.'

Lunchtime came and I sat alone in the staff room, eating a sandwich and reading a book. It had become usual for me to isolate myself in this manner – my presence was as fleeting for the staff as it was for the students, and they obviously saw little point in making much effort to get to know me. I didn't mind. The silence of corners gave me an opportunity to reflect on the day I had endured. And I was not, after all, out here to make friends.

I returned to my ICT suite for the final lesson. It had been an unproductive day for the kids I had taught, I knew that, but it had passed without difficulty. My last class – a large group of 12-year-olds – came in and seemed to know exactly which computers they should sit at. I took the register, wrote their task for the lesson on the board, and then sat at my desk to observe and see if anyone needed help. They were noisy, but from those screens I could see, they seemed to be on-task, and so I let them get on with it. One boy, a tiny thing called Ben with blond hair which grew up and then out and framed his face in unnatural right-angles, hunched over his keyboard and stared intensely at the screen a few centimetres from his nose. Unlike the rest of the class, he spoke to no-one, instead spending 10 minutes experimenting with different fonts for his title. I walked over to him.

'Are you all right?' I asked. 'Do you know what you're supposed to be doing?'

He looked up at me, nodded once, and then returned to his screen to try Rockwell Extra Bold.

I took a few circuits around the classroom and, though the volume was growing increasingly loud, they were all working. Sitting back at my desk, my attention was caught by Ben. He had finally moved on from the title and was typing, deleting and re-typing his first sentence with his left hand. His right flitted about his face, plucking hairs from his head, his eyebrows, his nose, his eyelashes, and then his head again. There was an agitation in that hand, and its movements sped up, his fingers forging pincers which moved from pulling single hairs to small clumps. He appeared to be muttering something at the screen, but I could not hear him above all this noise. An explosion was looking inevitable, and when it came, it did so cataclysmically. It was a single scream. Or maybe a howl. It broke from him with such force that his head was flung back and then down beneath the weight of it. He stopped and spun around to face the class who, to my surprise, were ignoring him.

'Shut up!' he bellowed. 'SHUT UP!' He ran from the classroom with his head in his hands. I followed.

51

Outside, Ben had started screaming again. I shut the door behind me and stood a few feet from him, assuming he might have Asperger's Syndrome, and that to approach him and invade his personal space would make matters worse. A female member of staff suddenly appeared around the corner. Ben saw her, and fled into her arms. She embraced him, picked him up like a baby, gave me an admonishing look, and carried him away.

I returned to the classroom, deeply confused. Perhaps it showed on my face: Karina left her group and came over to me.

'Don't worry, sir. That's just what Ben does. Are you all right?'

I looked at her. 'All right? Yeah... yeah... of course I am. But is Ben?'

She patted me on the shoulder. 'He does this once every few days. It's our fault, really. He hates the noise. You'll be all right.'

She returned to her friends, and I sat down at my desk, more confused than ever. Had this all just happened? Even more weirdly, had I really just been patted by a student and told it was all right?

The lesson finished and I walked out to the staff car park. As I unlocked the van door, I saw the teacher who had taken Ben away walking towards her own car. She saw me, too.

'Sorry for that. I wanted to talk to you, but I had to deal with Ben first,' she said.

'What happened? Does he have Asperger's? Is he on the autistic spectrum?'

'No, no, none of that. But Ben is a very troubled little boy. We all know him here. You should have been told about him. But I guess you weren't.'

'Told what?'

She inhaled, looked around her – possibly for Ben – and then said, 'Ben's currently in a home because his parents can't deal with him. He has issues, but no-one knows what. There's been plenty of tests, but none of them have revealed anything. What was he like before he blew up?'

I thought for a moment. 'Unresponsive. Obsessive. Agitated.'

'That's Ben. Set him a task, and he won't leave it until it's done. But he hates distractions.'

'That's what the other kids said to me. He couldn't deal with the noise. I guess I should have dealt with it myself.'

'You weren't to know. The thing about Ben is that, one-to-one, he's actually a very friendly, polite and articulate boy. That's why none of his tests have revealed anything. But when he gets angry about something, he can't leave it alone. His parents say he's been like that since he was a toddler. We have a lot of contact with them. They want him back.'

'Why was he taken from them?'

She looked around her again. 'Social Services did a drop-in one afternoon to check up on him. His parents didn't know they were coming. They said he was out at football practice, but the socials heard a weird howling noise coming from inside. They barged in, walked upstairs, and found Ben. His parents said it was the only way they knew to keep him under control.'

There was silence for a moment, and it was clear I had to ask before I would be told. 'Where was he?'

'In the shower, tied to the tap with binder twine.'

I drove back to my grandma's, mumbled a quick hello and something about needing a lie-down. Then I went upstairs, lay on the bed in my small room, and burst into tears.

* * * * *

After that, days passed without work, and I began to worry. With my bank balance slipping downwards, I was getting desperate for cash.

Even Grandma must have noticed, for she started giving me 'spends': a carefully folded five-pound note discreetly slipped into my hand each Monday morning. One afternoon, on the pretence of getting me to take her to the shops, she sneakily directed me to a nearby shoe-store, and bought me a pair of slippers.

It was early on the Monday of my last week in Manchester that my phone finally rang.

'Charlie!'

'Hi, Emma. Please tell me you've got some work for me.'

'You're not going to believe this, but I've just had four schools ringing me one after the other. There's a load of teachers off on training courses this week. Can you do today through to Thursday?'

'I'd love to,' I said. 'One school?'

'No, two days at one and two at another. Can I mark you down?'

'Please do. I'm pretty desperate right now.'

'Want to know what they're like?' she said.

I didn't even care, and told her so. I just needed the work.

'Fair enough. Be warned, though – they won't be easy.'

I had not expected them to be. Earlier, Emma herself had told me North Manchester had some of the most dangerous schools in the country. A friend of mine who had worked as a supply teacher in the city for a year described many of them as 'duck-and-cover' places and could talk ceaselessly about the number of knives he had seen confiscated from students. Even my uncle, on hearing I was in Manchester to teach, had laughed and advised me to carry a baseball bat.

'Thanks for the work, Emma,' I said. 'I really need it right now.'

'Not a problem. Good weekend?'

'The usual,' I said, the usual being a lot of tea with Grandma, followed by a lot of Bacardi with Auntie Sylvia, followed by a penetrating hangover (which Grandma would try to cure with the offer of a tripe sandwich). 'How about you?'

'Yeah, the usual for me, too. Managed to tick Greece off the list.'

'You went to Greece?'

'Not exactly,' she laughed, and I suddenly understood what she meant.

I struggled into my suit and left for work immediately. As it turned out, Emma had been wrong. The two schools I spent my final four days in Manchester in were far from challenging. Indeed, those days were little more than a few pleasant hours with some street-wise, but unaffected, students. I had a great week, and wondered just what all the fuss was about. Was Manchester really not as bad as people had made it out to be? Had I allowed misguided preconceptions to cloud my judgment? Or had I just got lucky?

I don't know. Perhaps it was the abundance of LSAs in each school (in one lesson I had three), which Manchester City LEA stretches its budget to accommodate, which made it easy for me; perhaps it was the fact that, already proud of their homeland and thus themselves, these students had nothing to prove to a transient supply teacher; or perhaps my expectations had been significantly lowered by Nottingham. Either way, what I do know is that the worst thing I had to endure from the kids during that final week in Manchester was little more than a comical aside.

I was taking a small Year 11 English class on the Wednesday morning. No work had been set, but I had some hand-outs with me, and gave the class a set of 'Writing to Persuade' worksheets intended to help them practice the techniques of persuasive writing. They got on with the task without complaint or sneer, leaving me with little to do save sit at the front and be ready to give any assistance to those who were struggling. After half an hour, between the quiet and acceptable conversations taking place around the classroom, I tuned into one between two girls, Sarah and Yazmin, when I heard the terms 'nipple-rings' and 'strap-on'.

At first, I pretended not to hear. They were not, after all, disturbing anyone else, and were continuing to work themselves as they nattered. But I kept one ear honed on them, just in case.

For the next five minutes, brief snatches of their conversation wafted across the classroom towards me. Yazmin said the word 'cock'. Sarah launched into a mumbled, and only slightly audible, query on what exactly 'rimming' was. Other students were beginning to disengage from their writing to tune into this contraband dialogue. Sarah said 'fingered'. Michael put down his pen and listened. Yazmin said, 'What did he want to go with that dog for?' Jordan and Josh stopped their own conversation and giggled.

I looked up. The class were getting off-task. I lifted my head and made ready to interject, but the two girls, as if sensing that the teacher had heard, promptly stopped their chatter, and lowered their heads to their books. Three minutes passed. Michael and Jordan and Josh were back at their scribbles. All was well. Until Sarah, turning around to face Carrie on the back row, suddenly said, 'What do you think, Carrie? Yazmin thinks that all girls like big willies. But I don't, 'cos I reckon that, if you have too many, you just end up with a bucket.'

The class exploded into a short-lived burst of laughter, quickly silenced by my loud, 'Sarah! That's enough!' Immediately, each student turned back to their writing. And stayed as such until the bell went.

That was the worst I got from the students in Manchester: an embarrassing but controllable spattering of inappropriate language. There were no knives, not even a belligerent walk-out, just two 16-year-old girls verbally exploring a rite of passage they evidently already knew more about than me. For the rest of the time, I found myself enjoying the company of these students: from the boys who tagged themselves Bez (and there are a *lot* of these) and danced about me like friendly monkeys repeating my name and asking if I could help them answer Question 7, to the girls who spent five-minute-long intervals from their work gazing at their on-screen reflections in the webcams of their computers. These were good kids who, though they came from fairly rough backgrounds, saw me not as an enemy, but as what I was – someone who wanted to help, and who wanted to teach them.

At the end of my final day, Jason stuck his head around the door. A supply teacher from a different agency to mine, Jason had been at the school for three weeks. I liked him a lot. The youngest teacher there, and the least experienced, he was filled with enthusiasm both in the classroom and staff room. We talked often during my time there and, since I was shortly leaving Manchester, Jason had offered that we go for a pint at the nearby pub.

'You ready, mate?'

'Nearly there. Let me just get my stuff and I'll meet you in the staff room.'

Jason saluted mock-clumsily, turned and walked off up the corridor. As I was packing the last of my things into my bag, I heard a ghastly voice echo up the corridor.

'Where the *fuck* is he?'

I stuck my head out the door to see a short fortysomething woman stride purposefully up the corridor. Bill, who worked the reception, trotted behind her, muttering something I could not hear but which seemed placatory, occasionally coming before the lady and trying to stop her with outstretched palms. The woman marched on regardless. She stopped in front of me.

'Is it you? *Eh*? Are you Mr Greene?' She pushed her face up close to mine while her finger jabbed itself at my chest. 'Are you? Do you teach my son?'

Bill managed to get between us. 'This isn't Mr Greene, Mrs Waterman. Now, if you'll just take a seat at reception, I'll fetch…'

'I ain't talking to no-one but Mr Greene. Where is he?' she screamed, marching off again up the corridor. I saw Jason appear from the staff room. Mrs Waterman saw as well, and quickened her step.

'Is it you?' she was shouting, her finger back to its old jabbing ways.

'Yes, I'm Mr Greene, Jason Greene,' he said, extending a hand. 'What seems…'

She ignored his hand and stopped inches from him. 'Are you my Daniel's tutor?'

'Yes, Dan's in my tutor group,' Jason replied, his voice level. I could see Mrs Shepherd, the Headteacher, appearing out of the staff room behind him.

'What's this you've being saying about him? Eh? *Who the fuck do you think you are?*'

In an instant, Mrs Shepherd had them both inside the staff room, shutting the door firmly behind her. A group of teachers, myself included, congregated by the entrance. Mrs Waterman's shrill voice was clearly audible, Jason's only occasionally. Feeling indecent over our eavesdropping, we began to slowly move away to the door and to a nearby classroom, where we sat and tried to work out what Jason had done. Twenty minutes passed, and then we heard the door open. Mrs Shepherd was leading Mrs Waterman out with her arm around her shoulders. Mrs Waterman was crying. Jason appeared behind and made his way towards us.

'*Fuuuuck,*' he breathed as he walked into the classroom. 'Get me to the pub.'

A fair assembly of teachers entered the local pub a few minutes later. I knew well enough they were not there to see me off. We all wanted to know what had just happened. Pints were bought and we found ourselves a table. A few remarks were exchanged, but nothing which might initiate a conversation. Attention was focused on Jason. He took a long pull of his lager.

'My fault,' he said finally. 'Completely my fault. Said something a bit stupid.' He took another drink. And then, 'Fuck.'

'What happened?' I asked.

'I stepped over the line. I admit it, I do. I realise it now. It was a stupid thing to say. Totally insensitive. Dan's been doing better lately, too. I feel like a bastard.'

'So what *did* you say?' Carla asked.

'Dan turned up late for tutor group again this morning. He always does, but it's been pissing me off a bit lately because all the rest manage to make it in on time. Anyway, he came in, and he was stinking of weed as usual. So I said to him, "Nice to see you at last, Dan. Hope you're not too stoned to do any work".'

Jason laughed nervously at that. I wanted to, as well. Was that it? Was that all he had said? Someone else at the table vocalised my thoughts for me.

'And that made his mother come in like that, shouting and screaming?'

'Yeah, yeah, but she had a point,' Jason said, to my surprise, defending her. 'The way she saw it, I was accusing her son of being a druggie. She's got six kids in all, the dad's never around, and then her son comes home from school one day and tells her his tutor had a go at him for doing drugs.'

'That's ridiculous,' the other teacher said. 'It's your job to point that kind of thing out. You only reprimanded him gently, and if you hadn't, you might as well be condoning his drug-use!'

'Don't get me wrong, I know that,' Jason continued. 'But I didn't have to say it the way I did, sarcastically and in front of the whole class.'

'Maybe you should have had a word with him on his own at the end and tried to find out what's going on,' another teacher chipped in.

'Exactly,' Jason replied. 'And I know that what I said didn't justify his mum coming in screaming at me, but I actually ended up feeling really sorry for her. She just broke down in the staff room, burst into tears, saying how difficult it was for her. She actually apologised to me, said it wasn't my fault, all that. But I still shouldn't have said it. I should have been more considerate.'

I finished my pint and left. I thought about what Jason had just been through. It reminded me of another teacher, a past colleague of mine. He thought he smelt marijuana on one of the boys in his class, reported it to the Deputy Head, and then found out that the boy's parents were threatening to take him to court for suggesting their son was a drug-user. That issue had been resolved, too, again inside the school, and again with a certain amount of tears and apologies.

There is a disparity which exists between teachers and parents in today's educational system. Any scan through a website or letters page of a newspaper which revolves around the subject of modern education will reveal this. Parents do not trust teachers, and teachers do not trust parents. It saddens me when I read anti-parent diatribes in teacher memoirs, and saddens me even more when I read (or hear) the same sort of criticism levelled at teachers from parents. It saddens me because such antipathy is not just unnecessary, it is also detrimental to the students and their learning. Such a tussle between the two main authority figures – typified in the nervous atmosphere of most school Parents' Evenings – smacks of the aftermath of a messy divorce. The parents may blame the teachers for their children's poor grades, the teachers may blame the parents for their students' poor behaviour, but, in actuality, the blame lies with neither and with both.

It is the former because really the fault lies in the lack of communication between parents and teachers, but it is the latter because both parties perpetuate it. Think of the school report.

The following is taken from a report written by one of my former colleagues for a Year 10 boy:

> *'Philip is struggling with his spelling. If he turned up to English regularly, he would receive the help he needs, and find spelling easier.'*

The extract is simple and to the point. Philip has difficulty in the written side of the subject, and his lack of attendance is not helping him overcome the difficulty. It is the kind of thing one would expect a teacher to say if needed, the kind of thing one would expect a parent to want to know about. But, after being handed in to the SMT, that report was sent back to my colleague, the given extract highlighted. Next to it, the Assistant Head had annotated: *'Re-write.'*

To claim this is a form of censorship might be a little hyperbolic, but it does come somewhere close. There is, at the moment, a strange sense in schools that we must not say anything which parents might construe as offensive. The reasoning is quite unclear to me: perhaps it stems from the fear of potential litigation instigated by the offended parents; perhaps it is that, in the current League Table-driven culture, where schools are pitched in competition with each other and where reputation has become increasingly important, it is too dangerous to offend parents and risk losing their younger offspring or their word-of-mouth recommendations to other parents. Whatever, this system – which keeps the truth shrouded – is, at the very least, an insult to both parents and teachers, as the majority of parents I've met want to hear the truth about their children, and the majority of teachers I know want to tell it. But at the worst, it has forged a negative disunity between both parties, based upon the potential liability of semantics. As a result, the absolutely vital communication between parents and teachers has been reduced to a back-and-forth system of doublespeak.

School reports now detail what National Curriculum Level Philip is achieving and how he can improve by 'making positive contributions to classroom discussions', rather than pointing out that things would be a lot more harmonious if he would stop swearing at his teachers. Statistics and national averages are used to explain why Philip has been placed in a given set, when the truth is he cannot be with his friends because he keeps starting fights with them.

It is true that parents must take more responsibility for the actions and behaviour of their children, but it is also true that teachers must stop fearing the consequences of their words and start telling it like it really is. However, as long as Senior Management Teams continue to nudge us away from the truth in favour of the semantic void, we won't. And so the parents will remain in the dark as to the actual performance of their children. And so the teachers will be forced to re-word their true opinions in spin. And so the students, hapless pivots to two such disconnected scales, will lose out.

I left Manchester late on a Monday afternoon. Reversing carefully from Grandma's driveway, I glanced into the living room window, expecting to see her standing there waving me off. It was a tradition she kept up with every member of the vast family: if you didn't wave to Grandma as you left, you might not be welcome back again. I waited, engine rumbling, but there was no sign and, since wild Mancunians could not have dragged her from her cheerful gesture, I started to worry a little. Suddenly, she appeared through the kitchen door and began tottering towards me, wrenching open the van door, despite the fact that I had already wound down the window.

'Here,' she panted, throwing the slippers I had carelessly left behind into my lap. 'Don't forget these. I bet you don't get them down there, do you?'

I started to thank her, but she was already off, scuttling back to her fire and the *Daily Star*. A few seconds later she appeared at the window. We waved, and I left.

Thick rain spattered incessantly off the windscreen as I drove down the M6 towards Birmingham, trickling and dripping onto my head through a small hole in the roof of the van and splashing through onto my lap every time I wound down the window to de-mist the windscreen. I had to focus hard on the road and the traffic about me. Forty miles on, the sun was already setting, but the rain had stopped and the cold and miserable day was turning into a cold and clear night. The gritters were out in force, spewing out phosphorescent swirls and plumes of sand and salt on to the road and filling the air with flickering orange light. The twilight took on an ethereal quality, a strange mix of pinks and blues poking through the bare and spindly branches of comatose trees. The cold was so dense it was like a bank of mist through which everything is seen dimly: even the dying sun looked cool. As the night fell, I saw Birmingham, my new home in silhouette on the horizon, and pushed on towards it.

BIRMINGHAM

I WAS LATE – uncomfortably, excruciatingly, stupidly late.

Enamel was ground; fingers left indentations on the steering wheel. I was supposed to meet the cover co-ordinator of Gilbert School at 8.30am, but instead I had spent the last 20 minutes following a tractor along an impossibly narrow rural lane. It was now quarter past nine, and I was still at least a mile away. I had already been warned about this a few days ago by Emma, my tardiness having become something of a ritual in Manchester.

'It doesn't look good, Charlie,' she had said. 'Keep turning up late and you'll get a reputation worse than mine.'

Yet here I was again. I had really made an effort that morning, rising at six o'clock, waking myself with hot coffee and toast, and then setting off for this school at the very limits of Birmingham with what I had thought would be plenty of time to spare. But I had not reckoned with the Black Country's myriad winding lanes, closed roads and wrong turns. Or that tractor.

I pulled into the school's car park at half past nine, racing through the labyrinth of Fords and Vauxhalls and Peugeots, the van lurching and whining and protesting as I pushed first gear for all it was worth. After a series of dead-ends, wild reverses and screeching, many-pointed turns, I realised that there was not one parking space left. Revving the engine, I pulled up on a patch of grass, slammed on the handbrake and leapt out of the door into a cloud of oil smoke and roasted clutch.

A hundred students, outside for their PE lesson, stood in silence, mouths describing perfect Os, staring at me. The PE teacher jogged over.

'Supply?' he said.

I grinned sheepishly. 'Sorry about that. Couldn't find anywhere to park. Little bit late.'

He grinned back. 'Don't worry about it,' he said. 'We all enjoyed it. Didn't realise a campervan was capable of manoeuvres like that. But if you work here again, you could do me a big favour and not drive across the cricket pitch.'

I looked back at the van and beyond it, noticing for the first time the diagonal swath my tyres had cut across the close-cropped turf.

'Sorry,' I said, and hurried inside.

As I signed in at reception, the Deputy Head walked past and stopped. 'Mr Carroll, is it?' he said cheerily, shaking my hand.

'Yes. Look, I'm really sorry…'

He cut me off. 'No need to worry. You've got a Year 10 class to start with. The rest I'll fill you in on later. We'd better get up there, the lesson started 15 minutes ago and the Head's covering.'

This was not good. In secondary schools, the Headteacher — having endless managerial and bureaucratic responsibilities — does not teach. Even Deputy and Assistant Heads have one or two periods per week, but the Headteacher should (indeed, must) have none. If he or she *does* take lessons, it suggests that the school is dangerously short of staff. I dreaded the phone-call from Emma that afternoon. I had clearly gone too far.

The Deputy opened the door of the classroom for me, and I entered nervously. Thirty students sat scribbling with ferocity at their *Romeo and Juliet* essays, a stern and ageing gentleman standing before them with arms folded. He came over to me.

'Look,' I began again. 'I am so…'

He grabbed me by the shoulder and shook it gently. 'Not a problem, old chap!'

I stood amazed. *Old chap?*

'I always welcome the opportunity to spend a bit of time with my students. You must have got stuck where they've closed that roundabout off and diverted the traffic.'

'Yes. I did. And elsewhere…' I mumbled.

'I probably should have told the agency to warn you about that one. Oh well! These lot all know what they're doing. Don't you, folks?'

A crisp 'Yes, sir!' punctuated the room.

'Good. Good, good. Then I'll leave you to it, Mr… er…'

'Carroll,' I said.

'Mr *Carroll*!' he cried with relish. 'A fine name, old chap! A fine name indeed!'

With that he strode out of the classroom. The Deputy threw me a quick wink and then followed.

Alone now, I surveyed the room. The disappearance of their Head seemed not to affect the students in the slightest, and they continued assiduously with their work. I waited. Some form of rebellion had to occur soon. It was only a matter of time. After a few minutes, one girl raised her hand. I was ready for her.

'Yes,' I said.

'Mr Carroll, would it be too implausible to suggest that the use of religious imagery within *Romeo and Juliet*'s shared sonnet is Shakespeare's way of implying to the audience that they are a match made in heaven?'

It took me a moment to answer. 'No,' I finally said. 'No. I don't think that would be too implausible at all.'

The girl breathed what seemed to be a sigh of relief, and fell back to her work with even more vigour than before.

There followed a near-perfect day at this near-perfect school. During the second period, a group of Year 7s entered and stood in silence behind their chairs. It took me a few uncomfortable minutes to work out what was going on.

'Er... you can sit now?'

They did so, and worked like ants. For the remaining three lessons, each class beavered away just as voraciously, the only interruption being the odd question. One boy asked if he could take his blazer off.

After the final class left, I took five minutes to look out of the window. A bank of close hills rippled the horizon, down them slipped an ancient church and graveyard, and, nestling in the base of the valley, a heather-flanked railway along which slow trains cut a lazy curve. Gilbert School sat in an area as immaculate as its own pupils. Its OFSTED report described it as an outstanding school, but I could not believe that this was all down to the exquisite surroundings, or the small and communal catchment area. The exemplary behaviour, it seemed, came from the hard work of a team of happy and involved teachers who were plainly valued and supported by their ever-present Headteacher. I saw him all day – he patrolled the corridors during lesson transitions and respite periods; he poked his head into some of my lessons, not to check on me, but to check that the students were behaving as they ought; he was often to be seen chatting to both teachers and pupils alike, always with an air of approachable affability. He was clearly proud of his school, and he was quite right to be, for it worked, as so many secondary state schools could work with the right ingredients.

As I left the classroom at the end of the day, I passed him in the corridor talking about matters Aston Villa with a Year 11 boy. He stopped short when he saw me, and caught my shoulder again.

'Was everything OK?' he said. I could see he was genuinely interested.

'Wonderful,' I said. 'Really lovely kids all day. I'm so sorry about being late this morning.'

He laughed. 'From what I've heard, you did well today. The pupils liked you. Thanks for your time.'

I shook his hand and left, crossing the dwindling maze of cars to my van and climbing in. A few scattered students shot out the way as I started the engine, and I was off, energised with the heady atmosphere of a good school.

* * * * *

I had hoped Gilbert would ask me back for the following day. Instead, Emma woke me with a day's work at Mitchell High School. This one was not in Birmingham, but in Walsall. Indeed, most of my work 'in Birmingham' was not in Birmingham at all, and I spent a large portion of November working (or, as Emma liked to put it, being 'whored out') across much of the West Midlands.

Mitchell turned out to be as immaculate and successful as Gilbert. It is one of the few remaining schools which still has a sixth form, and this is one of its finest assets. Polite, respectful and respected 17- and 18-year-olds are everywhere, managing to set impeccable standards within the school. There are university posters in every corridor, and the students hold doors open for passing teachers. I had an easy day, working on general cover for a range of varying subjects. The students were cheeky, in a harmless and compliant way – gentle kids who teased but never stepped over the boundary. They were fun to work with, and, again at the end of the day, I found myself feeling refreshed and invigorated, rather than downtrodden and exhausted.

In fact, I was even looking forward to my next assignment.

'There's something I should tell you about this next school, Charlie,' Emma said to me the following morning.

'What? Is it going to be a repeat of Tompkins?'

'Oh no, it's nowhere near as bad as that. It's just …' She paused. 'Well, it's just that it's an all-girls' school.'

'Oh,' I said.

'Have you ever worked at one before?'

'Never. Are they difficult?'

'Put it this way. I used to go to one. Just be careful, that's all.'

I hung up, considering the day ahead and worrying slightly at the caution in Emma's voice. When it comes to teaching, girls are far more frightening than boys. Boys are silly, effervescent creatures: they manifest their misbehaviour in loud and physical bursts, and can be quelled with something as simple as a carefully-chosen compliment. Girls, on the other hand, are complex and brooding, with labyrinthine skills of manipulation. While boys are inherently tactile, girls are verbal masters, and one sentence from the mouth of a girl can be more soul-destroying than any swing from the fist of a boy. In much the same way as the most terrifying teachers are always female, so too are the most perplexing pupils.

For once, I managed to make it in for morning briefing. As I sat in the staff room, I counted the number of male teachers. There were only four. Collecting my pack of lessons for the day from the cover co-ordinator, I ventured towards my room, hugging the wall as I went so as not to be knocked over by the oestrogen I convinced myself I could smell. Freud could have written a whole thesis about my body language.

Lesson one started. Thirty-two Year 8 girls piled into the classroom, most of whom took one look at me, emitted a brief and high-pitched giggle, and then sat down wherever they wanted. The noise was intense – with no bass or tenor to underscore, it was a thin band of soprano which seeped into my nerves and worked its way out through my pumping sweat glands.

'Right, Year 8,' I tried to say, but in fact squawked. A shriek to match my own ran through the classroom. I cleared my throat. Manly, like. 'Right, Year 8. Books out, please. Your task today is to write the opening chapter to the sequel of *Skellig*. Any questions?'

The girl who had chosen to sit directly in front of me raised her hand, her arm straight and clear.

'What's yer name, sir?'

'Mr Carroll.'

'No,' she said, blinking eyelashes that looked far too long to be a 13-year-old's. 'What's yer *real* name?'

Another collective giggle speared the class. Other girls began to loudly guess, and before I could answer they had already seemed to agree upon the name Chad. I didn't mind so much. It was better than Norman.

'My *real* name,' I said, 'is Mr Carroll. And I'll be happy to answer any other irrelevant questions during a break-time detention. As for now, it's time for some work.'

The old detention trick. Boy or girl, it rarely fails. The class begrudgingly opened their books and began their chapters. As they set to their task, I walked around the room taking names for the register. After scribbling 30 down, I reached the very back of the classroom, where the remaining two students sat, detached from everyone else.

'What are your names, girls? I need to tick them off the register.'

The one closest looked up, smiled, and said, 'Bethany Johnson'.

The other, a tall and thin girl whose lank, matted hair obscured her face from my view, continued staring at her closed book.

'What's your name?' I tried again, moving behind her.

'Have you got a tissue?' she grumbled, shifting in her seat so that her angular shoulder-blades faced me.

'What's your name?'

'Have you got a tissue?'

'Sorry, I don't have one. Now, what's your name, so I can mark you on the register.'

'I need a tissue.'

She still had not looked up at me.

'Look,' I said, using my 'genuine' voice. 'If you don't tell me your name, I can't mark you as present, and it'll go down as an absent mark. And then you'll get into trouble.'

'Let it. I don't care.'

'All you have to do is tell me your name.'

'Can I get a tissue?'

I could feel my patience dwindling. Having to ask the same question repeatedly is one of the teacher's prime frustrations. 'Come on, what's the point in getting into trouble over something silly like this? Just tell me your name.'

'I need to go and get a tissue.'

Reaching out, I turned her book over and looked at the front cover. 'Rebecca Pinder,' I read.

'*God*,' she suddenly spat, turning and glaring at me with eyes barely perceptible through the thick liner caked around them. 'If you were going to do *that*, why did you bother asking in the *first* place?'

I stood for a moment, marvelling at this pure rudeness – this unnecessary, uncalled-for, provocative obstinacy. I had to deal with it: to let her get away with this would be to invite all sorts of trouble, would be a swinging signboard which informed the other students that Mr Carroll could be walked all over.

'OK, Rebecca,' I said. 'To be honest, I don't really like being spoken to the way you're speaking to me right now. I suggest that you settle down a little bit and stop acting so rudely towards your teacher, otherwise you'll be forcing me to send you out.'

She narrowed her eyes even more. 'I need…' she breathed, 'a… fucking… *tissue!*'

I sent her out.

Following Rebecca's departure, things improved. I had one lesson from each year group that day and, though none were especially enjoyable, none were especially challenging, either. I was continually asked my age and whether or not I was married. Twice I was told I looked the spitting image of a character from *Eastenders*, once another from *Prison Break*. I spent at least half of the last lesson intercepting a Proustian volume of notes passed from hand to hand. Most I discarded into the bin, but one I kept to read after the lesson:

> *Whats she goin out with him fr?*
> *I no. Hes a fuckin dog!*
> *So is she! Her face = my ass*
> *LOL! + he is a retard*
> *Its like Shrek and King Kong*

At the end of the day, I walked up the stairs to the cover co-ordinator's office to get my timesheet signed.

'Would you be able to come back next Friday?' she said.

'Sorry, I'm afraid I'm already booked,' I lied. The school had not been that bad, I thought, but the prospect of spending another day amidst all those girls was just too frightening.

* * * * *

There ended my first week in the West Midlands. Leaving the gaggle far behind, I drove back to my campsite. After a month at Grandma's, it was fun to be living in the van again. I had always wanted a VW Campervan, ever since my eldest brother bought and restored a delicious 1972 Bay when I was a kid. He gave his life to that machine and I loved it just as much, daydreaming of the

Volkswagen I would someday own: an immaculate Split-Screen, light blue with an interior fitted out with eight duvets, a portable TV and – if I was really feeling decadent – a Sega Mega-Drive. I would drive this beast down to the *Run to the Sun* VW Festival where, at just the right moment, five of my friends would appear from doorways and tailgates and wound-down windows to splash the adoring crowd in water-pistol beer.

Such dreams: my early cars were instead Austin Metros and Ford Fiestas with three months' MOT, six figures on the milometer and a plethora of skittering head gaskets, voluminous oil leaks and detachable exhausts. But, at the start of this journey, my fantasy had become reality. After weeks of searching, I had found a 1983 T25 model with the old, air-cooled engine and blue panels dotted with a starscape of little rust-bubbles, and handed over £1,300 for the right to call her mine. I fell in love with her instantly. Inside, she had everything I needed to live: a gas-cooker (two hobs and a grill); a sink with a spitting tap; a range of cupboards and a small wardrobe in which I could hang my cheap suit; a fridge which, though it didn't work, was insulated enough to ensure that beers chilled on purchase would remain so; a tiny vanity cabinet and shaving mirror; and, most importantly, that fundamental VW design, the Rock and Roll bed – a seat which pulls out into a comfortable double sleeper.

I was amazed at how habitable my little bus was – especially when compared with the far more expensive motor caravans and mobile homes other peripatetics lived in. For my first week in the West Midlands, I checked into a campsite on the northern edge of Birmingham. The owner of the site was a jovial Brummy who greeted me with a warm handshake and a number of loving references to Volkswagens, and then promptly sent me to pitch up behind the site's workshop where I was well out of sight of the grander static caravans.

I was wedged between a 1980s Ford Campervan and an even older caravan, like the dunces of a classroom, the untouchables of our little subcontinent, hidden in the outskirts where our rust could not spread. A young couple called Rebecca and Rhys lived in the caravan: it was far cheaper than renting a house or, the unthinkable, buying one. They worked as bartenders in Birmingham, and drove off into the city every afternoon at four o'clock to begin their shifts. They would often return, drunk and giggly, just as I was waking up at six in the morning, and my breakfasts were often eaten to the sounds of their painfully audible sex.

To my right were the Franklins, a sixtysomething wife and husband who lived in their motorhome with two elephantine dogs. They were a friendly pair who came round to greet me on the Saturday with a packet of chocolate digestives.

'Welcome to Butlins,' said Mrs Franklin, as she poked her nose inside my van. 'Hey, it's a bit cosy in here, isn't it?' She was wearing a dressing-gown. It was four o'clock in the afternoon.

She climbed in, followed by her husband and their two dogs, who were dripping wet and who quickly made themselves at home on my bed. The Franklins sat in the driver and passenger seats. I tried to lean on the cooker.

'How long are you here for?' said Mrs Franklin, the talker of the two. Her husband seemed content just to coo at the dogs and occasionally remark upon their good looks.

'About a month,' I said. 'I'm doing a bit of work up here.'

'Really? What are you in?' Mrs Franklin asked, lighting up a Superking.

'I'm a teacher. I'm doing some supply in the area.'

'Oh, how nice! Well, you'll love it here.' She inhaled deeply.

'He likes you,' said Mr Franklin, pointing to the dog who was already asleep and drooling on my pillow. 'He doesn't usually feel so comfortable in a new place.'

There was a 10 second silence while we all stared at the dogs.

'Have a biscuit,' said Mrs Franklin.

'OK,' said Mr Franklin.

'So, how long have you been here?' I asked.

Mrs Franklin emitted a phlegmy laugh. 'Christ! Fucking years!' she said. 'We love it here. Have you met Roger the owner?'

I nodded.

'He's a bloody darling. A lot of people don't like him, but we like how he keeps the place. Don't we, Gavin?'

'We do,' Mr Franklin replied. 'Aww, just look at Doughnut. He's so content.'

'It's nice and clean here. We've lived in campsites before, and they were never a patch on Roger's place. Never as clean.'

'So you pretty much live here?'

'Oh yes,' she said. 'It's the perfect way to spend your retirement. No bills, no council tax. And the perfect thing is, here you have all the facilities you need. Don't you, Gavin?'

Mr Franklin made an agreeing noise and chomped on a biscuit.

'What we especially like is that they keep the heating on in the shower-block all the time.'

Mr Franklin looked at me. 'All the time,' he repeated.

'And the toilets and the laundry room and the kitchen are *so clean*,' said his wife. 'And he doesn't charge you for water. Yes, the facilities here are lovely. I mean, we may look like pikeys, but we don't have to *live* like them!'

This produced a great rasping laugh from both Franklins, so loud that it made the sleeping dog wake up with a sudden yelp and then proceed to flap the spit from its sodden jowls all over my curtains.

Mr Franklin gave a soft chuckle. 'Oh, he likes you, he does.'

I soon learned that most of the people on the campsite were not just visitors like me, but, like the Franklins, actually lived there. This was true for many of the people on the campsites I visited throughout the year. There is a subculture of folk – mostly the old and retired or young but too poor to buy a house – who live like this permanently. They are an interesting and surprisingly home-proud bunch, their mobile homes as static as brick houses, adorned with kooky solar-powered garden lights, heated awnings and all-weather deckchairs.

But campsite life was not for me. For one, it was too expensive. To spend a month on a campsite could cost as much as renting a house for the same time and, in some places, was more so. It surprised me how short of money I was. I was averaging a daily rate of between £90 and £150 pounds, and a lot of the time I was paid the higher rate – in my opinion, a very good wage – because I often worked in schools others wouldn't. My only bills were fuel and food, but the VW drank petrol at an alarming rate; after a sudden hike in fuel prices across the country, my bank balance was quickly slipping towards zero. The lack of work in Manchester had not helped.

Leaving the campsite was a good way to conserve my dwindling funds, but it was not the only reason why I did so. I also had a vague notion in my head – though no idea where it came from – that I ought to spend this year as vagrantly as I could, like a latter-day Kerouac on a 21st century apocalyptic binge of *On the Road* poverty. And so, after my first week of finding my feet in the West Midlands, I left Roger, Rebecca, Rhys, the Franklins and their two dogs, and moved once again into the lay-bys.

I found two which were ideal. If I was working in Birmingham or further south the following day, I stayed in a long and dusty pull-in to the east of the city; if I was to work further north, it was a smaller and more rural spot, ringed with beautiful low hills, directly outside a Waste Disposal Site. The latter was the more peaceful, but this was off-set by the smell of hot stone and rancid meat which lifted off the landfill on wet nights. Every now and then, I would return to the campsite, park the van up the hill, and sneak down on to the site under the cover of darkness to fill up my water bottles illicitly and have a long, warm shower.

I grew used to living in the van: from being a novelty, it quite quickly became my home. I learnt to change it from house to car with a smooth rapidity, packing up the bed and hiding my uncleaned pots and pans each morning so that, when I arrived in school, students wouldn't peer inside to see an unmade bed and remnants of a soupy dinner and then ask in the middle of a packed classroom: 'Do you *live* in that van, sir? Are you *homeless* or something?'

I was, of course. But I didn't want them to know that.

* * * * *

To begin my second week, I spent the Monday at a school in Tamworth, returning to my pungent lay-by that evening. Rolling out my bed and arranging the furniture just as I liked it, I settled down with my hot-water bottle to write in my daily journal. It had not been an easy day and, as I wrote, I wondered if my time in the West Midlands was going to be a slippery slope, a trajectory which pushed downwards from the pinnacle of Gilbert School to the very bottom of the educational mire. Though it was little more than a supposition at the time, it came true. That week went from middling to severely uncomfortable, and the two weeks which followed became more and more hellish, lowering me steadily down the grand spectrum of the educational rope.

Emma had called that morning, despatching me off to Boscombe Heights Technology College. It was a fairly tough school, she warned me, but endurable. And she was right. Monday was not an easy start to the week, but I got through it, managing where I could and ignoring where I could not.

I was taken to my classroom for the day where I was to cover for the teacher who was covering for the teacher who had been off for the last four months. During the weekend, someone (students were suspected, but there was no evidence) had broken into the school and started a fire in one of the corridors – my corridor, as it happened. The fire brigade had arrived within minutes, and the damage was minimal, but the entire block was laced with the heady aroma of stale smoke, and I often had to allow students outside for some fresh air when they were overtaken by coughing fits.

The classes were tolerable until I came to Period 3 just after break-time. As the students entered and sallied towards their desks, one boy hurled his planner away, hitting me in the face with it. He looked at me, wide-eyed, and then said, 'Josh just threw it at me!'

'Are you going to apologise?' I said.

He turned to Josh and said, 'I'm sorry, Josh.'

From there on, Period 3 was a nightmare. With 33 students before me, all 14 years old and desperate to prove it, I spent a whole hour doing my best to turn the unbounded chaos into something resembling a mere tumult. One boy in particular, Liam, saw the lesson for what it was – a terrible excuse for classroom control – and set about turning it to his advantage. Each time I tried to make some sort of indentation, to turn the lesson into something an OFSTED Inspector might recognise, Liam would do his best to incite a riot. After 20 minutes, I had to send him out, only to find that the classroom I had sent him to – manned by the Head of English – was also so chaotic that he was sent back to me again 10 minutes later.

Like a horde of gremlins intent on creating overwhelming mania, these Year 9s pushed and pulled me in every direction so that, as the changeover bell for Period 4 finally came along, I was content to let them spill out into the school and carry on their drama without even asking them to put their chairs back where they were supposed to be.

Thankfully, a sage Year 11 class came in after them, and rearranged the chairs so they could sit in their chosen groups.

'Tough lesson, sir?' one of the girls asked me as she took her books out.

'No, no, they were just a bit excitable,' I said.

She laughed knowingly, and two of her friends joined in. 'Don't worry, sir,' said someone else. 'We know how hard it is for supply teachers in this school.'

Feeling like I was back in my PGCE year – though this time comforted by mentors younger than me – I decided to be honest.

'All right, so they weren't the easiest group I've ever had,' I said. 'But I'm still here, aren't I? And as for you lot, I believe you're just beginning your 20th Century Drama coursework. Willy Russell's *Our Day Out*. So let's make a start on it.'

'Are you a real English teacher, sir?'

'I am, yes.'

'Could you talk us through it a bit? We've had supply teachers for the last month. We don't really get it.'

Perhaps the gesture was merely a placatory one, but I appreciated it nonetheless. I spent the lesson talking through the play with the class, giving them advice on what the essay demanded, showing them how to structure their paragraphs, and suggesting quotes to use. I even offered a few synonyms they could insert here and there to impress their standard teacher. And, like a collective of little saints, they listened and made notes all the way, probing me only on related additions.

At the end of the lesson, just as the bell was going, I felt compelled to tell them, 'Thank you, Year 11. You've been a wonderful class today, a real credit to your teacher. I'll make sure she hears just how fabulous you've been for me.'

One young man from the back row piped up: 'To be honest, sir, it was just good to actually be *taught* today. It's not often it happens.'

I thanked them again, and let them go. I was under no illusions. They were a lower set, the work left for them was minimal, and the choice to spend the lesson off-task would have been an easy one to make. The fact that they had not done that was not down to my teaching abilities. It was more to do with their growing empathy, their developing awareness of others, their maturity. Boscombe Heights was undoubtedly a challenging school, but it was also a school where students made their own choices, some of which were very positive. I encountered some feverishly uncooperative children there, but I also met some wonderful young adults, the kind it is a pleasure to spend time with.

*****

An inescapable, spiky cold set in. It was now getting close to December, the West Midlands were beginning to freeze over, and I was weathering my non-working hours inside an unheated van. I began to notice a problem with the big toe on my left foot. Within minutes of being back in the van, it went numb and turned so white it was hard to believe it belonged to me. The nail seemed the fleshiest part. Fearing early frostbite, I started to wear three pairs of socks.

I was living in a perpetual dusk. It was dark when I drove to work, dark when I returned. I began getting into bed before eight o'clock, trying to sleep through the cold. Daylight flashed in on school-hours, but I rarely saw it. Most of my classroom-windows had blinds. Once, I opened some because the sky was clear. Sunlight flooded the room and a boy called Rhys complained about the glare off his computer screen. I tried a joke; Rhys got up to close the blinds himself. I sat down.

One evening, the rain stopped and the sky cleared for the first time in weeks. Arriving at the lay-by in time to watch a thin sunset,

I retreated into the back of the van and left the curtains open, slipping a cold beer from the fridge and watching the passing cars. Their headlights began to flick on, and the beer got difficult to hold: I had to pour it away. In the passing intervals of an hour, I put on an extra jumper, a thick coat, a pair of gloves, a hat, and the hood my brother had bought me as a joke. I rolled out the bed and got under two duvets and three blankets. I lit the gas-hobs and boiled up two kettles to fill my hot-water bottles. Eventually, it became tolerable. Alongside the hot-water bottles, my body pumped out enough heat to be comfortable, and the day's exhaustion soon turned to sleep.

I woke abruptly a few hours later. My face felt like it was coated in snow. I was shivering, that was it. I was shivering so hard it had woken me up. My bottles were still warm, so was my body. It was my face. I pulled the duvet over my head, finding solace in the claustrophobia, and eventually slipping back into sleep.

I woke at five. It was the shaking again. I pulled myself up and lit the hobs, brewing anything that might warm. I turned on the light to see ice, ice everywhere. Ice on the outside of the windscreen, ice on the inside. Ice coating the ceiling, ice thickened around the rims of the sink. Ice on the towel I had left out to dry, ice on the corner of my duvet. I pulled at my pillow. It had frozen to the back window. I rose from my bed, dressed and shivered as I made soup for breakfast. Then I waited, teeth chattering, until I could go back to school, where the heating would be on.

The next school, begun the day after Boscombe Heights and then endured until the end of the week, was Taylor College in Birmingham – the same Taylor College of the Introduction, which featured interior water-bombs and the unsociable Ben Street.

As I drew close on Tuesday morning, I began gauging the area. Taylor sits between three rough council estates: the kind where you would not walk alone after dark or leave a pushbike unattended; the kind where car-wheels turn into bricks overnight; and where toddlers yell 'Daddy!' at passing blokes in the local supermarket because they think the word is a synonym for 'man'.

The school itself is an unsightly and depressing building, disintegrating through a mixture of age and vandalism. Across the road, a new school is currently being built (this was before the end of the Building Schools for the Future programme) though this is not without its problems. Recently, the building contractors considered a strike after they were stoned by the students at lunchtimes. When I heard about this, I decided to take a quick walk out of the school gates one lunchtime. I saw no stone-throwers, but I did see, right at the entrance, three teenagers surrounded by eight younger students. I noticed something change hands, and then something else. One of them spotted me approaching: all hands quickly shoved into pockets, and each of the teenagers walked off in a different direction. It was not hard to see what was happening: a drug deal had taken place, virtually on the school's premises. Yet I seemed to be the only adult around. There were no members of the Senior Management Team patrolling the area, and certainly no police. That same afternoon, I overheard one Year 10 boy snarling at another in the corridor, 'You tell that fucking Adam to stop spreading lies about my stuff – he hasn't even tasted it.'

My lessons were not lessons at all: instead, they were 50-minute intervals of blocking exits and taking tables and chairs from the hands of teenagers and placing them back on the floor. I often 'taught' from the door rather than the whiteboard – if I did not bar the way, the kids would get up and leave. Assaults were common. One boy strode out of the classroom to return a minute later with a long plank of wood with which he intended to 'batter' a girl – another girl physically restrained him. During a Food Technology lesson, one 14-year-old boy waved a sharp knife menacingly in front of another's face – I told him to 'Put down the knife', and only realised the import of such a sentence once the lesson was over.

Racism was just as common. Slurs and derogatory names were whispered under the breath, or written with an anonymous poison-pen and then left indiscreetly. They came from all directions, and no ethnicity was safe. In one memorable Year 11 maths lesson, I encountered Lucy McNally, who had just returned from a fixed-term exclusion for bringing a pint of vodka into school in a plastic bottle and then passing it around her history class. She had been loud and obnoxious throughout my lesson, and I had to send her out when she screamed, 'Go back to your own country, you foreign fucks!' at two small and quiet Polish boys sat at the front.

As she left, her two best friends called out to me. 'Why did you send her out? That's not fair!'

'I sent her out,' I replied, 'because of her offensive racist language.'

'She wasn't being racist!' one of them shouted. 'We're her witnesses! We'll say you were lying! We'll get you sacked!'

Fortunately for me, though not for the two Polish boys, Lucy burst back into the classroom at that moment, as another member of staff was trying to escort her to the Inclusion Unit.

'It's true!' she screamed, as she splashed dramatically through the door. 'Those two foreign, smelly, hairy bastards should piss off back to their own country!'

I spent four days at Taylor, and they were masochistic. Each evening, I wondered if I could go back the next day. One night, just to try and relax, I got so drunk on cheap red wine I was sick. I grew hazy and uncertain of why I was doing all this, why I had ended up here, in a school where I was not just appalled, I was sometimes frightened. I thought about Harriet Harman being photographed walking around her South London constituency with a group of local policemen, all

– including her – wearing stab-vests and then I thought about the staff room of Taylor College. There had not been a stab-vest in sight. These teachers, who had to enter such an area every day, wore only their cheap, easily-washable suits.

* * * * *

The weekend came, and depression with it. I walked out of Taylor on Friday afternoon contemplating giving it all up and going home. I was tired, and so strung out I wanted to stab balloons. Crawling into the comfort of the van, I slotted the key into the ignition and emitted a deep and cathartic sigh. I was feeling stifled, and needed to get out of Birmingham for a few days. I scanned my road atlas, and then set off immediately for the Black Country.

The Black Country is a West Midlands National Park for industrialism, and it spreads into parts of Birmingham, Wolverhampton and Staffordshire, taking its name from the coal so abundant in the area, and the heavy industrialism it instigated. I knew the area from paintings I had seen in the past: heavily-blotted, Goya-esque representations of indefatigable darkness, pierced only by the faint yellows of risen lights which look like they too will soon be consumed. But as I drove out into it, coursing along thin single-carriageways and B-roads, I found that it was not what I had expected. This was a land much closer to West Yorkshire than those doom-laden paintings: a spread of heaths and low villages, punctuated by a decaying sense of small-town industrialism. The foundries run down, the factories long since closed, the Black Country was, dare I say it, sleepy, and far more green than it was black.

I drove for miles and hours that weekend, delighting in all I found. I walked around the Kingsbury Water Park and visited the splendid cathedral in Lichfield. I stopped and stretched and then drove some more, discovering in my own way this land which is often called the Heart of the Country. It seemed that someone had clearly taken umbrage at this accusation and had decided, in the Heart of the Country Shopping Village, to remove an O, an R and a Y from the large sign at its entrance. As I passed, three teenagers stood beside the sign with wide, cheeky grins, while a fourth took a photo of them on her mobile phone's camera.

I came out of my Black Country weekend with a feeling akin to euphoria. Taylor had been well and truly clawed out from beneath my skin and discarded into the landfill I spent Sunday night beside. I was ready for the next challenge, ready for whatever Emma had to throw at me. I knew by now that my time in the West Midlands was one of educational calibration, and I was eager to see the next act in the play. This, after all, was what I had set out to do. I was experiencing the secondary system like I never had before, and – though I was losing weight, was drinking too much, was letting my shoulders subsume my neck – there were yet a few more rungs left to climb down. Taylor was not the bottom. There was still more to be seen.

Emma called me on the Monday morning.

'I've got two weeks on offer,' she said. 'There's nine days at a place called Bruller, and then one at Turnbull.'

I could not have asked for better, or for worse.

The Bruller Centre, a Pupil Referral Unit (PRU), is lodged deep in the molar of a small West Midlands town.

Every Local Education Authority has a PRU. It is the 'school' which takes in those children who have been permanently excluded from mainstream education. The average PRU will have between 20 and 30 students at any given time, and will offer them a chance to work towards their Key Stage 3 exams (taken at the end of Year 9) or their GCSEs (taken at the end of Year 11).

PRUs are small and intimate institutions whose main purpose is to keep a child versed in the ways of the National Curriculum so that they will not be behind when re-integrated back into mainstream education. If re-integration is not an option, students will remain at the PRU and take their exams there. PRUs are a kind of purgatory, a halfway house where teenagers are given the all-important 'second chance'. They are a back-up to the national hard-drive, a momentary respite and check for those kids who have found that being with a large group of their peers is difficult, and who need some space to get to grips with themselves.

The atmosphere of a PRU is far different to that of a mainstream secondary school, and I found that I needed to adjust to Bruller quickly. With fewer than 30 students and 10 members of staff, no class was larger than five pupils, and some had only two or three. There was no uniform, either for students or staff. The teenagers called me Charlie (that is, if they were being nice). The morning was composed of four half-hour lessons and a long break; the afternoon given over to activities such as sports, pool tournaments, or skills-based learning.

The PRU *had* to function this way. To try and recreate the environment of a generic school would not just have been futile. These were children with a record of causing fights, vandalising property, and playing truant. If Bruller was ever going to do anything for them, concessions had to be made. A blind eye was turned to the blatant smoking, a deaf ear to the constant swearing. Students were given breakfast and lunch for free – for a lot of them, it was all they ate each day. And, in fact, the system worked very well. Most of Bruller's teenagers leave with a number of qualifications that they otherwise never would have achieved.

But it was hard work for the staff. Bruller's teachers seemed to spend every lesson engaged in a rigorous system of coaxing, wheedling and gentle verbal prodding to ensure that the students did any work at all, whilst, at the same time, enduring a steady stream of threats and casual insults coming the other way.

For my first lesson, I had just one student: James, a bulky 16-year-old who, it was rumoured, was taking steroids. He had been in and out of a number of schools across North Yorkshire until his mother had given up and sent him to the Midlands to live with his father. After two weeks at his first school, he was excluded for fighting, and moved immediately to Bruller.

I was instructed to get him to complete a computer-based maths programme.

'What do ah get if ah do this work then, Charleh?' he asked.

'What do you get?' I said. 'How do you mean?'

'There must be summat in it for me?'

'Well, how about, if you work on it for 20 minutes, then for the last 10 minutes you can go on online games.'

He thought about this. 'Nah,' he said. 'How about, if ah do this... ah... ah get t' chin yer.'

He chuckled to himself at the thought of such a prize, then turned to his computer and began working.

I covered the Time Out Room on my free periods. Students came in sporadically and went to sleep, or they would question me on my favourite football team, why I didn't get a nicer car, or why I didn't get a better job. Whenever I turned the questions on them, they evaded answering, not wanting to reveal anything about themselves. I played pool with them in the afternoon, and got thrashed each time.

One day after lunch, Frank the English teacher took two girls to a nearby amusement arcade, and I accompanied them. On the way back in Frank's car, Tara described an area we drove through as 'where all the Pakis live'. We dropped her off at her house, and I saw that the windows had been broken and were held together with Sellotape.

Jeremy called me a 'fucking prick' when I praised his work.

Robert winked at me when the attractive receptionist passed the classroom and said: 'Nice her, ain't she? I'd give her one.'

I spoke to the other members of staff whenever I could, trying to find out how they liked it here, and why they had chosen this particular avenue. Some had fallen into it, starting as supply teachers and never leaving. Others enjoyed the constant diversity the job entailed. All were passionate, staunch defenders of their choice.

'These lot need my help and attention far more than kids in mainstream schools,' said one of the latter, Harry. Harry taught humanities, and I liked him a lot. He was a down-to-earth bloke in his 40s whose teaching style was devoid of either arrogance or maudlin sentimentality. He cared about his students and wanted them to do well in life, but he refused to take any shit from them. He was clearly the favourite teacher of all the kids – the authority figure that many of them did not have at home.

Harry had been at Bruller for a decade. He couldn't even imagine going back into mainstream education, he said: this was what he wanted to do until he retired. The PRU was his favourite conversational subject, and he could talk about it at length. His stories were magnificent and expertly told, and I loved hearing them as much as he loved telling them. His best ones were always about a girl called Stacey who had graduated a few years ago. She was positively wild, and Harry related her tales with a kind of wide-eyed awe, as if he still could not believe she had done such things. Amongst her many triumphs, she had managed to bully some OFSTED inspectors, had thrown a brick through the staff room window during the morning meeting, and had once brought a pitchfork in for the day. But her crowning glory came one day in her last month.

'It was just her in my lesson,' said Harry. 'She wasn't having none of it, and stormed out. I followed her out into the corridor, saying the usual, that if she didn't come back in she would be excluded, like. She just kept walking, shouting at me to fuck off and leave her alone, and then she left the site.

'I went to get Bill (the Deputy Head), and we walked out to see if she'd done one, or if she was just sulking somewhere. But we couldn't find her in the car park or round the back, she was long gone. So we're standing there, talking about maybe ringing up her carers, when I heard this faint rumbling sound, like a train or something. I asked Bill if he could hear it, and he could too, and it was getting louder and louder. We walked out on to the road to have a look and there, appearing at the top of the hill, was this bloody silhouette of a giant wheelie bin. It was coming nearer and getting bigger and bigger – bloody deafening, it was. We could see from where we were standing that it was overflowing with rubbish and a load of concrete, must have been taken from the building site up the road.

'Anyway, suddenly we sees this tiny little head – Stacey's – poke round the side of the bin. "This is for youse cunts!" she was shouting. She was pushing the bloody thing right at us! I saw her let go, and it just came hurtling down towards us, right through the gates. Me and Bill jumped out the way and it went flying past, right into me car! Bloody totalled the thing!'

Harry laughed hard and slapped his thigh at the recollection. 'Totalled it!' he cried. 'Ah, she was a character, that Stacey. But you know what? She left here with five GCSEs. I was so proud of her.'

'Have you ever seen her since? Do you know what she's up to these days?'

Harry was suddenly silent, and looked away from me. 'No,' he said, a little too quickly. 'No, I never saw her again.' I knew from his sudden change of demeanour, by the sadness which flashed across his face, that he was lying.

My two weeks came to an end at Bruller and I was left with one final day of work in the West Midlands. Emma had booked it for me a fortnight before, and I was ready to get it over with and leave this area for the next.

*****

I have never experienced so shocking a school as Turnbull.

It was an EBSD Specialist School for students with Emotional, Behavioural and Social Difficulties. There are only a handful of these in England. If children excluded from mainstream schools go to the LEAs' Pupil Referral Units, then EBSD schools are where those excluded from the PRUs go.

This is the very bottom of the teenage pool: an environment filled with students who have deeply upsetting issues. They are the ones for whom, sadly, little can be done: children with ASBOs; children on terrifyingly high dosages of Ritalin; children with criminal records and, already in their short lives, histories of violence.

Turnbull was staffed by what I felt was an absurdly low number of teachers, most of whom were young, male and energetic. They performed their jobs with an enthusiasm which was miraculous considering the constant strain they were under, not just from the rowdy students and the ridiculous lack of manpower on site, but also because the school was in Special Measures, and OFSTED were breathing ominously down their necks at all times. One can only wonder if those omniscient School Inspectors have ever done such a job themselves. The teachers were saintly, and so skilled it was enthralling to watch them work – and crushing to witness how much they were up against.

My first class consisted of two 14-year-old Year 9 boys, named the 'nicest, quietest group we have' by the assistant head. They worked well for the first half of the lesson, but for the second it was all I could do to stop them throwing their pens about and declaiming each other as 'gay as fuck'. My second class, likewise, were not so bad. But after break-time I was privy to how chaotic this school could be.

For period 3 I had three Year 8s. One, Will, came in and began his work. The other two, Craig and Simon, refused. My LSA tried to bring them in, but Craig ran off, and Simon climbed up into a hollow above the staircase where he was out of reach. I did not see him again. Craig, however, I did. He came back in on his own (the LSA was still outside trying to coax Simon down). He sat at a table.

'I'm glad you've come back, Craig. Here's your work,' I said, putting the sheet on his desk.

Eyeballing me, he threw it on the floor.

'Could you pick that up, please?' I asked.

'No,' he enunciated, staring at me all the time.

'Well, that's a shame,' I responded. 'I'll tell you what, I'm going to help Will for a bit, and then I'll come and see how you're getting on.'

A minute later, Craig stood up and plucked his folder from a table at the back of the room. Sitting down with it, he began ripping out the pages, tearing them in four, and throwing the remains on the floor.

'Craig,' I said, rising to my feet. 'Can you stop doing that, please?'

'No,' he replied, continuing to rip and tear, all the time staring at me.

'Craig, I'm going to ask you once more to stop. And, if you won't, I'm going to have to ask someone to remove you.'

He laughed, and carried on.

Perhaps the most telling factor of the school's challenging nature was the precautions put in place to deal with it. In each room and corridor were CCTV cameras, all of which were wired to two offices.

Those staff who were not teaching would be in the offices, looking out for any trouble brewing so they could pre-empt it. All the staff at Turnbull were specially trained to physically restrain students when necessary – they were licensed, if you like, to use force. This was, without a doubt, fundamentally necessary at Turnbull.

One of those staff – Gordon, a robust science teacher – had seen what was going on in my room on his monitor, and was already making his way down the corridor when I stuck my head out. We both entered to find Craig opening the window of this second-storey room, preparing himself to jump out.

Gordon raced over and grabbed him by the arms. As Craig struggled, a female teacher rushed in; they both tried to move Craig towards the door, but he was having none of it and began to flail about, screaming that he was going to murder the pair of them. As they kicked tables out of the way to create a clearing and lowered him to the ground, the second teacher turned to me and panted, 'Get support.'

I ran out of the classroom and called a passing teacher, who came in and pinned down Craig's legs. They held him face down on the floor for a good five minutes. I tried to continue teaching Will, but found myself unnerved by Craig's feral howls and threats from the carpet. Finally, his struggling subsided, and the second teacher said to him, 'Craig, I'm going to count to 10. If you haven't moved by then, we will release you, and we can all stand up and walk out of here together.'

She began the countdown. At six, Gordon loosened his grip on Craig's arm, and Craig suddenly lashed out. They closed down on him harder.

'Mr Carroll,' said the female teacher. 'Please go and get Mrs Vickers, the Assistant Head. I think we're going to have to get the police in.'

While I was gone, Craig did stop struggling of his own accord, and the police were not called. By the time I returned with Mrs Vickers, he was on his feet, dribbling. Outside the door, I whispered to Gordon. 'Were you really going to call the police? Or was it just a threat?'

He looked at me, and I could see he was pitying my naivety. 'We have to get the police in two or three times a week.'

Suddenly, the yelled command '*Support*!' echoed down the corridor, and Gordon sprinted off again.

Through Period 4, the chaos continued. I had four Year 7s: Matthew, Tim, John, and one of the few girls at the school, Caroline. Throughout the lesson, each was removed from and brought back into the classroom again and again, so that I never had more than two students in there at a time. Halfway through, Caroline returned from outside. She was a tiny thing with huge, pretty eyes, fat cheeks and an overall babyish quality which would have instantly endeared her to the sentimental adults on a TV talent show.

'Caroline, I'm glad you're back. Shall we have a go at this work?'

She turned and stared at me. 'Fuck off, you fucking southern cunt,' she slowly remarked.

I was taken aback. I cannot count how many times I have been told to fuck off by a student – from the faltering and nervous 'fuck *off*' of the young school bully uncertainly flexing his muscles, to the casual and jokey '*fuck* off' of the older student for whom swearing has become an everyday part of vocabulary, to the shouted and confident '*fuck off!*' of the student who is out of sight but not earshot, and who knows he will not be identified – but never before had it been so clearly directed and intentioned, and so devastatingly malicious.

'Pardon?' was all I could manage.

'Fuck off back down south. No-one wants you here. We all fucking hate you. So just fuck off.'

There was a calm and committed malevolence in her voice. I was so shocked that, for one brief but terrifying moment, I thought I might cry.

Pulling myself together, I said, 'Caroline, you've really hurt my feelings there. Those are some very nasty things to say.'

'Fuck your fucking feelings,' she said, standing up. 'And fuck you, you *fucking southern cunt*.' At that, she turned on her heel, and marched out.

I stood rigid, wondering if I had ever been spoken to like that in my life by *anyone*, anywhere, let alone by a tiny 11-year-old girl. Somewhere in my numbed brain, I heard one of the boys, busying himself colouring in the surface of the table, gently singing the repeated refrain, 'Fucking southern cunt', and giggling quietly at each repetition.

I quickly learned not to take Caroline's piercing remarks to heart. Ten minutes later, I heard her call an LSA a 'fucking ugly slut', pointing her finger into the woman's face with each syllable. Later still, I heard her refer to Gordon, who had a broad cockney accent, as a 'London suicide bomber'. She was really little more than a rifle filled with obscenities, aiming them at whoever happened to be standing before her.

Indeed, I learned not to take *any* of it to heart. During the staff debriefing at the day's end, I was muted as each teacher listed off the catalogue of ordeals they had endured over the last six hours. One member of staff had been assaulted four times, another had narrowly ducked a heavy ruler hurled at her face; a third, who rode a motorbike, had been almost knocked off his feet on arrival by a lad who had hit him over the head with a piece of drain-piping. The boy had wanted to check if the teacher's helmet worked.

The last to speak in the debriefing was Jayne, the LSA I had heard called a 'fucking ugly slut' by Caroline. In her early 20s, and only recently employed, she was not trained to restrain students, and so was not allowed to touch them. During an afternoon lesson, while the teacher of her class took one pupil outside for a quiet word, the remaining three students set upon Jayne and repeatedly kicked her about the legs. She fled from the room, but the students chased after her, out into the corridor and across the school. Jayne ran to the Assistant Head's office and banged loudly on the door. Mrs Vickers appeared to find Jayne panting and out of breath, the three students clustered behind her and smiling.

'When Mrs Vickers asked them what they were doing, they said they thought we were playing a game,' Jayne told us, and then rolled up one of her trouser-legs to reveal a series of thin bruises on her shin.

I left the debriefing with Gordon, still reeling with everything that had been said by the staff, and especially Jayne.

'What will happen to those three kids who chased Jayne?' I asked.

'Who knows? Probably nothing. They might get suspended for a day or two, but I doubt it.'

'But how can that be legal? They physically assaulted her. She's got the bruises to prove it.'

'Different rules apply here, Charlie. Think of it this way – you also saw me physically assault Craig this morning, or at least that's what he would call it. But, like I said, different rules.'

We reached the car park, and before Gordon left I had to ask him one final thing. 'Today was a bad day, right? I mean, it's not always like this, is it?'

He gave me the same look as earlier: his pity; my naivety. Though, this time, there was something else in there, a quiet sadness, perhaps.

'Actually,' he considered, 'today was about as average as you could get.'

* * * * *

If you are not in teaching, you may well never have heard of a PRU or an EBSD school, despite the fact that your Local Education Authority will have at least one PRU, and perhaps four or five. It may also have an EBSD school, or perhaps a tuition centre, or maybe a home-schooling group, to cater for those students who cannot cope with being schooled in the mainstream system.

Currently, thousands of children around England are working towards their exams in these unknown institutions. They are a vital part of our country's educational system, and something we should be proud of. Very few countries have the kind of educational provision that we have in England, where all children are guaranteed schooling, free of charge. Despite the numerous problems our system has, this at least shows that we have succeeded in rendering education as a fundamental entitlement for all.

Of course, within that bold statement there is plenty of controversy and argument. We may have free education for all, but there are thousands of children across the country who still manage to slip through the net and do not receive any kind of formal education. Likewise, it might also be argued that creating such a vastly expensive sub-system of PRUs and such like, funded by the taxpayer, in effect *allows* students to opt out of the mainstream. These are weighty arguments, but the one which seems to cause the most debate in educational circles is this: that the inclusion which PRUs, EBSD schools and all the rest rely upon supports the policy of *exclusion*.

'Exclusion' is a relatively new term which has replaced the older concepts of 'suspension' and 'expulsion'.

Until fairly recently, students whose behaviour made it necessary were either suspended (banned from the school for a number of days) or expelled (removed from the school permanently). Exclusion is an umbrella term which covers both areas.

There are three stages. The first is internal exclusion: a day where the student is removed from his timetable and required to spend the day inside the school, but in isolation. The second is fixed-term exclusion: the student will be asked to remain off the school's premises for a number of days. The term can be anything from, generally, two days to two weeks. Work will be sent home for the student to complete in his own time. Finally, there is permanent exclusion: the student will be asked to leave the school permanently. On the first exclusion, students will typically begin attending another school in their local area. If said student is permanently excluded again, he may try one or two other schools, or attend a PRU.

For those against exclusion, it does nothing but enhance the social disquiet of England. It picks on damaged children and encourages them along the path to poverty and crime, disenfranchising them to such an extent that they are left with no other option. Exclusion, this side of the argument states, can cause irreparable psychological damage to the excluded child, creating a resentment which will lead to the kind of wider social exclusion so many adults on the bread- and crime-line are experiencing today. School exclusion numbers tend to be highest in those areas where the number of impoverished single parents is also highest, leading some to question how exclusion can ever help such families and communities. In fact, say these critics, it is little more than conditioning, a means by which authority stamps into children that their lives are already pre-determined, that being an outsider is all they are fit for.

On the other side of the argument are those who see exclusion as not only necessary, but beneficial. They look to the other children in the classroom; if a child's behaviour is so disruptive that he is not only impeding his own learning but the learning of others, he must be removed from the classroom so that those others can learn as they need. It is a matter of free will: the misbehaving student has *chosen* to do as such, but his misbehaviour must not impact on the free will and the choices of the rest. A friend of mine, the writer Olly Wyatt, once gave me this theory on the subject. Paraphrasing the philosopher John Rawls, who said that the best society is the society that extends people's freedoms to the extent that their actions or beliefs are compatible with other people's freedoms, Wyatt suggested that school is a society like any other. And if one child is limiting another child's potential to learn, then he or she *must* be removed from that society, or that child will be imposing upon another child's fundamental right.

Those are the two sides to the argument. But what are the facts? Since the academic year 1997-1998, the rate of exclusions in English schools has fallen by 23%, leading to only 12 out of every 10,000 students being permanently excluded in the academic year 2004-2005. Since then, the numbers have continued to fall further each year. Taken at face value, this seems a good thing. It means, surely, that our schools are working. But, if you look deeper, this rather dramatic decrease seems to correlate to a target issued in 1997 by David Blunkett, then Secretary of Education. He announced that, by 2002, the number of exclusions in English schools needed to fall by 30%.

This was not just a request. To ensure that his target was met, Blunkett devised a twofold strategy: firstly, schools' budgets would be cut for each student excluded; secondly, a bureaucratic burden was imposed, so that any permanent exclusion would involve a lengthy and labyrinthine process of consultations, meetings and discussions – not to mention a forest of paperwork. Governors had to be worked around, and OFSTED were instructed to take a negative view of any school with just a few permanent exclusions each year.

During the academic year 2006-2007, these restraints became particularly telling: within that one year, the number of exclusions fell by 3%, while the number of successful appeals for excluded students rose by 9%. It is rarely worth the hardship for a Senior Management Team to exclude a child, and it is certainly not worth the loss of money. What matters is not how well the school is actually functioning: it is what is on the surface which counts.

It is perhaps obvious that I am very much *for* exclusion. This is because I have seen how beneficial it can be for a school, and how detrimental its absence can likewise be. If a student is preventing others from learning, that student *must* be removed from the lesson. And, if such a sanction does not have an impact, if said student continues to disrupt the learning of others in the next lesson, then exclusion policies *must* be implemented.

For it is the teacher – alone, in a cheap suit – who must stand up and endure this behaviour, must deal with the consequences of this Exclusion Fear, while the David Blunketts and Ed Balls and Michael Goves – in concert, in Armani or Timothy Everest – sit back and enjoy the ever-decreasing statistics placed before them.

THE PEAK DISTRICT

EMMA RANG AS I was halfway down a bottle of £4.99 cabernet sauvignon.

'How was Turnbull?'

'Please don't send me there *ever* again.'

A dry laugh. 'That's a shame. They asked for you back. Shall I tell them you're already booked?'

'Tell them whatever you want. Tell them I took Caroline's advice.'

'Eh?'

'Tell them I went back down south.'

I was starting to feel a little better. I was glad I would never have to work at Turnbull again, but was also pleased that it was the end of the month. A new city beckoned.

'Any plans for the weekend?' Emma asked.

'Yes, I've decided...' I was interrupted before I could finish.

'I'm *dreading* it,' Emma announced.

'Really? Why?'

'I quit smoking on Monday. And I've been doing really well. Haven't had one fag. But I know that as soon as I go out tonight and have a drink I'll want one.'

'Why don't you just stay in this weekend?'

Emma snorted. 'Out of the question. I know for a fact that the cast of *Hollyoaks* are in town tonight, and I'm determined to get into Matt Littler's pants. So I'm just going to have to get through it, I guess. At least the smoking ban will help. But listen, Charlie, something's come up that you might be interested in.'

'Well, about that, Emma… the thing is, I've decided that I'm going to move again this weekend.'

'That's exactly what I thought. Don't think I haven't noticed that at the end of every month you piss off somewhere new. My colleagues have started wondering why you can't sit still – Ted thought you might be an undercover journalist or something!' She laughed cynically. I tried to do the same. 'There's a position just come up that's perfect for you. It's not too far from where you are now, over in the Peak District, tutoring a Year 11 boy who's been permanently excluded. It's for one month, up to the start of the Christmas holidays. After that he's starting at a PRU in Sheffield. What do you think?'

Wouldn't that be cheating? I thought. The Peak District is not one of the most challenging areas in England. In fact, it is one of the most comfortable. Difficult schools, as a rule, tend to be found lodged deep in inner-cities. Teaching in a place like the Peak District – a National Park, lots of tiny communities, an area of outstanding beauty – would be the antithesis of what I had set out to do. Yet I could not resist the opportunity. I had just spent three months in urban grime, three long months amidst the graffiti and tower-blocks and subways of Nottingham, Manchester and Birmingham. The Peak District would be a little holiday from it all, a chance to get back to the country, to exchange city chaos for hills and village pubs. It was either that, or I stuck to my plan and spent December in Leicester.

'I'll take it,' I said.

I drove up the next day, leaving my lay-by for good, relieved to put it behind me as I forged north and entered the Peaks. I took a long and circuitous route up through the park, along thin and twisting roads flanked by ageing drystone walls, their tops covered in a fresh, white lichen like a year-long snow cap. It is actually two discrete landscapes:

the Dark Peak in the north, a wilderness of high moors and crags where the cold is exquisite, nipping fingers and ends of noses, piercing and numbing; and the White Peak in the south, a gentle menagerie of undulating hills and rolling fields, one gigantic farmyard, spliced with drystone walls and fuzzy-felt sheep.

I finally arrived in my new old village and slept peacefully there through the weekend's nights. During the two remaining days before I was to start work, I walked the unhurried streets, dipping into shops here and there, admiring the minimalism of their advertising. 'We Sell Beer' boasted one off-licence, while a locally-owned supermarket sign said simply, 'Stop Here for Most Things'. This was a return to the country, a tiny mecca of fields, cottages and early closing-hours which, until I arrived, I had not realised how much I had missed.

I went to bed early on Sunday night, partly because of the new job the next morning, partly to avoid the ever-increasing cold. I found myself a gravelled exit off a country lane which seemed to lead to nowhere, just far enough from the village to ensure that no students would pass me on their way to school but close enough to allow me to lie in until eight in the morning – after Birmingham, a luxury. I caught a few moments of light before the night set in, and stepped outside to examine my new surroundings. My outdoor home was a sheltered crevice of rising fields, grazing cows and dry-stone walls. As the fingernail moon began to flash up a clear, unpolluted sky, I dived inside the van, and heated the kettle. I fell asleep that night happy, and dreaming.

* * * * *

Anstee Tuition is something of an oddity: an LEA-funded peripatetic unit comprising five teachers and one Head. Its staff do most of their work in the headquarters, which are lodged in the two airy rooms of a small village building, but they also work one-on-one with students in their homes or at other small institutions. In this, Anstee is a product of its environment. Given the landscape of the Peaks, it is difficult for students excluded from schools in the area to be able to journey to their nearest PRU – often 30 or 40 miles away over the hills and along winding B-roads and lanes. Hence, the LEA set up Anstee to offer a part-time solution until something more permanent can be found. The average pupil spends a month or two with the group before moving on elsewhere: sometimes to a PRU, but usually to another school.

Quite often, if their student quota outnumbers the staff, a supply teacher is brought in to help out. This time, an English specialist was needed, and I got the call. The student I was to work with was a Year 11 boy called Stuart. He came from the village, and had been excluded from the local school for drug dealing. After Christmas, he was due to move in with his mother in Sheffield, where he could attend a nearby PRU. Until then, Anstee would take him.

Stuart had discovered drugs at an early age. It is a sad fact that there are many children just like him throughout Britain's schools, who find themselves quickly and deeply habituated to various substances and unable to keep their addictions separate from their school lives. Stuart had developed a penchant for marijuana in Year 8, and by the end of Year 9 he had realised that he could sell the stuff as well as smoke it. He began making a tidy profit by selling dope to his schoolfriends, often during school hours, often on the school grounds. At the beginning of Year 11, his operation was unmasked, and he was permanently excluded. It didn't really bother him – his attendance throughout Year 10 had been less than 40% anyway, and he was making enough money, he felt, to forget about education – but he did confide in his social worker that he would have liked to get his GCSEs in the core subjects: maths, science and English.

Stuart was a bright lad, and he had done well in maths and science. But his poor attendance meant he had fallen behind on his English coursework (today, the two English GCSEs involve a coursework folder of five written pieces and three spoken assessments, as well as exams). Hence, it was decided that, while he was with Anstee, his time would be devoted to catching up on his English coursework folder.

I arrived at the Tuition Centre on Monday morning at nine o'clock, the beginning of the staff's day. That morning – a rarity, since it was common for one or two of them to be out on home-visits – all the staff were in.

They were five middle-aged, kindly and patient women, as was their Head. I was steered into a chair at the meeting table while the ladies fussed about me, plied me with sugary tea and digestive biscuits, and made me feel like I was back at my grandma's. The six students were due in at 9.30am (though most often arrived closer to 10am), so I had plenty of time to make my introductions and enjoy the welcome. I had expected a briefing on Stuart and what I was to teach him, but instead found myself embroiled in what Joanne, the maths specialist, termed 'a lovely chat'. Revealing I was from Cornwall set off a series of holiday reminiscences, and it was soon established that all of them had, at one point in their lives, been to Looe. I lied that I knew it well.

The students began to arrive, and the staff one by one withdrew from the table to begin lessons. I was left alone with Susan, the Head.

'Right, Charlie,' she said. 'I suppose we should get you briefed, shouldn't we? I'll just get us a quick cup of tea before we start.'

She went to boil the kettle and I poked my head around the door leading to the next room. Three students had arrived – two boys and one girl, each 15 or 16 – and were sitting around tables with their elected adults, working intermittently on various equations, spellings or historical facts. Every now and then, one would rise up to make a glass of orange squash, or put some bread in the toaster. It was an atmosphere far removed from a mainstream school, and I found myself absorbed. My odd rapture was shattered when a steaming brew appeared a few inches from my face.

'Tea,' Susan said. 'I forgot to ask if you wanted sugar, so I put three in, just in case.'

We walked into her office, and I was told all about Stuart, the reason for his exclusion and what I was expected to teach him. Stuart had started with Anstee at the beginning of the previous week, and had already continued his reputation by turning up on only two of the five days.

'He's a lovely lad,' Susan told me. 'Very quiet, but lovely. He probably won't say much to you when you meet him, but don't take it personally. After all, he'll probably be... you know...'

'No?'

'On the *wacky-baccy*.'

She was right. Stuart finally arrived at 11 o'clock, so baked that even his pupils looked bloodshot. He stumbled into the main room, tripping over his own feet and bashing his knee against a nearby table. Looking accusingly at the table, he noticed Joanne's half-drunk cup of tea and picked it up. 'I see you've had a coffee morning,' he intoned, seriously. 'Where were my invite?' Then he let out a falsetto laugh which was so strong it bounced him off two walls, before stumbling back out of the door, shrieking. We didn't see him again for several days.

At least Stuart's absence gave me the opportunity to prepare a full pack of resources and lesson plans which would see us through as many of his pieces of coursework as our time together would allow. I read through the scant selection of work he had brought from his old school, using it to gauge his level. I scoured the internet for titles and worksheets which might interest him. I devised short, additional activities related to the essays in case his mind wandered and he needed something to bring him back on-task. All of which, when he returned on Thursday morning, turned out to be useless.

He slunk into the building, baseball cap low over his eyes and the collar of his tracksuit top pulled up around the rest of his face. He fell into a chair without saying a word to anyone and sat there, sighing with apparent boredom.

'Morning, Stuart,' I said, sitting down next to him. 'My name's Charlie. I'm going to be going through some English coursework with you before you head off to Sheffield.'

He nodded his head so slightly I barely noticed. 'All right,' he mumbled.

'I've been looking through your coursework folder so far. I read your Media piece about *The Matrix*. I really liked it. It's obvious you're good at English.'

I paused, but he did not respond.

'I thought we might start with the Original Writing assessment. It's a pretty easy one and might be a good place for us to begin. What do you reckon?'

Stuart looked at me, blinked, and then looked back at the table. 'I don't feel like doing any work today,' he grunted.

'Why's that?' I asked, trying to sound friendly and interested. For our first day together, it didn't much matter if he did no work, but it was important that I got him talking and established some kind of bond.

'Just don't feel like it,' he muttered, shrugging his shoulders nonchalantly.

'Fair enough,' I said. 'Anything you'd rather do?'

'Go home,' he said.

'How come you came in, then?'

'I was bored at home.'

'Well, why don't we try something different? It's not part of the coursework, but it's a good way to do some creative writing if you're stuck for ideas.'

He looked up at me. 'Go on,' he nodded.

I pulled two sheets of paper before us. 'What you do is write your first name vertically down the margin. Then you write down the first words you can think of which start with those letters. It's called free writing. Here, I'll do it first.'

I demonstrated, writing *CHARLIE* down the page and then adding in:

> *C – CREAM*
> *H – HEART*
> *A – ALSO*

'Oh yeah, I get it,' Stuart said before I could finish, scrawling his name on to the page and then chewing the tip of his pen thoughtfully. He considered for a moment, and then leant forward to scribble next to the first letter: *SPLIFF*. He chuckled, 'That's me!' and then threw the pen down. He stood up and began walking out.

I walked after him.

'Where are you going?' I asked as we entered the corridor.

'Off,' he said over his shoulder. 'Can't be bothered today.' Walking out of the front door, he took a rolled-up cigarette from his pocket and sparked it up. 'Bye,' he said, and stepped out on to the road. He did not come back in for the rest of the week.

'But can he just do that?' I asked Susan later over another cup of tea.

'Officially, no. All our students have to be in here five days a week, six hours a day. But, unfortunately, we don't have the sanctions in place to ensure that anything happens to them for not being here. The best you can do is just make the most of it when he turns up.'

'But that's ridiculous!' I said. 'Can't we phone his parents?'

'We've tried. His dad has less control over him than we do.'

'Well, how about we get him to make up the time he's lost with detentions or extra time at the end of the day?'

Susan chuckled. 'Oh, Charlie,' she said. 'How on earth do you propose we do that? We can't even keep him here when he's *supposed* to be, let alone when he isn't.'

I struggled for a comeback. Susan was right, of course – there was nothing we could do. But I could not help feeling frustrated, not so much with Stuart, but with the very system which engendered this hopelessness, and which effectively allowed an intelligent young man to throw away his chances of a good education.

'I just feel a bit bad about it,' I said. 'I've been here nearly a week, I'm being paid to teach Stuart, and yet I've hardly done anything.'

'Oh, that's not true,' Susan cooed. 'You've put together that lovely scheme of work which we can use after you leave. And you're extremely proficient with a kettle!' She was only half-joking.

* * * * *

I spent that Saturday and Sunday on the roads of the Peak District, loving the feeling of travelling through my country. Roads are savage, impersonal things, I know, but they still have that lustre Kerouac once discovered upon them, if only you look closely enough. Tarmac may well be mind-numbing, but I still feel a thrill every time I coast along a country road in bright sunshine, or slip into the glaring circus of a night-time motorway. While the rambler might be afforded the slow beauty of a hill and river conquered, in the same time a driver can skirt through scenery whose magnificent changes never cease to exhaust.

My favourite road was Snake Pass: a long climb which rises and rises up from the eastern border of Manchester into the Dark Peak. The road escalates at a giddy rate, rounding a curve at the top to present a view of water and hills, backed by the indomitable and smoggy Manchester skyline. At its summit, Snake Pass is a barren wilderness: bleak and cold in colour and climate. It is an icy and treacherous place, often augmented by a pale sky and weak sun. Up here, one can feel the altitude in the bones. Instinct kicks in, warning you to leave, to search for lower ground. This is no place for man, nor for blood.

The road follows the instinct, heeds the innate call, and plunges back down from this shivering, windswept desolation into a thick pine forest which grows to a line ruler-straight. Shelter is immediate, and, at certain times of the morning, life presents itself again in the form of rabbits and badgers. The birds in these trees are smaller and more nervous, familiar, not the muscular and predatory beasts with wingspans the size of a child which circle the deadzone above. The water which rests in stagnant pools is calmer down here, a place of respite for the gushing streams which sprint from their sources. The hinterland is gone, and with it the adrenalin one feels from just standing in such an alien place. The Dark Peak slowly drifts into the White Peak: roads pop up like veins through a wrist; hills flatten and nurture small hamlets; tranquillity prevails.

On the way back, I stopped in a tiny village. Here, in the village's church, there is a permanent second-hand book sale, with everything priced at 50p and an honesty box for payment. I browsed through the well-thumbed copies, accompanied only by a middle-aged lady who told me she came here every week to see what treasures she could find. I noticed she picked up a Martin Amis and a Louis de Bernières, and then put a pound coin in the box before quietly slipping out, as if not to disturb me. I stumbled upon an early edition guidebook of England, and snapped it up for half a pound.

Monday came around again, and I was back at work.

For the first three days, Stuart turned up only for fleeting five-minute visits: sometimes, to tax a cigarette off one of the other students; once, to eat an obscurely large pizza he had bought from a takeaway down the road. On Tuesday, his appearance was so quick that we only noticed him as he disappeared out the door. Susan explained that he had probably come in to sell some weed to one of the girl pupils: he was rumoured to do this regularly, but although the staff were as vigilant as they could be, they had never managed to catch him in the act. If they had, the police would have been called instantly.

On Thursday, he arrived towards the end of the day and plonked himself down in a seat. He had the same air of indifference he had affected a week before, but I sat down next to him anyway.

'How's it going, Stuart? I barely get to see you each day.'

He looked up at me and blinked. 'Been busy,' he mumbled.

'I wish I could say the same,' I replied.

'I thought teachers were supposed to always be busy,' Stuart said.

I took this as a good sign, it was the longest sentence he had uttered in my direction for the best part of two weeks. 'We're only busy when we've got students to teach.'

'Oh yeah,' he muttered. 'You're *my* teacher, aren't you?'

'I am. I'm here to get you through your English coursework folder. If you'll give me the chance.'

He looked up at me and, for the first time, rather than blinking, he grinned. 'Here. Have a sweet.' He produced a crumpled bag of Haribo from his pocket and took out a warm fried egg. Hoping this might be an opening, I took it and popped it in my mouth. Susan suddenly appeared.

'*Stuart!*' she shouted. 'I've told you before. You are *not* allowed to eat sweets on these premises!'

He feigned a look of remorse, enough to send Susan away. Once she had gone, his sorrowful countenance changed to a wide grin. He giggled, and I realised that I had stopped chewing, and that he had made me complicit.

'I'll catch you tomorrow, Charlie,' he whispered, and then legged it out the back door. It may not have been much, but it was a start.

Stuart was first to arrive the next morning. I was sitting at the meeting table with the ladies (by this point, I had very much become one of them, and would sometimes catch myself uttering things like, 'Two sugars today, Joyce, or just one?', 'He should have been voted off *Strictly Come Dancing* weeks ago', or 'I love that sweater on you, Sally'), and felt a sense of pride that mine was the first student to arrive. I waved to one of the tables in the next room – Stuart seemed, for once, completely in command of his senses – and we sat down.

'Cup of tea?'

'Eh?'

'Sorry. Force of habit.'

'Nah, nah, it's all right. I'll have a hot chocolate.'

I made us our drinks and came to sit back down, producing the pack of work for Stuart to get started on. I had already gathered that he had not been keen to start on the essay of my choice, and so decided to give him some freedom in the matter. We scanned through each of the assessments he could begin.

'Oh, I don't know,' he said, stretching his arms out and then clasping his hands behind his head. 'Can't we do something that's not so boring?'

'All right,' I said, reasoning that any work done would be a start. 'What do you want to do?'

'I don't know.'

'Well, look at this one, the Original Writing piece. The great thing about it is, essentially, you can do it on any subject you want.'

'So?'

'So … what could you write about? What are you interested in?'

'Eh?' He looked up at me, and held his gaze. I knew that I finally had him.

'What are you interested in? If you could be doing anything right now, what would it be?'

He looked at me for a moment. Then he looked around to see if anyone was listening. 'I'd sing,' he whispered.

'You'd sing?'

'I'd sing.'

It was not the reply I had expected, and it took me a moment to formulate a response.

'What would you sing?'

'I *do* sing.'

'You *do* sing?'

'I sing.'

'When?'

He looked about him again, as if he were about to impart some grave secret. 'I'm an MC,' he finally said.

'Oh, so you rap.'

'Fuck off, you twatting muppet, I ain't no fucking rapper!' he shouted, loud enough for Susan to poke her head around the door.

I looked over at her and made a face which I hoped would signal I had everything under control.

'Sorry, Stuart,' I said. 'I'm probably a bit behind the times. What sort of stuff do you do?'

'*Don-keh*,' he said.

'Donkey?'

He laughed. 'Not bloody *donkey*, you lemon. *Don-keh*.'

I asked him to spell it for me: D-O-N-K-A.

'Never heard of it,' I said.

'You wouldn't,' he said, settling back into his chair with an air of authority. 'It's from the streets. It's raw.'

'What kind of music does it sound like?'

'It's like …' Here he paused and considered. 'It's like… it's like a cross between grime and clutch-dance.'

Though I was only 27, and I consider my taste in music fairly up to date, but this definition flummoxed me.

'*What?*'

'Here. I'll show you,' he said, taking his phone from his pocket and pressing some keys. A fast-paced bass drum overscored by syncopated synth-chords scratched out of the phone's tinny speakers, while a cockney voice shouted semi-rhyming epithets to pussies, breast-jobs and cars over the top of it all.

'That's Donka?' I asked.

'That's Donka,' he nodded. 'That's what I sing.'

I hated Donka from the first second of my introduction to it, but for Stuart it was a passion. We chatted for the next hour about his love, and he admitted that he often improvised performances at the Open Mike night in the nearby town's only night-club, and had already established himself at one of Sheffield's clubs as the youngest person ever to win their weekly MC competition.

Stuart was chatting away like I had never seen before, lovingly detailing the ins and outs of his chosen scene. I took the opportunity, and challenged him to write a song. He grabbed the pen I presented with relish and bent his head down to score out some new lyrics. I left him for half an hour to pursue his work, and when he was finished he came and found me, tugging on my jumper and waving the piece of paper before me. I chuckled as I read through the 'song'. One couplet stood out so vividly that I recorded it that night in my daily journal:

'You're nothing, mate, but I'm famous,
Your mum looks like Frank from Shameless.'

'All right, then, Stuart,' I said. 'How about some coursework?'

'Depends what it is.'

'An account of the night you won the MC competition. Write about it.'

He grinned. 'Easy,' he said, sitting back down at the table, and snapping up his pen. He wrote uninterrupted until lunch time and finished his Original Writing coursework that Friday afternoon, re-drafting his first essay on the computer by the end of the day. It was not a stunning piece of literature, but neither was it altogether bad, and I thought I saw a sense of pride flash across his face when I read through it at the end of the day and marked it with a solid C grade. I felt proud, too. I was here to help Stuart write and finish his GCSE coursework folder, and we had just completed his first piece.

I began my weekend happy, driving all about the Peaks. By now, the end of the year was only a few weeks away, and a thick frost had settled on the national park and set hard. The short days were bright and blue, the nights star-filled and open, but, always, the land remained a thin white. I stopped in pretty towns such as Buxton or Castleton, juxtaposing them with the no-man's lands of the Dark Peak. I ventured out to the park's borders at Chatsworth or Matlock, overtaken by convoys of bikers for whom it was never too icy to ride. I climbed ethereal rocky outcroppings at Hathersage Booths and watched steam trains pump along ancient tracks. I took pints in bustling and cosy pubs, and then sipped whiskey under the duvet in my van upon pitch-black lanes. I walked to the top of hills to see no sign of civilisation for miles around, and then washed my face in a dozen streams so cold I gasped.

Those winter peaks brought the promise of Christmas and a much-needed holiday in the company of those I love, and any festering negativity left over from Birmingham was rinsed from me, shouted out and then lost inside the echoes of the land's undulating acoustics. I breathed the Peaks in like a virus, exulting in the troughs carved by the River Wye and its numerous tributaries, riding the rollercoaster roads to be posited in strange and beautiful lost-lands.

* * * * *

I returned to the village in good spirits to find, on Monday morning, Stuart present and in much the same mood. 'Here, Charlie, look at this,' he said as he entered, revealing a large rip in the side of his coat. 'I'm getting rips in all me clothes these days.'

'It's because you're a growing lad, Stuart,' I said, arranging the work for the next essay on a table. 'You're like the Incredible Hulk.'

He turned on me with a piercing glare and whispered, 'What the fuck did you just call me?'

'Er … the Incredible Hulk?'

'And what,' he grimaced, 'the bastard is that?'

'You know,' I said. 'The Incredible Hulk. Big green bloke. Rips his clothes and grows enormous when he's angry. From the comics.'

He was nonplussed, but the explanation seemed to be enough. 'Never heard of him,' he said, and then started busily fingering the rip in his coat again.

For the next three days, Stuart worked hard on his Shakespeare essay, gaining another credible C grade. On Thursday, I was worried he had had enough when he did not arrive on time in the morning. At half past eleven, he finally turned up.

'Where have you been?' I asked.

'Police station,' he said, throwing himself into a chair.

'What did you do this time?'

'Nothing,' he said, with a grin. 'I was the victim. I got mugged by this bloke I sort of know. He nicked me wallet and I've just been reporting him at the station.'

He was pleased with himself, and I could see why. Stuart had been inside police stations many times, but never before in this role. After taking 20 minutes to inform all the students and staff of his morning adventure, he sat down next to me, and we read through Act 1 Scene 5 of *Romeo and Juliet* – on the condition that I read Juliet's lines.

Our final week and a half passed and, by the end of it, Stuart had completed most of his coursework folder. It was up to his next teachers to finish it off, and then begin preparing him for his exams. I have no doubt that – as long as he turned up – Stuart will have passed. He did not come in on the last day of term, and I was sorry, because I had bought him a Christmas card. But I did have my farewell of sorts.

I saw him the evening before as I walked through the village to buy dinner. A police car raced past and, following it with my gaze, I saw, not far from me, Stuart and two of his friends hollering at it as it shot past.

'Fucking pigs!'

'Oy, oyyyyy!'

'*Wankaaaaahhhhh*!'

They began swaggering towards me, three towering teenage boys who I would have found intimidating had I not known that Stuart was amongst them. As they drew close, one of them looked over at me in my suit. 'Hellooo,' he intoned in a mocking accent.

I laughed at him, then nodded over at Stuart. 'Hi, Stuart,' I said.

Stuart turned and recognised me, guilt distinguishable on his face. 'Oh. All right, Charlie?' he said, turning bashful and chewing on a fingernail.

'Causing trouble?' I asked.

I heard his friend, the one who first spoke to me, whisper, 'Who the fuck...' but Stuart silenced him with a look. He turned back to me. 'Nah,' he said.

I grinned and carried on walking. That was the last time I saw him. It seemed a fitting final meeting – an acknowledgement of the eventual success we had forged together. Stuart was neither malicious nor unintelligent, but was disaffected with education to the point of indifference, and had been for some time. I could see why he had not made it through the mainstream system. Life outside of school was too enjoyable to miss – all his friends were older, he was able to party uninterrupted, he was even employed. There was no chance any general school could have enticed him away from that, sadly; there was nothing they could have offered which would have encouraged him to return to the fold.

I knew students like Stuart from my own experience. As part of a class of 30, they were impossible. Desperate to be anywhere else, they would cause havoc just for something to do. Squeezing work from them was confounding, a perpetual frustration, and days of my time had been lost trying to accommodate them. In the average classroom, Stuart would have been rude, aggressive, obstinate, the winner of a reputation he should not have had but did not care about. Yet, within the confines of our little one-on-one environment within Anstee Tuition, I watched him thrive, producing three creditable pieces of GCSE coursework in the time it takes most classes to emit one.

The reason for his success was uncomplicated. With no other students around us to expend our energies on, I was able to interact with Stuart at exactly the right level necessary for his learning. His previous teachers had not done so because, through no fault of their own, they did not have the same opportunities I was given. Stick Stuart, or any child like Stuart, into a class of 30, and you will lose him. It is a humble truth, yet one which goes ignored in almost every mainstream school in England today.

The average class in a current English state secondary school consists of 30 pupils and one teacher, a ratio considered unworkable in most developed countries. Not every student can be taught one-on-one, but it is fundamentally necessary for class sizes to be reduced if teachers are ever going to be able to interact to the appropriate level with each student, and if each student is ever going to get the education they deserve.

Why is this not happening? Why are teachers constantly finding themselves lost in a melee of packed classes, instead of the ten-pupils-to-one-teacher ratio found in the independent sector? Well, in order to come anywhere close to that in the state sector, over 100,000 new teachers would have to be introduced to the system in the space of one year – an increase which even the idealists laugh at. But this is no reason to abandon the argument. Perhaps we will never hit such low numbers as those in independent schools (and perhaps we never should – for me, a class of ten is too small: to learn effectively, pupils must be able to interact with their teacher, but they must also have sufficient peers to interact with), but this does not mean that we cannot attempt to reduce our class sizes to some extent.

The problem is that the notion of class size carries no real weight in modern educational debates. There are more pressing matters to be dealt with first: student behaviour, attendance, targets and, of course, money. Any appeal to class size is brushed under the carpet – not by teachers, but by the authorities – and is done so for a very simple reason.

With the steady decline in the UK's birth-rate between 1965 and 1976, England's student population fell considerably throughout the 1980s – for example, in 1980 there were 30% fewer pupils in primary schools than there had been in 1970. Instead of valuing the effect this could have on national class sizes, as I have said Margaret Thatcher's government took the opportunity to save money, and got rid of 50,000 teachers. During this time, class sizes were held at a constant, despite the fact that, during the same time, every other Western country and a substantial number of Far Eastern countries succeeded in improving their average class sizes.

Such a course of action is not a 20th century relic. Very recently, it was revealed that the government, faced with another reduction in the pupil demographic, is continuing to act in the same way. During the academic year 2007-2008, 792,000 spare pupil places were 'discovered' throughout the country. Responding to this stroke of good luck, the government and its local authorities have preferred not to rejoice in the falling class sizes the situation would inevitably entail, but instead have begun drawing up plans on which schools can legitimately be closed.

The issue of class size is different from that of exclusion in that not only is it uncontroversial, it is barely even considered. Though it is an incontrovertible fact that students learn more effectively within a class of 20 than a class of 30 or more, the latter size has been kept at a constant for the last 30 years. Spurning the examples of other developed countries across the globe, the British government has refused to do anything about the issue, choosing instead to close schools, cut back funding, and force teachers into taking on classes far too large to manage. In consequence, the teachers are responding in kind. For this is the sad truth behind it all – it is not just England's schools which are disappearing, England's teachers are, too.

SHEFFIELD

JANUARY CAME, AND I felt refreshed from the Christmas break, ready to get back into my journey.

I had been offered a room for the month in the house of a friend of a friend in Sheffield, and was pleased to be escaping the cold which had so dominated the last two months of my life. I quickly found another reason to be grateful. After the impermeable frost and blue skies of December, January turned into a month of solid, unforgiving rain. Driving up to Yorkshire from the south west where I had spent the last fortnight, I saw England as it often is: underwater. The fields stretching out from the motorway embankments were rippling, dirty lagoons which forced sheep to huddle in corners or climb walls, and each river I crossed was bursting and spilling. Even my van was doing its bit to blend into the environment, springing hidden leaks in the ceiling so that, by night, I had to lash a tarpaulin over the roof and, by day, place numerous saucepans in various spots on the floor. I often came out of school to find the pans had overflowed hours before, spilling rainwater into the soaked carpet which had started giving off a nauseating aroma. Mould grew on the curtains. In times of real downpour, the driver's footwell turned into a rock pool, and I had to drive to work in wellies. I was glad I did not have to sleep in the van.

My landlady, though not a student herself, lived in the student area of Sheffield. I rented the attic room of her house; it was large but cosy, and it was wonderful to be able to stand up straight in my own bedroom, and not to have to brave the cold and the wind and the rain every time I needed a piss. The view from the window was of the city's ski village, and the whole thing gave me the giddy feeling of staying in a resort. That was soon knocked out of me. Orwell was scathing about Sheffield in *The Road to Wigan Pier*, and while he experienced it during the terrible 1930s, when the once-thriving steel industry was in serious decline and the city was devastated by poverty and unemployment, it is not much more pleasant now.

The steel industry is long gone, replaced – we are told – by a modern and sparkling new Sheffield, a benefactor of the Great Northern City Regeneration Scheme, on a par with Manchester and Leeds. Sadly, I did not find this to be the case at all.

Unlike much of the rest of Yorkshire, Sheffield has not aged well. Effort has been made in the city centre, where poems by Roger McGough, Andrew Motion and Jarvis Cocker adorn the walls of buildings in gigantic letters, and ambitious water features spring up everywhere. The Peace Gardens – a kind of miniature Eden Project – are lovely. But despite all the strange industrial-looking works of public art and sculpture dotted about, and the portentous squares and pedestrianised thoroughfares, Sheffield is now a generic mediocrity projecting itself through the medium of shopping; all the town planners have really done is to turn it into a large and characterless retail park.

At the forefront is the huge Meadowhall Shopping Centre underneath the M1 at Junction 34. This complex would be daunting if it were not overwhelmed by the decaying industrialism which surrounds it: miles of cranes and rubbish tips, industrial units and 'modern warehousing facilities', dying factories and dirty workshops and the two 250-foot-high Tinsley cooling towers. After living and working in the city, the association remains. This *is* Sheffield. This is what now defines the city: some shops, a ring of industry, and very little else. I tried to like it, looked for its hidden beauties, but I could not find them.

At least there was plenty of work in Sheffield. Emma called me on my first morning.

'Charlie!'

'Emma!'

'You've got a choice for today. Murray College covering Science, or the same pay for being an LSA to a single boy at Stockton School.'

'Why is the LSA role the same pay?'

'He's an interesting lad. Philip Pugsley. The LSAs at Stockton refuse to work with him, and I've had a client doing it for a month until he dropped out yesterday.'

'Why?'

'Pugsley lit up in a lesson.'

'Is that all?'

'He lit up a spliff.'

'I see. I'll take Pugsley.'

'You got a Sat Nav yet?'

'Of course not.'

'Then get your A-Z out, you bloody Luddite.'

Philip Pugsley – an apt name for such a big-faced boy – was waiting at reception for me. One of the Assistant Headteachers was there, too, but it was Philip who marched towards me when I arrived, held out his hand, and said: 'Pleased to meet you, Mr Carroll.'

I liked him instantly.

He had just turned 16 and wanted to drop out of school, but his tutor, who he was close to, had encouraged him to at least attempt his GCSE exams.

'What've they said about me?' Philip asked as we walked through the school towards his first lesson.

'I've only just got here,' I said. 'Maybe the Assistant Head would have said something, but you got in there first.'

Philip laughed. He seemed to like that.

'Okay, Mr C,' he said. 'Don't worry. You're with me. I'm safe, I am.'

Safe he was. I spent the whole day with Philip and, unlike other students who do whatever they can to evade their school's adult presence, Philip seemed to take mine as some sort of mark of authority, and I couldn't help feeling that I was being treated at best like his security staff, and at worst like a member of his entourage. It was rare I ever spoke to another teacher, for Philip always made sure I was nearby, but I soon understood by his actions alone – actions which he never made any pretence to hide from me – that he was the school's dealer. I wondered why he was still at Stockton, why he had not been permanently excluded like Stuart had been. Perhaps it was his charisma, which he oozed with the confidence of a celebrity; more likely, it was Exclusion Fear.

In his English lesson, he showed me his first draft of an essay on *Much Ado About Nothing*. I underlined one sentence: 'Benedick looks up to Don Pedro because he has him on tick.'

'I don't get this bit,' I said.

'What?' Philip said, grinning at me. 'On tick?'

'Yes. I've never heard of it. What does it mean?'

He thought for a while, trying to conjure a way to explain this slang to a layman. 'On tick is like... it's like... like if you go to buy some weed, yeah, but you don't have any money, then the guy will give it to you on tick, and you'll, like, pay him later.'

On tick. Philip's means of expressing himself through the semantic field of narcotics became a theme for that day. After leaving him for two minutes in maths, I came back to find that he had written his email address out on thin lengths of torn paper and was distributing them out to the class like cheap, homemade business cards; in ICT, every time I looked away he logged on to his email account. When I confronted him about it, he responded, 'Just checking my appointments, Mr C.'

Finally, at the end of the day, we had RE. There were 34 in the class, and the teacher was evidently exasperated with the lot of them, and so set them two pages to work from out of a textbook, and let them get on with it. Leaving Philip, I went to talk to her for a while.

'I've taught this group since the beginning of last year,' she said. 'I've really tried with them, but as they've got older they've lost interest more and more. The problem is, they didn't even choose this. RE is a mandatory subject here, and they have to do it whether they like it or not. I hate to admit it, but I've given up with them. Don't get me wrong, I love my subject, but when they get to this age I only want to teach them if they choose it. What's your specialism?'

'English.'

'So you're the same. They have to do your subject, whether they like it or not.'

'True, but I think it's right English is a compulsory subject,' I replied. 'Whether they like it or not.'

'Oh, I agree, but RE shouldn't be. Just listen to them now. They're not talking about their work.'

We looked out over the large class, who continued their chatter oblivious to our supervision. I looked at Philip's group, a cluster of nine boys who had positioned their chairs into a rough circle. Philip was talking, and the rest were leaning towards him, rapt.

'... so Kev fucking turns up with a knife after that... I just grabbed my bottle and threw it at him...'

'See?' the RE teacher said to me. 'How am I supposed to compete with that?'

I tuned back into Philip's narrative.

'He fucked off... I'd had 15 beers... he knew I was fucking out of it... I was fucked, mate.'

Philip evidently expected silence to commemorate his feat, and such silence was appreciated by all but one, the challenger to Philip's triumph.

'I can down 20 bottles of WKD!' the imposter unexpectedly squealed.

There was a moment of quiet, and then all-embracing laughter. 'You drink W... K... *D*?' Philip chortled. 'You fucking twat!'

The rest joined him in the deprecating merriment, and then Philip began to speak in whispers, which the others reciprocated. I could make out no more of their conversation.

At the end of the lesson, the last of the day, Philip came up to me and held out his hand. 'You back tomorrow, Mr C?'

'Unfortunately not, Philip. I'm booked at another school.'

He dropped his hand as I was about to shake it, and without another word walked away.

* * * * *

Following Stockton, I spent the rest of the month teaching at five different schools dotted about the area, and two further south in Chesterfield. There was one school in particular – Hocking Technology College – which always seemed to be short of staff. I worked there at least twice a week.

Hocking was a brand new school. It had state-of-the-art equipment and resources, clean classrooms and corridors, and the students' uniforms were impeccable. Yet the standard of behaviour there was atrocious. A large percentage of the students were downright nasty and spiteful people. They were vile to the staff and cruel to each other. Most of my classes seemed to be dominated by bullying boys and bitchy girls, who took verbal and sometimes physical swipes at each other with a vitriolic relish. When you work with children, even the most vicious, you can usually find something redeemable about them. I found this hard at Hocking.

There were Matthew and Ahmed, who would shout and holler from the back of the classroom at any instruction I gave as if they were at a football-match and I was the biased referee. I felt especially unsympathetic towards Matthew, a short and self-righteous boy who would fling his arms into the air and squeal '*I didn't do anything!*' and '*Are you stupid?*' in a voice so high-pitched and screechy it made me shudder.

There was Georgia, who would refuse to turn around and face me when I spoke to her. When I decided enough was enough and sent her out, she protested, 'Sir! It wasn't my fault! They said that if I turned around I was a lesbian!'

There was Jhan, who spent an entire ICT lesson testing all the permutations of an internet porn search until he found one naughty picture which had escaped the school's filter: an extreme close-up of a large pair of breasts. Hitting the full-screen key, he shouted over to the quiet and bullied Sameera, 'Hey, Sameera! Bet you wish you had these, ya flat bitch!'

There was the register I passed around one lesson for the students to write their names on, and which came back with the word 'darky' scrawled next to Mohammed's name.

One day, a 16-year-old came up to me at the end of a lesson to sign the daily report which monitored his behaviour. He had done no work throughout the lesson, and I had written as such.

He looked at my comment, said, 'You're a fucking prick, you are,' and strode out.

The LSA supporting me laughed as the door slammed shut.

'We get that a lot here,' he said. 'You'll get used to it.'

Another day I was asked to cover a Drama lesson. It was disastrous. Halfway through, I took a moment to stand back and watch what was going on. Children were throwing bags at each other, giving piggy-backs and running around the studio. There was fighting, there was screaming. It was chaos. I had no control, and I was well aware of it. Each time I made a suggestion or request it would instantly be challenged by a fired-up and indignant child. This constant need for confrontation was wearying. I lost count of the number of times a teenager shouted – no, *screamed* – in my face. By the end of the lesson, when it was time for them to show their performances to each other, I told them they would not. I told them that I could not trust them to be quiet enough to watch each other, to allow others to be heard. I told them that I had never met a bunch of students who were so mean to each other, and I meant it. A girl who leant against a wall to the side raised her hand.

'What was that? Didn't hear you.'

The class burst into laughter, picked up their bags and left before the bell sounded. I drove home, prey to bouts of road rage along the way.

There were no moments of harrowing severity at Hocking, no individual instances which stood out with shocking clarity, but the persistence of this general low standard of behaviour made it by far the most challenging school I worked at in Sheffield.

When I first began planning this journey, and this book, I wanted to find out why so many teachers were leaving the profession, but I was adamant that I did not want to write a clichéd lament about the behaviour of teenagers in England today: 'When I was a kid, the summers were hotter, the music was better, and we knew how to behave.'

Bad behaviour has always been an issue for teachers – it is part of the job, no matter what school or year you teach in. Why else would PGCE courses devote whole units to the acquisition of management techniques and disciplinary tactics? Why else do heads of department spend so long observing how their NQTs pre-empt behavioural issues? Why else are the education sections of bookshops lined with titles like *Behaviour in the Classroom* or *Getting the Buggers to Behave*?

I remember appalling things happening during my own school-days, some of them perpetrated by me. Even my mother, a woman who devoted her working life to teaching, was a self-confessed 'troublemaker' at school.

But it is not something which can be ignored and, from my own experience, and from reading and researching, what strikes me is that it is not the *quantity* of poor behaviour which has led to the decline in teacher numbers but the *quality*. Teachers are now dealing with issues which cannot just be glossed over and laughed about later in the staff room; they are up against behaviour which has become personal, and meaningful. One particular problem stands out. Though 'cyber-bullying' only surfaced in recent years, it is prevalent in many of England's schools today, aimed at both pupils and teachers.

Using social networking websites, text messages, chat-rooms and emails, some youngsters are tormenting their peers, bombarding them with messages and threats which can be as psychologically dangerous as a fist-fight in the playground. You have probably read about this kind of thing in the papers. What is less well known, however, is the extent to which staff fall victim to cyber-bullying. YouTube is filled with videos of Sirs and Misses being publicly shouted down and besmirched. Bebo, Myspace and Facebook have a huge number of groups dedicated to the defamation of unwitting folk just trying to do their jobs. And Ratemyteacher is a website specifically set up to allow students to denigrate teachers, anonymously and often viciously, and leave the remarks in cyberspace forever.

It may sound relatively harmless, but cyber-bullying can actually be extremely vitriolic and hurtful, and extremely influential. Teaching union surveys suggest that around 17% of teachers have fallen victim, and there are many cases of people retiring early or suffering psychological harm. In Kent, an art teacher received sexually explicit comments from her pupils on a social networking site; she raised this at school during a lesson, and was dismayed to find that new, worse comments were added that evening. In Yorkshire, a science teacher received a tumult of threatening phone calls and voicemail messages and when she tried to address the problem at school, she began receiving phone calls for fake pizza deliveries which demanded her home address. Another teacher discovered a webpage dedicated to her on Bebo which was full of comments so disturbing she considered resigning. Finally, one particularly nasty case-study from a female secondary school teacher – taken from the NASUWT's magazine – is worth citing in full:

> A pupil got my mobile number and... I received 68 malicious phone calls over a period of three weeks threatening to rape me and rape and kill my mother. Initially, senior staff told me to ignore the calls as they were 'just kids'. A male police officer told me there was a 'lesson to be learned here: don't bring your phone to school'. After receiving six calls in 30 minutes one day, I called the police and was finally interviewed by a female officer who put a trace on my phone and applied for my phone records, a process which takes up to ten weeks.
>
> I was told not to change my phone number and not to answer any anonymous calls until further notice. After receiving 16 calls one Saturday evening, I finally gave up and changed my number. The police have advised me they may not be able to prosecute those involved. I have remained in school throughout, despite feelings of severe anxiety and stress.

Bullying is found in all professions and all social-groups, but rarely do adults suffer it from children. What makes it worse is that no-one does anything about it. The quantity of teenage behaviour in the twenty-first century has not increased, but its severity assuredly has. This is what really grinds, what upsets and disorients and ultimately *hurts* the modern-day teacher: the quality of the behaviour, followed closely by the system's reluctance to act upon it. The above example says it all. When threats of rape and murder were issued to a teacher and her family, she was told only one thing: she should not have brought her phone into school.

WEST YORKSHIRE

I WENT TO VISIT GRANDMA in Manchester for the weekend, recuperating from Sheffield with adult conversation and Bacardi. I finally left on Tuesday – another grey, wet afternoon – re-packing the van and setting off for Bradford and Leeds. I had managed to fix the irritating little leak in the van roof – pretty important, given that I would be spending the next month on the road again.

Of all the lists I made during my research into the most challenging areas in the country, Bradford came high on most. Oddly – given that the two cities are so close together they are almost one – Leeds did not appear once. I drove towards Yorkshire with different impressions of each. Bradford I knew only from apocryphal, often disturbing, stories; Leeds I had visited once before, enjoying a drunken weekend in the company of a good friend who was a student of the city. I had already decided that, although I would spend as much of February as possible working in Bradford, I would live it in Leeds.

I found my way on to the M62, out of the limits of Manchester, leaving behind the decaying mills and factories which sit on the edge, and lifting up along the folds of that great wall which separates Manchester and Leeds: the Pennines. I have driven the M62 at all hours of the day and night, and have always been caught up in at least one traffic jam. Yet the M62 is one of our country's most beautiful stretches of motorway, a ribbon of tarmac rising to its summit – at 372 metres, it is the highest motorway point in England – and then falling back down to the urban sprawl in the east. At one point, the east and

131

west carriageways split around a small farmhouse and its chopped fields. The sheep here have grown used to the sound of high-speed motor vehicles, and graze nonchalantly; the men who work this land, men I have seen many times from a fleeting 60mph vantage point, get on with their work as if unconscious of the many thousands of eyes that watch them every day. Driving past this house, you can't help but wonder: amidst this rural scene of jagged hills, browning pastures and sloping lakes, can these men talk of anything other than the vast, multi-laned patch of concrete, cars and traffic cones which bisects and pollutes their birthright with tinny lights, Doppler sounds, and insidious fumes?

By the time I passed this farm, the sun had already set and night-time was spilling in. I saw the moorlands and lakes I passed only by the headlights which flashed off them, enjoyed Huddersfield only by the winking street-lights which bound together to form a menagerie of orange in a faraway Pennine dust-bowl. At Junction 27, I left this strange and beautiful motorway to join the M621, which would take me into the heart of Leeds. I drifted down a hillside, and the city opened up before me: a confluence of high-rise buildings, neon letterings, digital thermometers and lights, lights everywhere. Leeds is best entered by night. Like a Las Vegas oasis after Nevada blackness, it is an ethereal factory of pinpoints and flecked skybursting cuboids, a tantalising shimmer of appropriated electricity, a recreation of the same starlight it obscures. And, for the next month, it was to be my new home.

I found a likely lay-by and called Emma. She answered the phone in a state of breathless confusion. 'Yep… er, hello… who's this?'

'It's Charlie, Emma.'

'Charlie? I… er… Charlie?' I heard a male voice murmuring in the background. 'Shh,' she said. 'Oh, *Charlie*! Of course. Charlie.'

'Is everything all right?'

'Yes… I just… er…'

'Sorry – did I catch you at home?'

'No, no,' she said. 'It's fine. I'm still in the office. Just hang on a second.'

There was a barely audible exchange of words, followed by the sound of something moving. A desk, perhaps. Then a door opening and closing.

'Sorry about that, Charlie,' she said. 'You caught me at a delicate moment. What can I do for you?'

'I just wanted to let you know I've arrived in Leeds,' I said. 'I'll call back tomorrow morning, if you'd prefer.'

'Leeds!' she shouted down the phone. 'Yes! Of course you have! And I'm very glad about it. I've got the perfect place for you. Can you start tomorrow?'

I had wanted to take Wednesday off, to give me a chance to explore my new home. But I was reluctant to turn work down. 'Why?' I said. 'What kind of place is it?'

'Just the kind of place you like. *Exceptionally* challenging. Most of the supply teachers in the area refuse to work there. There's a post we've been trying to fill for the last month, but no one will do it.'

'Is it long term?'

'Ideally, yes. But I'm sure they'd be happy to take you for as long as you'll give. They're a bit desperate.'

'Thanks,' I said.

'Only problem is it isn't actually in Leeds. Or in Bradford. It's further out into West Yorkshire. Shouldn't be too bad a drive for you, though. Do you fancy it?'

'Why not?' I said, taking out a pen and paper to get the details.

'Fantastic.' She gave me the directions. 'You'll be teaching maths. The school's called Varka.'

* * * * *

I arrived early on the Wednesday morning after a miraculous lack of wrong turns, pulled the van into the empty staff car park, and stepped out. The school was an austere, 1920s redbrick building with separate (though no longer enforced) entrances for Boys and Girls, and the place reeked of the cane and old-fashioned rows of desks.

I was greeted at reception by Darren Fleming, a short, springy man who pumped my hand enthusiastically and welcomed me with what seemed a sigh of relief. He filled me in on the situation with the maths department as we walked to his office.

The situation with the maths department was that there *was* no maths department.

A month ago, at the end of the Christmas holidays, the seven members of the faculty had returned to begin their new term. Their 'department' – actually an old and weathered building stuck at the bottom of the sports field – was not the most enticing, but they were seasoned, stalwart and ready. Life was difficult at Varka, but it always had been – such was the nature of the estate the school tilted upon; most of the kids were doing fine and the teachers were finding ways of keeping quiet and under control those who were not.

But they were in for a shock that morning. As they had arrived at work, the Headteacher had announced that a nearby school had been closed 'for legal reasons', and that a third of its students were due to transfer to Varka that morning.

'Not an ideal situation as you can imagine,' said Darren, handing me a coffee.

There was little else for the seven maths teachers to do but accept this new challenge and get on with it.

The morning passed without serious incident, but things went awry during Period 4: the pre-lunch lesson. At 1pm – 20 minutes before the lunch break – two of the new girls ran out of one classroom and tore down through the block, smacking loudly on doors and barging into the classrooms. They were quickly joined by other pupils from the closed-down school, and within five minutes all of the students were out in the corridors. The block became a heaving throng of 14-year-olds. Some were swinging from the pipes which ringed the ceilings; others were play-fighting, though with full-blown punches and kicks; a group of girls were smoking; one lad was being beaten up by six others with a length of moulding torn from the walls; another was destroying a door.

The seven maths teachers tried to restore order, but the children, sensing safety in numbers, ignored them. Things came to a head when one of the adults was knocked to the floor by rushing children. Fearing for their safety, the teachers left.

One went to notify the Headteacher, and another called the police; members of the Senior Management Team hurried down to the maths block, but were also unable to restore order. At 1.20pm, the lunch bell went, and the students dispersed, flooding out on to the field and playgrounds. By the time the police arrived, the situation was over.

After the lunch break, the school closed early and both students and staff were sent home. The following day, the seven maths teachers were suspended indefinitely for 'gross misconduct', in that they had left nearly 200 students for an extended period of time without any adult supervision. Nothing at all happened to any of the students.

'After that,' said Darren, 'the Headteacher agreed to resign, and I was sent in to do his job.'

He was a 'Super Head', of the type brought in to turn round failing schools by LEAs once they have gone into Special Measures after an adverse OFSTED investigation. These are highly talented teachers and managers who are often able to name their own salaries. Darren was immensely successful – he had been known to bring a school out of Special Measures in the space of a single year – but this meant that his life was as peripatetic as mine. He had worked all over the country as acting Head, saving a number of schools and PRUs and Centres from extinction.

'I started three days after the incident,' he said. 'Since then, we've effected a number of positive changes. I think most of the teachers would say they're pretty happy with what we've done. My main failing is I still haven't managed to sort out the maths department. I want to be completely honest with you before you start.' I sipped my coffee. 'The school is still officially under investigation. None of the maths teachers have been allowed back yet, though two have formally handed in their resignation and from what I've heard I don't think the rest of them particularly want to return. Right now, the department is made up of supply teachers. Since that day, only two have stayed on for the whole month. We've been through 14 supply staff in that department alone. Most work for a day and then don't want to come back. Currently there are only five teachers – yourself included – working in the place of seven.'

He exhaled deeply and sat back, allowing me the chance to assimilate this information. I thought about it.

'Can I ask,' I said, 'why they all keep leaving?'

He leant forward and clasped his hands. 'I think the problem is the location. The maths block is just a run-down building at the far end of the sports field. The new students finally seem to be accepting that they can't misbehave around the main part of the school, but when they get down there they still see it as a free period. I try to man it with as many members of SMT as I can whenever I can, but there's so many issues going on – plus the fact that most of the SMT are teaching to cover others, even the Deputy is practically on a full timetable – that I just can't guarantee that there will be someone down there.'

'Right,' I said, nodding slowly.

'And the way the kids see it is that they might as well be on a different site altogether, staffed only by supply teachers. And you know as well as I do how kids feel about supply teachers.'

I did: I remembered all too well from my own schooldays how they offered little more than a joyous opportunity to see how far you could push them.

'Look, I'm not trying to put you off here,' Darren continued. 'That's the last thing I want. I can't stress enough how much you're needed. But I also don't want to lie to you. The staff down there are still finding things extremely difficult. And you will too. So ...' He paused. 'Still want to work here?'

I laughed. 'I'll let you know at the end of the day.'

'Please do,' he said, serious once again. 'I'll be around as often as I can, and I promise I'll be as supportive as I can. But you need to remember that we're all under investigation here, and our hands are tied in a number of ways.'

I was grateful for his honesty. Though I could not help the odd shuddering thought that this was going to be a school just like Turnbull, I was ready to at least give it a go. I looked up at the clock and noticed that the school day was about to begin.

'One last thing before you start,' Darren said as we stood up to leave. 'And this is of the utmost importance. The LEA has enforced a new condition to the school policy: any time a student leaves your room, you absolutely *must* go out after them. I've managed to get CCTV cameras installed in the corridors in case anything happens again, so if you go out you'll be covered. But it is imperative that you do. What the LEA are most worried about is any litigation that may arise as a result of the old staff leaving the students unattended. So if a student leaves your room without permission you *have* to follow them and try and bring them back in.'

'What about the 29 other students I'll be leaving behind in the classroom? Won't I be leaving them unattended?'

He laughed. 'I know. Ludicrous, isn't it? I brought the same thing up with the council and suggested they could install cameras in the classrooms as well. They said no, on the basis that it would be infringing the students' rights. But, to be honest, the problems never seem to occur in the classroom, they're always in the corridor. And, unfortunately, if a student leaves your classroom unattended and causes havoc, the LEA will blame you. I'm sorry it has to be like that, but... well...'

'Them's the rules?' I said.

'Yeah,' he chuckled, forlornly. 'Them's the rules.'

We left his office together for the staff room and morning briefing. As we entered, I was surprised at the atmosphere – there was no tension and, when I approached the circle of maths supply teachers Darren motioned me towards, they all greeted me with a hearty camaraderie. I shook hands with each of them and introduced myself, joining in with their jokes about fresh meat and the you-don't-have-to-be-crazy-to-work-here-but-it-helps clichés. Darren began the briefing and silence fell instantly. He had the same air of friendliness and informality with which he had spoken to me that morning. I could see he was well-liked and well-respected.

Notices were asked for, and one teacher raised his hand.

'Just to let you know that I've had to suspend Harry Calvino for the next five days,' he said. A murmur of agreement went around the room. 'Yesterday, Helen took him and his tutor group down to The Bowling Alley after school. As you all know, that group has been a bit of a problem recently, and it was actually me who suggested it might be a good idea to get them to bond with each other a little better.'

All eyes turned to Helen, a young art teacher, who nodded.

'Unfortunately, halfway through their game, Harry decided to order some chips but, because they didn't come fast enough, he took it upon himself to go up to one of the waitresses and unleash... well... what can only be described as a foul-mouthed tirade.'

The teacher sat next to me leaned over and whispered into my ear, 'He called her a cunt.'

'Needless to say,' Darren said, 'Harry's been banned from The Bowling Alley for life. And to be honest, if he keeps going the way he is, the same thing's going to happen here.' A Mexican nod went around the room.

After the briefing, John – the acting Head of Maths – led me down towards the block. It was as Darren had described: a messy conglomeration of seven dilapidated classrooms joined together by a roofed but windy corridor. The main building was a good five-minute walk away, and could barely be seen from most of the classrooms. Behind it lay a low hedge which formed a border between the school and the housing estate.

John led me to my classroom and, with a quick 'Good luck!' left me there. I did not have a tutor group, and so was able to get myself settled before Period 1. I sat down at my desk and had a look around. There were a few displays stapled to the walls, but most had been scrawled over with words like 'Gay' or 'Wanker'. The tables were covered with graphic depictions of phalluses and open-legged ladies, and a number of the chairs were broken.

John had said that only the Year 9s were still causing trouble – the same group who had created such problems a month earlier. Since my day began with a Year 7 group followed by a Year 11 class, things did not seem so bad. The students were surly and uncommunicative, treating me as if I was not there, but they all stayed in their seats and all at least attempted the work set for them. By break time, I was feeling rather chipper, and sat in the maths office consuming the free coffee and toast with a smile on my face. Compared to some of the schools of my last five months, it had been an easy morning. John came and sat next to me.

'ow's it HHow's it been?' he asked.

'Actually really good,' I spluttered through a mouthful of toast. 'They were all right.'

The three other staff entered looking pensive.

'It's Year 9 next,' John said. 'These are the ones.'

John had been there since the beginning, along with a female teacher called Sally; the others were Callie and Yusef, who had started a week before me.

'Is anyone coming down today?' Sally asked, referring to the Senior Management Team.

'Not today,' John said. 'They're all teaching. It's just us.'

As the bell went for Period 3, each of the teachers positioned themselves outside the doors to their classrooms. I copied them, ready for the onslaught. I was expecting a wave: a heaving, pulsating throng of students coursing through the corridor with the persistence of a riot. Instead, they came slowly and one by one. Fifteen minutes into the lesson, I had only ten students inside my room. I looked over at John, whose room was opposite mine.

'Is this normal, John?' I asked. 'We're a quarter of the way through the lesson already.'

'Follow me, if you want,' he said, leaving his door and heading out of the block. I walked after him, unsure what to expect. Outside, nearly 200 14-year-olds swilled about the tarmac patch which led off the field. John barked a few orders at them, but they ignored him, engrossed in their socialising. John turned to me. 'That's pretty much all we can do. From here, we just hope they come in.'

It was a full half-hour before I had all my students in my room. It was, perhaps, one of the advantages of this disorder: the lessons for this most difficult of year groups were reduced. I had given those sat inside a task to begin working on, but since the school policy dictated I needed to remain at the door and keep an eye on those students outside of the classroom rather than those inside, the latter understood that they effectively had no teacher, and did nothing. Everything was upside down.

Once all my students were present, I tried to begin. It was impossible. This was not a lesson. The few who would sit down preferred tables to chairs; the others wandered listlessly around the room, talking loudly and occasionally knocking over chairs or scuffling. The room teemed with life, life which went its own way and ignored any remonstrations or appeals. In the space of 30 minutes, I succeeded in getting three students to write the title in their books. The rest were too busy chatting and play-fighting.

A girl left the room. I did as I had been told and followed her out into the corridor.

'What do you want?' she spat. 'Fuck off!'

'I need you to stay inside the classroom,' I told her. 'Go back in, please.'

She laughed, ambling up the corridor and then back down again before returning to the room, clearly making a point that to do so was her decision, not mine.

Moments later, a second pupil got up, threw his book on the floor and walked out. Again, I followed. He took a brief moment to laugh at me before lighting a cigarette and vaulting over the hedge to freedom. (Over the coming days, I would lose count of the number of times I would see children escaping over that hedge towards their homes, often lighting up on the way. I always made a point of reporting each of them to Darren as soon as possible, but, as far as I knew, nothing ever happened to them.)

The rest of the class spilled out five minutes before the bell for their lunch. I was left to right the tables and chairs and read the new graffitied additions to our learning space.

* * * * *

My first week at Varka followed this pattern. Though far from a joy, the other classes were tolerable and my days began to hinge around the Year 9s. It did not take long to discover that the most challenging students were all from the closed school. They hated Varka, did not understand why they had to go there, and did everything they could to cause trouble. As I learned their names and their characters, I learned their histories from Darren.

There was Sophie – one of the two girls who had sparked the whole affair by walking out of the classroom back at the beginning of term. Her father had just come out of prison and her mother had just gone in – while pregnant. In a moment of candour, Sophie said one day, 'The babby's due when she's still inside. That's so cruel to the babby.'

The other girl who had joined Sophie on that infamous day was Chloe. She happily admitted that her own poor behaviour often stemmed from an amphetamine comedown. Chloe took speed because it was given to her by a 19-year-old friend who lived alone in a squat, and who exchanged the drug for Chloe's friendship. Her biggest score came when she accompanied this woman to the abortion clinic because no-one else would. Chloe was 13 years old.

Amongst the boys was Sam. He was at such risk at home with his father that Social Services demanded he instead stay with his brother and his wife and their baby in their one-room bedsit. Sam slept on the floor. His defence mechanism led him to take offence at the most innocuous conversations. Once, after he had behaved exceptionally well during a lesson, I tried to reward him with a 'treat' to conclude the lesson.

'You've done really well today, Sam,' I said. 'Do you want to play Monopoly for the last 15 minutes with Joe and Kerry?'

'Yeah! Let's play Monopoly!'

'OK, then. Do you know where Miss used to keep it?'

'It's in the cupboard, you fucking stupid twat!'

There was Tony, whose recurrent mood swings twanged him back and forth between benevolence and hostility. During one lesson, after working studiously for 20 minutes, he raised his hand. I walked over to him, and when I reached his table, Tony beckoned me close.

'I fucking hate you, you cunt,' he intoned, levelly.

'Why?' I asked.

'Because you're a fucking prick who needs to get some fucking friends.'

'I don't understand what I've done wrong,' I said.

'See this?' he shouted back at me, rising up and grabbing a metal tin filled with felt-tip pens. 'This is your face.' He punched it, leaving a large dent in the centre. 'And see this?' he continued, rotating the tin and then delivering another resounding thump into the opposite side. 'That's your bollocks.'

At that, he emptied the tin over Ryan's head. Ryan jumped up and chased Tony out of the room. They were both laughing. I followed. Outside the block, I found that Ryan had jumped the hedge, leaving Tony alone slumped against the wall, about to cry.

'Are you all right, Tony?' I asked.

He looked up at me, and it was like he was seeing me for the first time that day.

'I'm all right, sir. Why?'

'I just thought that, after what you said in there, you might be feeling a bit angry towards me.'

He seemed startled by the idea. 'No way,' he said. 'You're safe, you are.'

I came to discover that most of the class were typical teenagers, but that a few of these volatiles were able to ignite them.

Will kept a tally of how many times he could scream in a falsetto voice, '*Fuck yooooooo!*'

Vicky had a penchant for smacking her maths textbook as hard as she could over the heads of boys she fancied.

Michael, with a randomness I could never put a pattern to, would take a chair to the corner of the room and shut down, allowing no entreaties to penetrate his robotic immobility.

And then, of course, there was Ralph. But we will come to him later.

It was a horrid three days. I fought my way through them as best I could, but I could never shake off the dread of those Year 9s. Callie had enough and left on the Thursday, to be replaced by another supply teacher who taught through Friday, and then did not turn up the following Monday. I sat with the maths staff each break and lunch time, and the pervading feeling was inescapable. This was the hardest job we had ever done.

* * * * *

I needed a weekend of exploration to take my mind off Varka, and rose at 7am on Saturday morning to drive into and wander the two enormous cities of West Yorkshire. Almost every guidebook of England describes Leeds and Bradford as a 'conurbation'. This word signifies an aggregation of two or more cities or towns, and, topographically, this is indeed what has happened to Bradford and Leeds. Over the years, the two cities have spilled into each other so haphazardly that endings and beginnings are blurred. Today, there is only, in the south, one area which keeps them from forever binding into one discrete super-city: the small town of Pudsey, which diligently keeps each of its larger neighbours at arm's length.

In almost every other sense, Bradford and Leeds could not be more distinct. Leeds is all designer shops and polished surfaces, England's Milan; Bradford, weathered and earthy, is our Naples. If driving into Leeds is like entering a sparkling North American metropolis, arriving into Bradford is quite different. Its motorway – the M606 – drops you off on the outskirts and watches gleefully as you attempt to penetrate the mesh of grey, rainy suburbs which, from a distance, seem to drip down the side of the hill like a Rio de Janeiro slum.

But the cities did not seem enough. On the Saturday night, with another cheap bottle of supermarket wine drained, I scanned my road atlas, and then set off the next morning for the Pennines. I squeezed Varka memories from my mind with long bouts of driving and fish-and-chip meals in towns and villages which soothed with their pretty rurality: Hebden Bridge, Heptonstall, Haworth, Todmorden, Lydgate. I visited the parsonage of the Brontes and the grave of Sylvia Plath. I walked country lanes and climbed hills so steep they made my gums itch. I breathed in the fresh Pennine air all around me, and I relaxed.

I rose from my pit on Monday morning ready for my second week at Varka. I boiled my kettle and took a long, hot wash. Inching the van out of my lay-by, I drove back to school.

I met Darren outside the staff room. He was as bouncy and effervescent as when I had first met him. He lived in the depths of North Yorkshire, and had to leave at five o'clock in the morning to arrive at work by half-past six. 'It's definitely worth it,' he said. 'Just to get away. In the country. That's where my life is.'

During my free period I was asked to cover the Time Out room for that hour. I obliged, hoping it might be a chance to put my feet up and read a book. It was, until the last 20 minutes. An irate teacher poked his head through the door to inform me that Sophie would be spending the rest of the session with me due to her poor behaviour in his history lesson. She sauntered in and plonked herself down on one of the seats.

'All right, Sophie?' I asked as the teacher left.

'No,' she said.

'What happened?'

'*God*! Your voice goes right *through* me!' she said, leaving it at that and turning to face the wall.

Ten minutes of silence passed. I read my book. Sophie gradually turned away from her vantage point. I looked up to see her watching me. She was scratching casually at her head, and my gaze followed her fingers. Her hair was saturated with headlice.

'So what happened?' I said.

'Chloe,' she said. 'We had a fight. She said I was ugly. *Fuck*. I've seen better-looking people than *her* at Poundland.'

'Is that why you were sent out? Because you had a fight with Chloe?'

'Yeah,' she replied sullenly, scratching her head again.

'I thought you two were friends.'

'She's not my friend. I fucking hate the little bitch.'

That seemed to be that. She turned to face the wall again, angrily burrowing for more lice. I returned to my book.

The following day there was only a smattering of students present, and so Sally and I decided to collapse our two classes into one. With 23 kids and two of us, it seemed a good idea. The lesson began well, and continued so until the last five minutes when, with a shrill cry of '*Fuck yooooo*!', Will jumped up from his seat and began pounding Joe. That was the signal for chaos to erupt. Sam immediately joined in, picking up anything he could get his hands on and throwing it at everyone in sight (including me and Sally); Ryan jumped up and down on the centre of a table; Ralph leapt up and started to swing from the thin, bending pipes which flowed around the back wall; Sophie stole a board-pen from my desk and wrote 'Suck dick you motherfucking cunt. Sophie' on the wall, with perfect spelling.

There was a moment when Sally and I looked at each other, and I could see that she was thinking the same as I: 'What are we supposed to do?' The moment was interrupted when Chloe sneaked behind me and began to hit me on the back with her fake designer handbag and the rest of the students stopped to watch. Sally intercepted the swinging bag, took it off Chloe, and escorted her from the room, while the other students laughed and pointed at me until the bell went. At which, they sprinted out.

And then Wednesday came, and, with it, Ralph. Ralph was another of the Year 9s moved from the closed school into Varka. Although only 13, he was a stocky and well-built boy with blonde hair which was already thinning; he was known for levels of behaviour more hostile and thuggish than the rest, and for often taking an instant dislike to male members of staff. Darren had spent a lot of time with Ralph, trying to find a way through his surliness and succeeding in unmasking the personality behind the hostility. He had warned me about him on my first day.

'Just let him be,' he had said. 'He won't like you at first. And he'll make sure you know it. But give him some time, use humour whenever you can, and he'll eventually come around.'

Unfortunately for me, he didn't. In fact, Ralph took a greater disliking to me than to any other member of staff. He began referring to me as 'that posh cunt' – mostly when I was in earshot – and liked to retreat to the back of the room during a lesson to sit on the floor and proclaim my failings to the class.

'Mr Carroll stinks of shit.'

'Don't listen to him. He's only a supply teacher. He don't know nothing.'

'Sir's a virgin.'

'Posh cunt.'

If I told him to be quiet, he spoke louder; if I ignored him he laughed at me. I wished I could send him out, but Darren had made it clear that once they were in, we had to do our best to keep them in. So I was left with no choice but to endure him as he slowly chipped away at my resolve to stay calm.

On the Tuesday, he crept up behind me during my break-time duty and yelled 'BANG!' so loud into my ear that it rang for the next half-hour.

On Wednesday, he walked out of the room during a lesson. I had to follow him, and not only because of Darren's instructions – I had let Ryan slip from the room unnoticed the day before, and he had managed to get into the school office and take another boy's personal files from a cabinet. I left the classroom to find Ralph pacing back and forth across the short width of the corridor.

'Leave me alone,' he said without looking at me.

'Ralph,' I began, knowing by now the script off by heart. 'I need you to come back into the classroom. I can't continue the lesson until you're in there with us.'

This was exactly what Darren had told me to say. I had used it a few times before. It had generally worked.

'I'm not coming back in. Leave me alone,' Ralph responded. His step quickened; and I saw I could not encourage him back into the classroom. A different approach was required.

'Ralph,' I said in a placatory tone. 'That's fine. You need some time to cool down. But I need you to stay out here, in this corridor. Will you do that?'

He stopped pacing, and turned to face me. 'I said…' he hissed, '*leave… me… alone.*'

The vein in his forehead was beginning to pump. I noticed that it proceeded all the way up his scalp. His eyebrows were furrowed, and he was staring at me, motionless.

'Ralph,' I said, taking one step towards him. 'That's fine. You need a bit of time to yourself. I understand. Just please, for my sake, promise me you'll stay outside the classroom.'

Ralph lowered his gaze from me to the floor. He breathed out again, and resumed his pacing.

'You take all the time you need, Ralph,' I said. 'And then come back in when you're ready.'

I turned and walked back into the classroom. I knew I had broken the rules by leaving him out in the corridor, but I felt it was the best thing I could have done. I walked back in, thinking perhaps I might have gained some ground with the boy. The lesson continued for two minutes, until Sam – Ralph's best friend – decided to get up and leave. As per my orders, I followed him out into the corridor. He had sat down on the floor next to Ralph. As soon as Ralph saw me, the hostility was back in his eyes.

'I told you to fucking leave me alone!' he said.

'I'm not here for you, Ralph. I'm here for Sam.'

'Fuck off and leave me alone, too!' said Sam.

'Sam, I need you to come back inside the classroom, please.'

That was where it all ended. Ralph jumped to his feet. 'I'm gonna break your fucking *jaw*, you posh cunt!' he shouted, landing inches from me, and drawing his arm back to swing, fist clenched.

I reacted on instinct alone, immediately raising my arms up to chest height with palms facing outward. Submissive. Accommodating.

'All right, all right, I'm going,' I said, backing into the classroom, hands still in the same position.

The rest of the class were doing what they wanted. I sat down on the edge of a nearby table. I was shaking. I could hear Ralph and Sam outside the door. Sam was laughing. Ralph was ranting.

'I'm gonna smash that fucking posh twat's face in! Fucking following me everywhere, the *gay prick*! I'm gonna break his *fucking jaw*!'

I could not think. A lot of students have threatened me with a lot of things over the years – from the hollow 'I'm gonna get my dad in to see you!' to the equally impulsive and unrealistic warning of physical harm ('I'm gonna break your nose') like Luke from Nottingham had attempted, to suggestions that I'd find my car vandalised later or I'd be reported for 'unfairness' to the Headteacher or even sued. None of these ever came to anything; now, for the first time, I believed a pupil could, and would, go through with his threat. I have no doubt in my mind that, had I not immediately backed down, Ralph would have hit me, and hit me hard. It was only by luck that Elliott, the Deputy Head, turned up at that moment and looked around the door. I motioned him in and told him everything. I remember that moment now: how I described the events of the lesson with something akin to hysteria; how close I was to collapse; how I had just become a victim in my own workplace.

Elliott escorted Ralph away. Sam returned to the room. I stood at the front and tried to mutter a few imperatives. It was no use. I was drained. The class saw, and took advantage, rising from their seats to throw pencil cases at each other. Too numbed, I slumped into my chair and let them get on with it for the last 10 minutes of the lesson. When the bell went, they piled out. Sam was the last to go. As he reached the door, he turned around and hollered, 'Pussy!' And then he ran along with the rest of them.

I had a few minutes before the next class were due to arrive, and so I hurried over into John's room, still shaking. He looked up from the book he was marking, obviously concerned at my state. I explained to him as carefully as I could that Ralph had just physically threatened me and that I could no longer work with him. I talked slowly through the events that had just occurred, leaving out nothing.

John took a deep breath. 'All right,' he said. 'Right now, there's nothing I can do. The Year 10s will be here in a minute.' I looked out the window and could already see the first few arriving. 'Can you manage the next lesson?'

'I'm not sure.'

'Well, you'll have to. At lunch time, the two of us will go and see Darren together.' He passed me an Incident Report form, a generic sheet of A4 on which I had to record what had just happened. In every school, there are thousands of bits of paper just like this, scrawled over with whatever poor behaviour the school's teachers will have had to endure from their pupils throughout the year, and then usually locked away at the bottom of a filing cabinet, never to be referred to again. 'Fill this in when you can,' he said.

I barely spoke to my next class. I handed them some textbooks (one between three was how far the limited resources stretched), wrote the page numbers they were to read, and then sat back and let them get on with it.

At lunchtime, John and I went to see Darren. I explained what had happened, offering the Incident Report as some kind of evidence. Darren listened to it all solemnly. After I finished, he stood up. 'Wait here,' he said. 'I'll go and get Ralph. I think the four of us need a little chat.'

I stayed in Darren's office, receiving gratefully the tea his PA brought me and finding some solace in the peace and quiet there. I was thankful for Darren's immediate support, and hoped it would result in the exclusion of Ralph. Ten minutes later, Darren and John returned. They motioned for me to follow them. We walked over to a nearby art room. Through the window in the door, I could see Ralph sitting in there on his own. As the three of us entered, he laughed.

'I wondered why you brought me in here,' he said.

'So you do know, then?' Darren asked.

'It's because of what I said to him, innit?'

'What did you say?'

'I told him I'd break his jaw.'

'And why did you do that?'

'Because he's a fucking div. I hate him.'

The discussion lasted for 15 minutes. Ralph was unashamed and open as Darren and John probed. I said nothing. Once, Ralph turned to me and said, 'Stop looking at me. Go on, fucking stop looking at me.' I recognised the tone, it was the same as the *What you looking at?* of a Friday night in a rough pub. Later on, he laughed, 'He ran away, the fucking pussy!'

The meeting finished. Ralph promised that he would never threaten or intimidate an adult in the school again. He did not apologise. It was agreed that he would be moved from my class to John's. As Ralph walked out the door, he called back over his shoulder, 'Posh cunt.'

He was not excluded.

He should have been, and perhaps would have been, but Darren's hands were tied by the ongoing investigation. With the LEA watching carefully for any hiccups or discrepancies within the school, Darren was doing his best not to rock the boat. Attempting an exclusion would have been met with even more bureaucracy than usual, and doubtless the governors would not have honoured it anyway, despite what Ralph had done. All this meant, of course, that, for the staff, the investigation itself was making it far more difficult to teach effectively at Varka than even the new cohort of students were. I remarked as such to John on our return to the maths department.

'You're learning quickly,' he said.

Back in the maths office, we joined the other teachers. They already knew about the incident, and it was discussed at length, numerous theories tossed into the conversation.

'You probably remind him of someone, and he's reacting against them, not you.'

'He's just projecting his anger, and his fear, on to you.'

'He's becoming an Alpha male, and he sees you as competition.'

'He's showing the girls in the class that he's physically the strongest. It's primal.'

But I cared for none of this. What mattered to me were not causes, but consequences. My physical safety had been compromised, and I no longer felt secure in the school environment. Despite all the verbal abuse and aggression I had previously experienced, I had never once felt myself or a colleague of mine to be in physical danger. Now, at Varka, I did. Worse still was the fact that any minimal authority I had assumed with that class had been stolen from me. Ralph now knew that all he had to do was threaten me, and I would back down. Other students, Sam especially, would have realised the same. From the moment it happened until the next morning, it was all I could think about.

That night, I barely slept. The scene ran around and around my head, infiltrating my fitful dreams. The following morning, during the drive into work, I thought myself into near-hysteria, getting to the point where I feared Ralph might bring a knife into school (not too implausible, but more on knives later) to use on me. Every time I saw him over the following two days – and especially when he would walk past my classroom on his way to John's maths lesson and, in a sing-song voice, call out, 'Dick head!' – I felt sick.

* * * * *

The Thursday and Friday passed, and then came the weekend, which I drank my way through. On the Monday morning I awoke and drove with reluctance back into school. I still had two weeks to go. I was dreading every tick of the clock. As it happened, I made it only through that day. By the end of it, I left Varka for good.

My Year 9s arrived at 10.20am – Period 2. I had nipped off to the toilet straight after the previous lesson, and had come back to find Ralph sitting inside my classroom next to Sam.

'Ralph,' I said as I entered, doing my best to sound breezy but failing irrevocably. 'You take maths with Mr Bull now. His room's next door.'

'And what the fuck you going to do about it?' he asked, settling an unnerving gaze on me.

Without saying a word, I walked out to inform John. He came back in with me, appealing to Ralph to get up and go to his room. Ralph steadfastly refused.

'Fine,' John said. 'Then I'll teach this class, and Mr Carroll can teach mine.'

I nodded and walked across the corridor to his room, the effect being that I had just been removed from my own lesson instead of the student. I took John's class, realising with some relief that he had a group as challenging as mine. When the bell went, I dismissed them, walked out into the corridor and came right upon Ralph and Sam in conversation. Ralph turned to face me.

'That's it, keep moving,' he said, flicking his hand dismissively, like a member of the nouveau riche patronising a waiter.

I was faced with a dilemma. I could not allow Ralph to tell me what to do, but I did not want another confrontation. Suddenly, John appeared.

'Mr Carroll's not going to go anywhere if you talk to him like that, is he?' he said.

'All right, then,' said Ralph. 'Move.'

'Say please, and I might,' I said.

'Move… *please*.'

I did, walking over to my classroom. John left, and Ralph stuck his head through my door as he walked by. He looked at me with loathing. 'You fucking cunt,' he said, shaking his head, almost as if he pitied me. And then he left.

I knew right at that moment that I had to leave Varka. Ralph had finally disempowered me. He knew he could speak to me how he liked, and knew that I would always back down. That was enough, because – and here's the thing, here's the red-faced, cowering, shameful thing – I had become scared of this 13-year-old boy. I am deeply embarrassed to admit it, but it is the truth. Around Ralph, I did not feel safe, and this robbed me of my confidence which, in turn, stripped me of my professionalism. I could already see what was happening: Ralph, with the cause-effect mentality of a thug, was beginning to bully me.

At the end of the day, I went to see Darren.

'I have to leave,' I said.

He looked at me with an expression of disappointment. This conversation was becoming all too familiar for him.

'I'm really sorry,' I continued when he did not respond. 'But I can't work here anymore.'

'Why not?'

'Ralph,' I said.

'Ralph promised he would never threaten you again.'

'It's gone deeper than that now. He taunts me whenever I see him. This morning, he refused to leave my classroom, so I had to. *I* had to leave, not him. When he's around, it's useless me trying to teach, because to him I'm not a teacher anymore – I'm his victim. And it won't be long before the other kids realise that, too. Some already have. So I have to go. I'm sorry. I know you need staff more than ever. But I can't work in an environment where this kind of thing is allowed to happen.'

I stood up, and Darren rose to shake my hand, telling me he understood, and even offering to write me a reference should I need it.

I felt awful. I liked Darren. I liked all the staff. I respected everything they were all doing at this most troublesome of schools, and I hated the fact that I had become yet another supply teacher to let them down. I had run away from problems that they would have to clear up themselves, stretched for staff as they already were. I was also ashamed of myself. I was doing something which reduced my personal and professional integrity: I had left work because I was scared of a child. It did not feel good. I had been bullied, and not stood up to the bully.

Yet as I sat in my van that night and gulped down a bottle of cheap red wine, I found myself realising that the biggest disservice I had done was to Ralph. When I failed to show up the next morning, Ralph would understand exactly why. As a result, he would come to believe that, by intimidating someone, by using the threat of violence, he would be able to get his own way. Looking back on the whole experience now, months away from it as I write these very words, I still cannot escape that. It is what I, a teacher, have taught him. And I feel pretty devastated about it.

*****

In a way, I was lucky. One in 10 state school teachers have been actually physically injured by a student; 75% have been threatened with violence. Within my first year – within my first month of teaching – I was among the latter percentage, though I have yet to enter the ranks of the former. I felt worryingly close to that in the presence of Ralph.

But I have discussed violence in schools already; the whole experience at Varka School led me to contemplate another reason why so many teachers are leaving the profession. That reason is litigation.

Ralph did not like me from the start, but what pushed him toward potential violence was what happened when he insisted on walking out of the classroom. He wanted to be left alone, and this might have been the best thing. It is a common tactic to offer certain children – particularly those with anger management issues – 'time-outs' when they need them: to keep such students within a lesson against their will can often lead to unnecessary confrontation, whereas a few minutes of peace and solitude can allow them the chance to calm down and return to the classroom of their own accord. The problem with Ralph was that, when he needed these moments to himself, I had been ordered to follow him. He hated that.

This directive had been formulated by the Local Education Authority. Why? Because as a teacher I am *in loco parentis* – literally, in the place of the parent. In the eyes of the law, when I have children in my classroom I have the same legal responsibilities, and liabilities, as a parent.

This is a logical concept, ensuring that students can be safe within their school environment and will not be subject to the passing mood-swings of a volatile figurehead. It provides comfort to parents sending their five year olds off to a place apart from them, and the knowledge that if the school does not look after them, then the law will. Similarly, it gives the authorities a recourse should the safety of a child become suspect.

Unfortunately, it has been taken advantage of, thanks to our insidious litigation culture.

During my PGCE, I attended a series of seminars entitled 'Pastoral Care'. These dealt with the responsibilities and duties one has in a school outside of teaching – from the realtively minor, such as what it was to be a tutor, to how to deal with a girl who has just found out she is pregnant, or what to do when a student approaches you and admits that he has just knifed someone. But, above all, we talked about the law. Teachers exist in a minefield of liability. If a student falls over and breaks his leg whilst on a day trip, you may be liable; if a student takes a sexual liking to you and you do not deal with it correctly, you could also be liable; if three boys walk into your classroom during your lesson and beat the living daylights out of one of your students then, again, you might be liable, on the basis that you had, paradoxically, 'allowed' it to happen. But, equally, if you try to intervene physically, you might *also* be liable. The list goes on.

When I have a class of 30 before me, I take on a parental responsibility for each of them. If one chooses to run out, or goes to the toilet, or walks across the hall to borrow some paper from another room, he remains my responsibility no matter what he decides to do or what happens to him.

I understand why: I am their teacher, after all. If I cannot keep them safe, I do not deserve my job. But it is those factors out of my control, environmental or intentional, which worry me, and worry an awful lot of us.

In an age where no-win-no-fee adverts and the like are daily injected into the public consciousness, it is little surprise that 'blame culture' is a frequent topic of conversation. People can be very quick to sue, and while litigation pervades every aspect of life, its looming presence in education cannot be ignored. It is not uncommon for schools to receive up to 30 claims a year for financial compensation for staff negligence.

This is why school trips are dying out: it is not because teachers no longer want to lead them, but because they are too frightened to.

Most unions have advised for a number of years now that teachers should not involve themselves with school trips as protection against the threat of litigation.

It was due to the stamped-in fear of legal action that I continued to follow Ralph outside the classroom when I knew I ought to leave him be. Litigation, based upon a wrongful interpretation of *in loco parentis*, is a threat, and many teachers are responding to the threat by fleeing the profession.

* * * * *

I wandered Leeds for a few days after leaving Varka. I was listless and despondent: Ralph had left me feeling sullen and unmotivated. I did not want to go back to work. I called Emma the next day to explain why I had left, and later realised with some considerable surprise that I had expected her to be angry with me.

It should not have been a surprise – I was angry with myself. I felt a failure. I knew that by leaving I had done the right thing, but I knew I had let Ralph run me out of his school. I tried to rationalise it, I made notes on violence in schools and the fact that litigation often leaves teachers powerless to deal with it, and I objectified everything that had happened a hundred times over, always coming to the conclusion that I had been left with no alternative. But it did not help. I could not shake the sense that I had shirked a duty inherent to teaching, and it became cancerous.

I told Emma I needed a couple of days off before going back to work elsewhere. The couple of days turned into a few, then the rest of the week, then the whole of the next, and then it was half-term.

I questioned for the first time the project I had set myself, wondered whether I was really cut out for it. I thought back to a conversation with a colleague at the school I left the year before, who I outlined the idea to.

'It sounds like you're actually going looking for trouble,' he said.

'I'm not *looking* for trouble, I just want to document the fact that it happens.'

'But what if you get knifed or something?'

'I know. It'd make a great story!'

The joke seemed hollow now. Here I was: not knifed, not even assaulted. The *threat* of a punch, and some casual insults, had thrown me. That was all that had happened, and already I was questioning whether I should just leave the whole thing as an unfortunate little test of my own courage. It was all I thought about for days.

I wallowed, shuffling aimlessly about Leeds city centre, my eyes blind to all around. Often, I would find myself in the grand Central Library: a beautiful and twisting building, outside of which stand two huge chess-boards upon which contestants of all ages and races meet and do battle. Inside it is as quiet and loveable as any traditional English library could be. There I lost myself in the welcoming staff, and the thousands of books organised with a slightly eccentric rendering of the Dewey system, finally scratching Ralph from the circuits of my brain. I spent three long and quiet afternoons in that library, reading everything I could get my hands on, and making sporadic notes on all that came to mind.

It was in there, reading Roger Deakin's *Waterlog*, and coming to a passage which lovingly spoke of the West Country, that I realised where I wanted to be. Home. I walked back to the van and drove it all the way down in a single evening.

I was sad to leave West Yorkshire, but the need to put Ralph and Varka behind me was urgent. I did not teach for the next two weeks. I wondered if I ever would again.

LONDON

I LOUNGED IN Cornish houses, convalescing. I went to pubs with family or with friends and drank in their comfort alongside the thick ale I was bought. I got a phone call from my old Head of Department who had heard I was around and wondered whether I wanted to come back to the school. There was a job waiting. I toyed with the idea. The last six months were forming themselves into a wintry hole in my memory. I was forgetting the good times I had experienced at schools like Mitchell and Gilbert, with students I had taught like Stuart from the Peak District, or with staff I had worked alongside like Linda from Coggan. Instead, all I could remember was a long sentence of confrontations and bleak estates, flattened at the end by the full-stop of Ralph.

I filled the half-term days with mini road-trips, driving off to old haunts I knew and loved. If I was going to give it all up, I thought, I would not miss the teaching. But I would miss the road. I stayed in one night and read my journals from the past six months. The words evoked memories – not just visual or auditory, but kinaesthetic and tactile, too – and they made me laugh. I re-walked the contours of Leeds, re-lived a morning in front of the TV with Grandma, re-drove the Peaks. I remembered all the campsites and lay-bys, the streets of Manchester, the curves of the M62 and the canals of Birmingham. I knew I had to give it one last go, if not for the teaching, then at least for the travelling it allowed me. London was next on my list and, though I did not for a second want to work there, I still wanted to go. To go and live it.

I left the next day. Ralph and Varka had been cast from my thoughts, but only temporarily: if I did not leave now, things would surface, would rear, and I would never leave the peninsula again. With only two motorways to navigate, it was the simplest journey yet.

Three of my closest friends lived together in London and they had offered me their couch, for as long as I wanted it. In fact, although they all now had full-time jobs and serious relationships, there had always been somebody sleeping on their couch, ever since they had moved in together. I was just another in the long line of Resident Hobos to whom they offered their collective charity. And though I paid them no rent, obstructed the shower and the kitchen and the television, left books spread across tables and clothes across floors, forgot to turn off lights, sequestered the broadband connection, made more washing-up than I cleaned, took up a valuable parking space, engaged them in stultifying conversation about my day at work when all they wanted was to spend time with their girlfriends, and left them short a set of keys so I could come and go as I pleased, they never once minded, never once said a word. They will make good parents one day, I've no doubt.

The boys lived in Dalston, a suburb of the borough of Hackney. Though West Yorkshire is over 100 square miles bigger than London, its population of 2.2 million pales in comparison to London's seven and a half million. Hackney itself has over 200,000 residents, more than the city of Newcastle-upon-Tyne.

Emma had nothing to do with the capital; supply placements were handled through the main London office and its sub-departments. As luck would have it, the boroughs with the most failing schools – Hackney, Haringey and Tower Hamlets – were within easy reach of the house. I was told immediately by the agency that finding work within any of them would not be a problem, and that, while we're at it, could I start tomorrow?

I put it off. I gave the consultants the excuse that I was still settling into my new home, but the truth is I was scared to go back into schools, more worried than I had been (I noticed with some concern) when I began the whole project back in Nottingham. Back then, I had imagined I would grow stronger and more immune as the journey unravelled, but Ralph had rocked me, shaking my confidence to its foundation. I did not want to go back to school.

But I had to. After all the time I had taken off, there was less than a hundred pounds in my bank account. To live, I needed to work. So it was with a mixture of dread and self-doubt that, on Tuesday afternoon, I accepted a job for the next day.

I awoke on the Wednesday morning at five, and could not get back to sleep. Eventually, I pulled myself up from the couch, padded down to the kitchen, and stared vacantly out the window at the desolate streets of Dalston as the kettle boiled and the toaster toasted. I returned to the living room with my breakfast, eating it in silent darkness, trying not to think but incapable of stopping myself.

After an hour, one of my new housemates, John, appeared from his en-suite bedroom.

'Ah! Morning, Charlie!' he exclaimed with that dawn brightness I remembered so well from when we had lived together at university. 'I've been lying in bed for the past hour, not sleeping. It was ridiculous. Literally. So I thought, fuck it, while I'm awake, might as well go for a run, eh?'

I stared at him wide-eyed as he made himself a gigantic bowl of Rice Crispies, attacking it with an animal lust and spraying milk-sodden cereal everywhere. Then he donned some latex shorts, strapped a miner's torch to his forehead, and pranced from the room on an early morning run. Watching his elbows as they butted and jerked their way out of the front door, I started by envying his spirit for life, and then finished by thanking him for taking my mind off the day I had ahead of me.

I had been commissioned to work at an all-boys' school. It was an average school for the area – though far below the national average – but as I set off I reminded myself that I was only booked for one day and that, no matter how bad it was, I would never have to return if I did not want to. I was also teaching English, and I found some solace in that. Though I had not struggled with the myriad subjects I had taught over the last six months, I was most comfortable with my specialism.

The school was a typical inner-city comprehensive, fraught with difficulties but dealing with them as best it could. The staff were a chirpy lot, but there were no illusions as to how much they struggled just to teach. Around the staff room, numerous posters showed graffiti tags and asked in stiff, undecorative language if you knew who was behind them. Around the corridors, similar posters adorned the walls, though these were directed at the students:

Drugs can get you killed
The police are always watching
Knives + Fear = Death

The students themselves were huge: towering, stubbly leviathans who spoke a street-patois I could not understand, emphasising important words with flicked gesticulations and rib-shaking laughter.

I stumbled my way through the first three lessons, all Year 7s and Year 8s, like a student teacher, lacking in confidence and throwing out threats of punishment I knew I could not back up. The students responded in kind, pushing me to see when I would capitulate, grinning defiantly when I did. They made the most of this stricken supply teacher, and one even asked if I would be back tomorrow, presumably so he could have another lesson off. Period 4 came, and I found myself in a mist of surly Year 11s. They were an intermediate set, and each one clocked me as he entered. No work had been set for this class, so I scampered over to the Head of English next door to see what I should do.

'Well, they've just had an exam,' she said. 'So it's not likely they'll do anything. Just tell them they've got a revision period.'

Fair enough. Once they all sat down, I stood before them and began to speak. An instant hush fell, one I had not been expecting. 'Right, Year 11,' I said. 'I know you've just had an exam, so we'll call this lesson a revision session. You know as well as I do what that means, but in case you don't, here it is. Get your GCSE Poetry Anthology out and put it in front of you. You can talk with those around you, that's fine, but I don't want to see anyone getting out of their seats or messing around. You've basically been given a free period here, so don't abuse it. Because if you do, you'll be forcing me into giving you some actual work to do. Are we understood?'

The collective and decidedly deep-voiced reply came: 'Yes, sir.'

They knew the system as well as I did. Occasionally in schools, a class may be given a 'lesson off' if their teacher is away and has not set anything. This is, of course, deeply wrong – particularly since it contains the implication that it is the students, rather than the teachers, who have made the decision that no work will be done – but that does not stop it from sometimes being the easiest answer. If the class is difficult and the supply teacher new to the school, it can be better to accept that no learning is going to happen, rather than fight it. It is telling evidence of the decline in teacher-authority within some schools.

The lesson started well, but after 10 minutes the throwing began. First it was a rubber, then a paper aeroplane, then a pencil case, and finally a chair. I should have stopped them when it was just a rubber, but I had left it too late: now there was no chance. Tables were upended and, before I could get out of my seat, one boy had grabbed another and was beginning to punch him gleefully in the thigh. My shouts to stop were so loud that the Head of Department came running in from next door. She removed the violent student, barked a few imperatives at the rest, and seats were returned to.

As she left, I looked about me. Order was restored, but only minimally. The students were now sitting where they wanted, brushing books off the tables and engaging in loud and provocative talk. I sat back and watched them. I knew there was nothing I could do about this, but also knew that if things got out of hand again, I had a resort, the Head of Department. Seemingly, the students realised this, too, and did not again return to their chaos. Instead, they were content just to talk. So I listened.

They split themselves into four groups. The largest was composed of about 12 lads who sat in varying directions to form a rough circle. They began talking about gang fights, referring to other boys they knew by nicknames and the names of the 'batch' they were in – Fatty Roger from The Homerton Crew, The Paki from Hackney, the Barnsbury Boys. They boasted loudly of bottling others, of bloody fights witnessed and gorgeous girls they had bagged. They seemed genuine enough, but I could not help wonder at their lack of discretion. This bandying of names and happenings seemed to suggest no intimate knowledge, but instead a crazy need to be recognised. If they were as deep into the gangs as their shouts suggested, I doubted they would feel the need to prove themselves so vociferously amongst their peers.

I noticed that one of the groups sat in the back corner. Three-strong, they had their hoods up, were talking quietly and doing nothing to draw attention to themselves. They were the ones you would not recognise in a line-up a few weeks later. They were the ones who, perhaps, these others were trying to impress.

Finally, lunch time came, and the Year 11s swaggered out the door. I ate my sandwich greedily, urging the final lesson to come and then go. I wanted to go home.

Period 5 arrived, and I found myself taking a top set of Year 10s. The lesson – I had one to teach this time – ran smoothly, save for one confrontation. He was called Jack, and was a red-haired, well-built, freckly young man with a quick tongue and an unfortunate sense of his own physicality. Halfway through the lesson, Jack jumped to his feet and grabbed Nabille by his collar. 'What did you say?' he screamed. 'What did you just say?'

I moved into action, but before I could get in the middle of them, Jack had released Nabille and was turning to face me. Nabille was shaken and looked close to tears. Jack looked the opposite. He glared at me as I quietly but surely told him that his behaviour was unacceptable, and would not be tolerated. Jack made to sit down, but then rose up again as if he had forgotten something. 'I'll just tell you this,' he said, flexing his shoulders. 'I don't like being told what to do. And when people start ordering me about I explode. That's what the last teacher did. I threw a chair at him. That's why he left.' He sat down.

A hundred thoughts flashed through my mind at once. Ralph slumped in the corridor. 'I'm gonna break your fucking jaw!' A fist raised and ready to strike. The sound of my feet back-stepping. The view over my fingertips.

I swallowed. 'Are you threatening me, Jack?' I asked. The question was not rhetorical.

'I'm just telling you. That's all.'

I thought for a second, and then spoke. I was surprised to hear my words calm and level as they came out. 'Jack, you'd better be careful. Threatening a member of staff is almost as bad as actually attacking them.'

Jack held my gaze for a few seconds, and then looked down at his work. He picked up his pen. He started to answer question four. I left him to it. Fifteen minutes later, I walked past his table, and Jack said to Aron next to him, in that kind of *sotto voce* tone which teachers learn to recognise as being used for their benefit, 'Once you get in shit you can't get out of it again. So you might as well not get in shit in the first place.'

There it ended. I left the school on the bell and caught the overland train home. I reflected. I had not enjoyed a second of the day, but I had endured it. It had been hard, a challenge, a pull. But I knew I could still do it, and that was something.

* * * * *

Over the following six weeks, work was regular. As time passed, I found myself rotating between five schools in Hackney, Haringey, Tower Hamlets and another borough further away, teaching only at them and never anywhere else. They were all, as I had requested, challenging, but as I grew to know them and the students who went to them, I found that each had their charms. I started to enjoy the work. My journal-notes for the period focused not on foul and outrageous events, but instead revealed anecdotal whimsies:

> 10th March: Just found out that the word 'bush' is now used colloquially to mean 'wanker' or 'prick', ie. 'Come on, ya bush!' Is this derived from George Bush?
> 19th March: In staff room for briefing. One teacher told a story of how he swore at a student. Laughs all round. Sudden silence as everyone noticed me in the corner. Teacher: 'You're not OFSTED, are you, mate?'
> 27th March: Covered a Science lesson Period 4 and watched a DVD. The narrator said, 'This substance is

called Gypsum'. Three boys at the front broke into a fit of sniggering, and one loudly giggled, 'Hur-hur-hur ... jism'.

29th March: Alistair, fellow English teacher, told me this joke – What's the difference between an OFSTED inspector and a plastic surgeon? A plastic surgeon tucks your features.

It was not long before I realised I was enjoying myself. Though I was working in three of the worst areas for education in the country, things were going well. I liked the kids, I liked the staff, and I liked the schools.

At least twice a week, I was asked to work at Boreham School. Nine years ago, this had been one of the most challenging schools in the capital. OFSTED had failed it, a Super Head had been brought in, and Special Measures imposed. Within two years, the school was out of Special Measures and the Head had made such a positive effect that when OFTSED re-visited in late 2006 Boreham was awarded Outstanding status, the highest mark a school can receive.

Boreham stands as an example of what a school can achieve when managed and run effectively. Nearly half of its students were on free school meals, slightly fewer had English as a second language, and nearly 40% had special educational needs: far higher than – and, in some cases, more than four times as much as – the national average (where 13% of England's school children are on free school meals, 9% have English as a second language and 17% have special educational needs). Situated on the edge of a poor estate, many of the feeder primary schools in the area have difficulties with their intake, difficulties which are then passed on to Boreham when the students turn 11 and move to secondary school. However, through a strong environment of rewards and sanctions, Boreham succeeds in turning these students around in the space of a few years.

I grew to understand within days that the younger the students were, the wilder they tended to be. The Year 11s were calm, kindly and respectful, while the Year 7s strutted around like tiny gangsters, practising pimp-walks in the corridors, and squaring up to teachers twice their size with gesticulating hands flapping wildly: "e was just dissin' you *like*!'

I often covered for the same English teacher, a woman who was fighting her way through the early stages of a difficult pregnancy and needed a lot of time off. I grew to know her classes, and grew fond of them. There was one of each cohort from Key Stage 3 Year 7 to A-Level Year 12. A fair and balanced portion of the department's timetable, together they hit every rung of the ability ladder. Overall, I spent over three weeks at Boreham, always with these same classes. The height of my problems with them came when Year 9 Arvin typed on to his PowerPoint presentation the words, 'Julius Ceser was a fat prick who liked to master bait'; or when Year 8 Redis took umbrage at my request to stop talking and start working, and said with a faltering uneasiness to his voice, 'Fuck off.' As far as consequences went, Arvin panicked when he realised I had seen what he was typing and promptly deleted it, coming up to me at the end of the lesson once everyone else had left and quietly apologising. Redis was excluded for a day for swearing at a teacher. How different, and how conducive to teaching, things were here, I thought, when held up against the confined prism of Varka.

One of my Year 8 lessons involved the pupils writing spells like the witches' curses from *Macbeth*. The new curses could have whatever result the students deemed fit – to kill, to split up a relationship, to make someone's hair fall out. Reece's was especially specific, revealing itself in his concluding couplet:

> *Listen to my curse and don't be silly,*
> *Or you'll end up with a half-inch willy.*

Reece presented the poem to me, and asked if he could illustrate it. I said that would be fine. He asked if he could draw a selection of willies. I said no.

'Oh, but sir, I'm really good at drawing them,' he protested.

'If I were you,' I said, lowering my voice, 'I wouldn't go shouting that around.'

Robbie, a Year 11 student who already had a beard I was jealous of, presented me with his finished Media coursework to proofread.

'Robbie,' I said. 'What does this sentence mean: "*Jaws* was a watershed in film-making history"?'

Robbie thought for a minute. 'It means, like, that *Jaws* was good because there was, like, loads of water in it.'

'No, that's not what it means.'

'Oh.'

'Did you copy and paste this from the internet?'

'Yes.'

During a DT cover, I noticed that James had been characteristically lazy all lesson. For doing so little work, I got him to collect in all the students' designs at the end. He asked Pouneh where hers was.

'I didn't do anything,' Pouneh told him.

'Respect,' James said, and they high-fived.

Boreham was by no means an easy school to teach in, but it rewarded its teachers. It was the kind of environment where one actually made a difference, and could see it. The students I taught were *grateful* for my presence, and made no attempt at hiding it. They loved their regular teacher, but they understood the difficulties she was going through in her personal life. Many of them, I dare say, had their own intimate experience of pregnancy. They also knew full well that having an English specialist as their substitute teacher was a privilege easily lost, so took care not to. On my last day, Tyrone brought me a bottle of Lambrini, concealed in four plastic carrier bags. 'Just wanted to say thanks, sir,' he mumbled as he left with all the others, pushing the package into my hands. I unwrapped it, and felt like crying. How sweet it was to feel that way through happiness rather than impotence.

* * * * *

It was at Boreham, four weeks into my time in London, that I first heard the term *shanking*. I had read it before, on the blog of a London state school teacher. But this was the first time I had ever heard a teenager say it.

A *shank* is a knife; to *shank* is to stab somebody. Student knifings have entered the English lexical and cerebral canon in the same way as the campus massacre has in America. In London, they are especially prevalent. Gangs have become an increasingly alluring prospect for many of London's poorer children and teenagers, and, as the size and popularity of gangs has grown, so too has the frequency of knifings.

It is not exclusive to London. In 2005, a 12-year-old girl slashed another across the face with the blade from a pencil sharpener in Sheffield. Even those areas considered 'safe and sleepy' have been affected: in 2007, there was a stabbing inside a school in Devon and four years before that a 14-year-old boy was stabbed to death in a school corridor in Lincolnshire. But London has seen the most, and worst, attacks. In 2008, 28 teenagers were stabbed to death in the city, and over 6,000 arrests for carrying a knife were made. Many of these incidents happened on school grounds, and knives have become a concern for anyone connected with education. Teacher knifings are virtually non-existent, but this is not where the problem lies. The mere possibility of a child carrying a lethal weapon whilst at school is a serious issue, and metal detectors – 'knife arches' – have now been installed at the entrances to hundreds of schools throughout London, Manchester, Birmingham and Liverpool.

At Boreham, the Senior Management Team had security wands with them at all times, and never hesitated to scan over and around a student if they felt it necessary. Random checks took place often, and it was not rare for an Assistant Head to enter my classroom during a lesson and walk through the students, casting his or her paddle about to the sporadic emissions of squeaks and pops while I attempted to continue teaching. It was a bizarre feeling: these intrusions were welcome, but they were still intrusions.

With the incessant media coverage, and with these security wands dancing up and down the school halls like props from *Star Trek*, I expected some exposure to knifings. As it turned out, I saw and heard of none within any of the schools in which I taught. The closest I got was when I overheard the student talking about shanking, and even he was denigrating it: 'See, if you got a problem with someone, and you end up shanking them, you don't get no respect for it.'

*****

As the weeks passed, the days gradually got longer, and the air gradually got easier. Towards the end of March, the first warm day of the year hit. I surfaced from the train on my way home from Boreham and, for the first time in what seemed like years, I felt the heat from the sun, not just the occasional ripples it had made through the cold for the last six months. The winter which had set in some time during the previous October had blown itself out with one final mother of a party the weekend before, feeding the country with snow and thunderstorms. Now spring began and brought with it a different

England. I had been waiting for it. The clocks were going forward two days later. My hat, stinking after not leaving my head in months, was going back in the cupboard.

Once I got home, I borrowed John's bicycle, riding it out into the streets of London – something I did every evening until I left. It is by far the best way to see the city. I entered the heart of the capital each time through a varied conglomeration of residential streets and avenues, coasting these quiet and leafy rows of Georgian terraced houses before hitting London proper, speeding through it with the feverish smugness of the cyclist in a traffic jam. London opened up to me on that bike, and I followed its contours gladly: around the pin-striped City district; through the 'centre' of Piccadilly, Leicester and Covent Garden; over any of the soaring bridges; along the gregarious, promenade-esque South Bank, weaving behind the skaters and BMX-bikers who knew the best way to cut through the tourists; and then returning via Shoreditch, snaffling late-night curries, and watching live music for free in dark Brick Lane bars.

I stopped when the fancy took me at expensive, well-placed pubs, enjoying solitary pints with a stillness exempt from the chaos always around. I loved the beer garden of the Founders Arms on the South Bank, where I could sit and enjoy St Paul's over the Thames, half-cast in gloomy light and shadow, still the clear centrepiece, the reminder that, no matter what is built around it, this will always be Wren's city. I freewheeled into Leicester Square, pulling up at a pub named after Orwell's 'perfect alehouse', the Moon under Water. Once, I pushed the bike through the Square to find it gridlocked with pedestrians. A Martin Scorsese film was being premiered, and so I took a moment to join the throngs who crammed themselves around the red carpet. An actor from *Eastenders* appeared, stopping to pose for the collective of paparazzi, and one of my fellow voyeurs shouted at the actor's girlfriend, 'Get yer tits out, love!'

A policeman appeared next to the shouter. 'Calm down, mate.'

'What?' the bloke protested.

'Well, it's a bit inappropriate, isn't it?' the policeman responded.

'Erm, I suppose. Sorry.'

There was an American girl stood behind me. 'That's *so* British,' she said. 'I *love* it.'

Over and along the pavements, in Covent Garden I claimed another favourite pub. Hidden above a tiny pasty shop in the centre, a Cornish-themed bar, the Cove, miraculously existed. A little ersatz slice of home in the middle of the gigantic cityscape, it sold beer from the Skinner's and St Austell breweries, and was always the place where I arranged to meet those Cornish I knew who had chosen this life. We would perch on stools in the outdoor terrace overlooking the main performance space of Covent Garden, and I would admit that I had got the London bug. They would laugh politely, and change the subject to ambitions and greatness. Evidently, they had the bug, too.

My final week passed easily. The Easter holidays were due, and so was my next move. All the five schools I had worked at in London had teacher-training days on the last Friday and I was not needed at any of them, so I decided to pay an old friend a visit.

* * * * *

Henry had been on my PGCE course. A lackadaisical and friendly fellow, he became infamous throughout our year group as the one who just didn't give a toss. While the rest of us toiled and panicked over our various written assessments, Henry always made sure to turn his in at the last minute with a reductive interpretation of the minimum word-count. While the rest of us gathered in cafés on occasional evenings to sip coffee nervously and discuss the tribulations of being a student-teacher, Henry would appear with a pint of cider and ask if anyone else had caught the rugby. And while the rest of us spent the other evenings fretting and cursing over lesson plans and evaluations, Henry would don his favourite 'I Love Chicks and Cheese' T-shirt, and hit the nearest Ladbrokes.

By the time it came to May of that year, we had all secured jobs. Even I, determined to find some sort of work in insular Cornwall, had succeeded. But June came around, and Henry was still unemployed.

'Aren't you worried?' I asked him one night.

'Worried, old bean? Don't know the meaning of the word.' It was possible that he did not.

'But we were told all the best jobs would be gone by Easter. And we're now almost ready to graduate. Have you even been looking?'

'Of course I've been *looking*,' he grinned, slapping me on the shoulder for effect. 'But nothing's come up yet that's right for me.'

'But if you leave it any longer, there'll be nothing left at all, let alone anywhere that's *right* for you…'

He dismissed me with an emphatic 'Nonsense!', and then rose from his seat. 'Pint?'

'No, I'll be all right, thanks. Got some marking to do.'

'Tosser,' he said, and marched off to the bar.

None of us expected Henry to find a job. June passed and, with it, the end of the course. One by one, we each began to leave Nottingham for whatever LEA we had nominated, steeling ourselves for a summer of preparation and sweating. Henry booked himself a holiday in Spain. And then, on my last day before I was to leave for Cornwall, I bumped into him in the streets of Nottingham. He had, just two days before, landed himself a job, and had done so with the opportunistic immoderation characteristic of only him.

Henry was public school-educated. An advocate of the independent sector in English education, part of the reason he had not managed to find work until so late was because he had decided that, now a teacher, he wanted to return to public schools. Our tutors warned him that very few took on NQTs, that he would be better off getting some experience first in state schools, and then trying again. But Henry was not to be deterred, and he finally achieved his goal, winning a job at a prestigious independent school in the south-east. It was exactly what he wanted.

'Can't bloody wait,' he said that afternoon in Nottingham. 'I'll get longer holidays than you, more money than you, and I won't have to deal with any of the bloody *oiks* you'll be contending with.' He gave a laugh and slapped me on the shoulder. 'Later, old bean.' He began to walk off, but then stopped and turned around. 'Stay in touch!' he called, framing the order with a salute.

And I thought, *I bet I'll never see him again.*

We did stay in touch, albeit sparingly. Each September, it became a tradition for those in our PGCE tutor group to send round-robin emails to each other. The emails were always full of changes: Eva had left her school and gone to work for another; Ruth had already been promoted to Head of Department; Elaine had packed up and gone to teach in Shanghai; Beth to Hong Kong; Charlie had got the idea into his head that it might be fun to write a book. And always, every single year, the drop-out rate increased. By the end of that academic year, seven out of the original twelve of us had left the English educational system.

The one person who never had any changes to report, however, was Henry. He stayed at his school. He saw no reason to leave. He liked teaching. By the time I reached London, I had become almost obsessively interested with Henry's contentment. How had his career ever managed to take such a straight line? What was so good about this school that he had stayed there for four years? Why on earth was he so *happy*? So I sent him an email, telling him of my project, and asking if I might come and visit him to have a talk about the independent sector. He replied, bettering my proposal – why not come in for a day to observe? With my impending day off approaching and Henry's school not far from London, the whole thing seemed fated, and so I set off into the south-east of England to find him.

Henry worked at Mabley, an all boys' school and one of the top hundred independent schools in England. Popular with the children of actors and football managers, it has just under 900 pupils, 15% of whom are sixth-formers. Parents pay around £10,000 in fees per student each year, plus an extra £1,200 for lunches. The school itself is a mixture of ornate, grandiose buildings and inane post-war classroom-blocks. The grounds are immense and breathtaking, like a university campus, with acres of woodland and a stretch of calm water. Most of the land has been transformed into various sports fields, and there are at least five full-size rugby pitches alone. For the first-time visitor, the whole thing is a hazy mirage of redbrick walls, weeping willows, and students referred to by their surnames.

Henry led me in to meet his form group at the start of the day, and we sat down before fifteen Year 7 and 8 boys. Six of them were writing in their books; one was playing air-piano dreamily on the table; another abstractedly fingered a protractor, his toy a tool for learning. The rest were chatting about school and sports. Two were discussing the crucifixion.

'If it had rained, the wood might have cracked and Jesus could have slipped away.'

'It's Jerusalem. How likely is rain?'

As Henry and I entered, they greeted him with a unanimous, 'Good morning, sir,' and ignored me. In any average state school, 'Who's that?' and 'Why's he here?' would have been asked in a flurry of shouts. Henry took the register and then left them to whatever they were doing, turning to me.

'Do you ever get any behavioural problems?' I asked.

'Never,' he said, with that penchant for absolutes I remembered from university. 'Of course, we've got our fair share of thickies, bullies and lazy twots – Finbar, that last one was meant for *you* – but nothing out of the ordinary. Above all, the kids here have a genuine respect for authority. For any adult entering the school, their authority is assumed.'

I thought about the schools I knew, where, for an adult entering, authority is earned.

I shadowed Henry for the rest of the day, placing myself discreetly at the back of the classroom to take notes during lessons and following him through the corridors at break sessions. For Period 2, the students were 10 minutes late. There are no bells at Mabley, so teachers often run over with their lessons. When the students finally arrived, they were all out of breath. They had sprinted. It was not that they feared Henry's reaction – understanding that this happened, he was forgiving rather than strict. They had run because they did not want to be late.

For Period 4, there was an assembly for the Year 7 cohort. Henry and I stood at the back of the hall. Each time the teacher-speaker in front said something positive, the students would applaud and cheer a thoroughly-enunciated 'Hooray!' I could not escape the feeling that I was looking at a future House of Lords, and I felt a little sick.

At lunch time, we ate good food in the refectory and then went to look around the annual Hobbies Fair in the sports hall. Students of all ages had gathered there to erect shrine-like stalls which displayed their favourite hobbies. It was here that you could see the money abundant within these walls, could see how rich these children's parents were. One had a brand new motorbike, another his sailing-dinghy, one a collection of expensive electric guitars, and yet another a 'Segway', a two-wheeled vehicle – like a sideways, stand-up motorbike – which had cost £3,000. Pupils clamoured around the stalls cooing and cawing, and I felt sorry for the Year 8 boy who stood, alone yet proud, behind his collection of polished rocks.

To finish the lunch break, Henry took me to the staff room. There was a veritable roar in there, the likes of which I had not heard in other schools. The teachers sauntered about, loud and confident, brash, even. I spoke to a few while Henry methodically collected plates of biscuits from each table and settled himself down to enjoy his strange dessert. Between all the teachers I chatted to, there was only one complaint, though it was common to all. The parents, they said, put a lot of pressure on them. Though they did not have to cope with the impositions of OFSTED or governmental criteria and curricula, this was made up for by the parents. One English teacher explained it to me. 'The problem is, they pay all this money, and then expect their kid to automatically get an A,' he said. 'They don't seem to understand that some kids just aren't capable of achieving top marks – the way they see it, that £10,000 should *guarantee* an A, should buy it. But it doesn't work like that. And it's very difficult to explain that it's all just genetic, that actually their kid is just a dozy Joe Soap.'

Henry had to stay on at the end of the day to coach the Year 10 rugby team, so I bid him farewell in his classroom, thanked him for the day and left, driving down the lane which joined the school to the main road. It had been an interesting day and, as soon as I found a lay-by to spend the night on, I reflected on it at length.

I have a deep prejudice against independent schools. I just do not like them, though I have never been sure why. Perhaps it is the socialist in me, rallying against those who charge for what I consider to be a fundamental human right. Or perhaps it is because, when I was a kid, I lost one of my best friends to an independent school. But that day with Henry at Mabley had made me realise something: namely, that my prejudice was rather abstract, and very ungrounded. It was based on concepts, on theories, with no hard evidence behind it whatsoever.

Not only had I never taught in an independent school, up until that day I had never even set foot in one.

By the end of that day, I still knew I disliked the independent sector just as much as I had before, but I at least had some sort of basis now. It was just a question of backing it up. The next day, I drove down to the West Country and parked up in the town I had left seven months earlier to start this journey. I paid a visit to my old local library, filling up on books, and then digging some of my own out of the van's literature cupboard, so that I could read my way through the weekend.

*****

It has been said that it is impossible to write a book about England without mentioning the class system at least once. Whether or not this be true, it is certainly impossible for anyone to write a book about education in England without mentioning the class system. The independent-state divide so clear in our country's schools is a product of it, a block of contemporary culture moulded by the hands of the tiers as they push and pull with each other. Whether you advocate its presence or rebel against it or are simply ambivalent, the fact that it is seminal to our country's society is inescapable – the independent sector is a force which any educational theory, doctrine or polemic cannot ignore. While there are only 7% of the country's children in independent education, 20% of those currently at university are privately educated, and a staggering 50% of Oxbridge students have come from the independent sector. Going one rung down the ladder to A-Levels, a recent survey found that 87 of the top 100 schools in England's league tables were private, whilst – in the field of GCSEs – 80% of independent school students passed five or more GCSEs at A* to C. In the state sector at the time, only 43% achieved the same.

The independent schooling system in England is clearly successful, and it is also an extremely lucrative enterprise. By the turn of the 21st century, there were 2,300 independent schools in Britain, generating between them £3.2 billion a year from the parents of 600,000 students. No other country in the world has a state-independent divide quite like ours. Indeed, it is only in developing, third-world countries – where any semblance of a decent education *has* to be paid for – that you will find any system remotely similar.

This flood of money becomes apparent when visiting an independent school. It was certainly clear to me at Mabley. Here there were only 680 pre-A level students (the average state school has 1,100), and the student-to-teacher ratio was 18:1 (rather than the 30:1 class size of the average state school). Over the past ten years, there had been no exclusions of any kind, and no more than three staff had left per year. The pay-scale – £23,460 for NQTs plus £1,700 each year for eight years – was higher than the public sector's (on average, £20,627 for NQTs plus £1,800 each year for five years) and here the percentage of students with Special Educational Needs was 1.4, whereas the national average in state schools is 17%.

Perhaps Mabley is not entirely representative of all independent schools across Britain, but I doubt it is as far removed from them all as it is from the average state school. I had seen children running to their lessons because they did not want to be late, had heard out-of-class conversations which suggested these children not just enjoyed school, but loved it, and had read the school prospectus' dizzying list of the extra-curricular activities on offer, many of which, Henry informed me, were full. The vast gulf which exists between independent and state schools became apparent to me at Mabley, and I finally realised why I did not like the independent sector. It was because I was jealous.

And perhaps this is another reason why so many teachers are leaving. Perhaps they are jealous, too. Perhaps they had noticed the same gulf I had, for many seemed to be fleeing the problems of the state system for the comfort of the independent. And, when I thought back over my day at Mabley and juxtaposed it with my time in schools like Varka, I found I could not blame them.

THE WEST COUNTRY

I WAS CHEATING AGAIN. Like the Peak District earlier in the year, returning to the West Country to teach for the next six weeks had not been on my original agenda. Though the area does include some tough schools – particularly in Bristol – the south west of England is by no means among the most difficult places to work. In fact, teachers often move there specifically for the easy life. Cornwall in particular is a notoriously difficult place to get a job.

But the truth was that I needed the respite. Seven months of teaching in demanding and draining conditions had exhausted me. I was tired of the inner cities, tired of turning up at a new school each day to assimilate brand new systems. The cloying, never-ending concrete had begun to suffocate me, and I was sick of my constant anonymity. I wanted to be near friends, to have the same classes each day, to know the rules not just of a school, but of a place. I wanted some stability.

After the West Yorkshire debacle, my old Head of Department had called to offer me work. I had declined his offer of a permanent position, but had accepted something more short-term. The female teacher who had replaced me when I left Somerset had soon become pregnant. Her maternity leave was due to start at the close of the Easter holidays, and the school's Senior Management Team was searching for a temporary teacher to take over her classes throughout her absence. If I wanted it, the work was there.

The West Country

I wanted it. These were my old classes, students I knew well and enjoyed working with. I negotiated terms with the Head and agreed to work for the penultimate half-term of the academic year. I would take on my replacement's entire timetable – including her free periods – along with all her responsibilities. It meant I had to return to the tiring cycle of planning and marking, but the school offered to pay me handsomely for it, far more than I was earning elsewhere. Truth be told, I would have done it for my usual basic rate. Six weeks of an easy life lay ahead, and I was looking forward to relaxing into it. Thoroughly spent from the last seven months, I saw the next half-term as a welcome little working holiday.

It was not just about the school, of course. I was also happy at the chance to return west for a time. The limits of the West Country are a matter of debate: for some, it includes Dorset, Wiltshire and sections of Gloucestershire; others say it extends no further than the Tamar. For me, the West Country is Cornwall, Devon and Somerset, the chunky peninsula which forms the tail of England.

I grew up in Cornwall, was a definitive West Country boy, but by the age of 13 I was already saving my weekly pocket money for regular train journeys to Plymouth, Dawlish, Exeter and Bristol. In many ways, my long history of travelling started then: all those splendid journeys through Europe and South-East Asia which defined my early 20s were born right there. I explored the region with a hunger, mapping out routes and pathways in the back of my English schoolbooks. Trains were my favourite mode of transport, but when I passed my driving test, my first car, a £180 Austin Metro, felt my wanderlust acutely, finally dying of exhaustion on Bodmin Moor after a mammoth Bank Holiday weekend road-trip. I still vividly remember the first time I caught a public bus alone, a three-mile journey from my village to the city of Truro. I was nine years old. I have been trying to re-capture the excitement I felt on that short journey ever since.

By the time I was 18, I felt I had seen the whole of the west and needed to move on. I left for six years, moving about Britain and Europe, but I always came back to visit, and I never forgot why I had loved the West Country so much. I moved back to Cornwall for my first teaching job, then up to Somerset a year and a half later. I left again to start the journey that forms this book, but after seven months my longing for home was immense.

I came back to Somerset in late April. Arriving on a day of blue sky and blossoming trees, I convinced myself that the clichés were true, that the air was cleaner down here, the life slower. London had been my city fix. For now, I was glad to be back where I belonged.

* * * * *

I started back at Pascoe Community School on a bright Monday morning, the first day of the summer term. I arrived early, greeted by my old English department colleagues with familial warmth, and took some time to walk around the school, dropping in on other friends from less than a year ago. It was a morning of smiles and handshakes and welcome-backs. Staff had left on maternity or paternity leave, or would soon do so; some had been promoted; new teachers had arrived. Everyone seemed, bizarrely, hairier. The students themselves responded to my reappearance in their own ways. Year 8s and 9s would spot me, double-take, shout out 'Mr Carroll!', come running up, and then suddenly realise that they did not know what to say. Others – especially those older – would nod over at me from their packs of friends in a fashion much more befitting their level of cool. 'All right, sir? Back, then? Thought you'd managed to get out of this dump.'

I poked my head around the door of the Headteacher's office to say a quick hello.

'Charlie!' he called out boisterously, jumping up from his desk and bounding over to pull me into the office by my arm, displaying the effervescent likeability I remembered so well of him, part of the reason why he made such an excellent Head. We sat down and chattered freely. It was the most welcoming and unawkward first morning I had experienced all year.

I was looking forward to Period 1. The class I was to take was one of the key reasons not just for my choice to return to Pascoe, but for the Senior Management Team's desire to have me back. They were a group of thirty-two 16-year-old Year 11 top-set boys: a collection of some of the smartest lads in the entire student cohort. I had taught this class through their Year 10, growing to care for them a great deal. They remain, to this day, my favourite class; when I left the school, one of my deepest regrets had been that I would not see them finish. Their current teacher – through no fault of her own – had left them at perhaps the most crucial part of their school lives: the final month before study leave and their exams. This was a worry for the SMT. A large portion of any school's reputation hinges upon how well its students do in their GCSEs, and so – as with any competition such as that which the league table culture in English education has created (but more of that later) – those who look set to do best are relied upon heavily. If their regular teacher leaves close to the final exams, this is verging on a crisis. To employ a non-specialist supply teacher to oversee such a class is unthinkable. Fortunately, I knew the subject and the students, and this was perhaps the main reason why I had been taken back on what were, in many ways, my own terms. The Senior Management Team got an established and reliable stand-in, the students got their old teacher back, and I got to watch the graduation of 32 of the most inspiring pupils I had ever worked with. Unusually, everyone was a winner.

I sat down at my old desk. The bell went. The corridor outside became a whirlwind of movement and noisy Somerset accents. I heard my Year 11s begin to arrive in clusters. I stayed in my seat. Perhaps unsure whether it would be decent to enter of their own accord, they waited outside, growing in number. Their voices seeped in under the door. 'I heard Carroll's back.' 'Bollocks, he moved to New Zealand.' 'Jamie saw him this morning.'

Once I was sure they had all arrived, I opened the door. There they all stood in a rough line against the wall. A cheer went up from Iain, quickly drowned out by an echo from all the rest. They piled in, slapping me on the shoulder or grinning toothily. Some had started to grow stubble, I noticed. Following them back into the classroom, I stood behind my desk while they pushed towards their seats and emptied their rucksacks on to their tables. I couldn't help feeling that I was not with a class, but with some old friends.

We talked for 10 minutes. I told them some of the more innocuous stories from my last seven months' travelling. They filled me in with football tournaments won and essays they had excelled in. Mike stood up and, with the encouraging cheers of those around him, welcomed me back in Klingon. Richard arrived late with a sincere apology and a plausible excuse, and it was time to start the lesson: a 45-minute practice essay under exam conditions. I handed out some A4 lined paper, wrote the title on the board, and they fell to it in absolute silence. I was shocked at this instantaneous switch, but then I looked at the bent tops of their heads and remembered that, with this lot, it had always been that way.

I had worked hard with them over the first months of the previous year, endeavouring to create an environment halfway between a boys' club and an academic hothouse. Intellectually, I had pushed them harder than any other class before, but I had also let them know it, and given them a resultant freedom of thought and speech with a lenience that is absent in my general teaching style. And, to my delight, it seemed to have worked. These were no longer the boys I had met at the beginning of their Key Stage 4 years, they were young adults. I saw Francis, a boy who started Year 10 reserved and self-conscious, but who was now so confident he could put the jokers to shame with his sharp retorts. There was Richard, who joined Pascoe later than the others but thrived in its atmosphere, becoming a clever and erudite in-house stand-up comic. There was Phil, who forgot to put paragraphs in his SATs, yet had recently sent a letter to an extreme sports magazine and won a prize for it. He proudly showed me the publication one day. 'See that, sir?' he said, pointing to one of his sentences. 'Personification.'

By the Wednesday of my first week, it felt like I had never left. In the staff room at break-times, colleagues asked for tales of the inner-city sectors, and traded them for horror stories of their own. Our gossipy conversations reached the same conclusion with a familiar consistency. Pascoe was wonderful, and we knew it. Here, we did not worry about violent confrontations or knife threats; here, there was no need for closed-circuit cameras in the corridors; the exclusion policy was fair and devoid of enforced fear; *we* were devoid of fear – we could teach, and enjoy teaching.

Much like Boreham in London, Pascoe is a clear example of how first-rate our state educational system can be. Its catchment area includes some fairly impoverished estates, its Special Educational Needs quota is far above average, and its exclusion rate is high, yet the school continues to be one of the top state schools by league table rankings in England. In 2006, it was awarded Outstanding status by OFSTED. Heads and Seconds of Department from other schools in the area have been known to take on basic teacher roles at Pascoe just for the opportunity of working there. Its staff turnover rate is low, and the morale throughout the school, of students and staff, is high.

When I first applied for my job there, I was sent its prospectus. One of OFSTED's comments from the last visit was that the students were 'proud of their school'. There is no higher recommendation.

But Pascoe is the exception, rather than the rule. Why is it such a success? It is true that, though the school may house those from disadvantaged backgrounds, it is still somewhat a product of its location, and could never contend with the intake of, say, an inner-city school. West Country life – in all its charming, clichéd backwardness – is rife here, from the rural softness of its people to the idyllic romances of country air. Time may not pass in reverse, but it certainly runs on a much slower clock. While in Birmingham I might have entered a school office to find myself in the midst of police calls and drug confiscations, at Pascoe the ladies in the office drank tea and ate thin slices of cake whilst looking out of the window at the duck who had chosen to lay her eggs by the school pond ('She's been sitting on those eggs for days without moving now… The drake comes along occasionally, but then sods off again. Typical man.').

It would be wrong, though, to claim that Pascoe does not have its own list of challenging behaviours to deal with. During my third day back, a Year 11 student, when asked by one of my colleagues why he had missed his already-extended coursework deadline, threw his bag across the room and screamed, 'You fucking twat!' at the teacher. That student was immediately excluded for a week, and he was excluded because his teacher was supported by those who run the school. The outburst was not brushed under the carpet or left to ferment; it was dealt with swiftly and correctly. And this is why Pascoe is so successful. The key is the Senior Management Team.

I've taught in schools where you rarely see the Headteacher or Deputy Headteacher outside of their offices, and perhaps the students did not either, for they seemed not to care whenever I invoked an SMT name in a threat against misbehaviour. But when I began working at Pascoe, I felt the Senior Management Team's positive presence acutely. The 'managers' who comprised the team all had individual talents which harmonised when implemented collectively. They were always present. It saddens me when a Headteacher spends more time out of the school than in, or more time shut up in his or her office than along the corridors or in the classrooms, but this is often the case. In the long list of schools I have worked at throughout my career, too many Headteachers have been little more than shadowy Big Brothers to the schools' networks, known only by name, face and reputation. And though they will doubtless refuse to admit it, their actions are a detriment to the success of their schools. The Senior Management Team of a school, you see, must be there to lead, but they must also be there to follow up, to shirk delegation and deal with emerging issues firsthand. The SMT of Pascoe does exactly this: they are not a 'last resort', but instead are colleagues, colleagues we all, teachers and students alike, trust in to decide what is right, and then to act upon it.

I could not give enough praise to Pascoe. It is a school so ideal I almost want to look for cracks. Yet it is real, and it stands as an example of just how good the educational system in England could be for all. For when an effective Senior Management Team are in place, teachers stay in their jobs because they are happy there, and students are able to learn (and learn successfully) in an atmosphere they are not just comfortable and content in, but one which they are proud of.

*****

Spring was now underway, the sun was eager to show off its charms after five months of hibernation, and I was out on the road every weekend. I wanted to check back in at favourite haunts: Wells,

Bath, Sidmouth, Dartmoor, Colliford Lake, Falmouth, Porthtowan. I shunned lay-bys for the luxury of campsites, cheap as they were before peak season hit. I left my trusty maps in the cupboard and travelled by memory alone, following the songlines of my youth.

I had dreamed of journeys like these during those frozen nights in Birmingham: long, exploratory voyages down the A30, flanked by convoys of VWs crawling over the lanes like flies, eager for a Cornish weekend. Horns blasted and saluted every few minutes. Even those broken down on the hard shoulder were surrounded by drivers and passengers in high spirits, who grinned and stuck their thumbs up at each Doppler beep.

I coasted through inland Somerset – a wealth of farms, woodlands, garden centres and red earth – pushing up to the coast and following the siren roads which lured me through leafy glens and confronted me with sudden dead ends, sheer drops, narrow tracks, and networks of clutch-burning, brake-melting hills. I frittered about the backroads of Devon before slamming into Cornwall, the change of landscape immediate. Hills lowered. Space grew and, with it, a sense of desolation. Granite prevailed.

I found strips of land I had once been intimate with, and rejoiced in the ancient Kernewek of the road signs. Water was everywhere, surrounding the peninsula and coursing under and through it. I parked up beside beaches, watched swell-lines as the wind whipped them into messy, closing-out six-footers, and retraced family walks up to solitary engine-houses on north coast cliffs. I absorbed wonderful sunsets from these coastal vantage points, feeling the environment in my skin: the calcium milkiness of the shallow waters; stones the colour of rust; the fragility of the sheer cliffs, so crumbling with sediment you could bore into them with your fingernails; the long line of queuing headlands, dotted here and there by thin, silky coves. And then there was the ocean, the thrashing, crashing ocean before it all, breathing and moving back and forth, sucking and licking, rolling out and out and out to a world of danger and curves. I came to believe I had manufactured all this for myself. Almost a year had passed since I made the decision to do this, to travel this country, to learn it as I had never before bothered. Much had hurt along the way, but it was all worth it.

*****

One week, Pascoe had a teacher training day. I was not needed, and so asked Emma to find me work elsewhere in the West Country. Bristol's Dell Community College was nominated, and I set off early to beat the city's rush hour traffic.

Dell was renowned as a challenging school and, though it was not as difficult as some of the others I had taught in throughout the country, the contrast between it and Pascoe was immediate. A general feeling of negativity permeated throughout: the students were rude and depressive, and so too were the staff. The dinner ladies served me my food with a miserable anger. There was a sense of all-pervading boredom about this school, the feeling that no-one cared about it, and that problems were sooner ignored than met. My cover for Period 1, the invigilation of a maths exam in the main hall, confirmed such thoughts. The pupils were allowed to use calculators, but most of them had not brought one. For the next hour, I and two other teachers ran frantically about the room swapping 30 calculators between 70 children. It was both comical and ludicrous.

After that, I entered Period 2 – Year 10 English – to find the students sitting working on practice essays for their forthcoming exams. The quiet was pleasant, and I needed to only introduce myself, offer some encouragement and take my seat.

Twenty minutes in, however, one boy sprang from his chair at the back of the classroom and grabbed his neighbour, wrenching him to his feet and securing him in an aggressive headlock. 'Don't talk about my mum!' he screamed. 'It's my fucking mum!'

I darted towards them, shouting at another boy to get a member of staff. He merely laughed at me, but fortunately a girl insinuated herself between the fighting pupils and broke them up. I ordered both boys outside and, to my surprise, they complied without argument. One walked around the corner of the corridor, and I could hear him making a soft noise which could have been either crying or giggling. I spoke to the other.

'What was that all about?' I said.

'I don't know,' he said. 'Anil just grabbed me for no reason.' I could see thick red marks on his neck. I sent him back inside and rounded the corner to find the other boy.

'What just happened, Anil?'

'A wind-up, sir,' he said emotionlessly. 'Just a wind-up.'

He walked back into the classroom and sat in a free seat at the front. Nothing more was said.

At lunch time, I found my way back to the staff room. Along the corridor, I passed the Deputy Head as he pulled four guilty-looking boys from a male toilet. The stench of cigarette smoke gushed out after them. He was shouting furiously. 'In the toilets? *Really*? I thought kids these days were more inventive than that! Even *we* didn't use the toilets!'

No-one spoke to me in the staff room.

My last lesson in this depressing place was Year 11 English. As I entered the room, an unfamiliar teacher strode up to me. 'You're Charlie, yeah?' she said. 'Great. Would you do me a big favour and swap lessons with me? I already had this lot before lunch, and I could do with having them again to finish off their work. Could you take my class instead?'

It seemed logical, so I agreed.

'Brilliant,' she said. 'Thanks. There's cover work on the desk. Don't worry. My lot are lovely.'

I followed her instructions to find her room. The students were splayed around the classroom creating a throb of noise, and I had to cross the space sideways in order to squeeze through the immoveable rabble. The cover work left on the desk was a single print-out of a PowerPoint presentation devoid of instructions or pedagogical context. I flicked through it, trying to work out how it might be used, and concluded that it was not only insufficient, but useless. Eventually, I managed to ascertain that it had something to do with a poem they were studying for their exams. Unfortunately, it was one I had never taught before, so I had no lesson-plans of my own to fall back on. The poem was Wilfred Owen's *Dulce Et Decorum Est*, and all the print-out seemed to provide was some information copied and pasted from the internet about the first World War.

Falteringly, I tried to start the lesson with a discussion on the poem and the war, but the students were either riotous or indifferent or needed Learning Support Assistants, of which there were none: one of the boys at the front had Tourette's Syndrome, and I realised that the quiet girl at the back was not refusing to work but had not heard my instructions because she was profoundly deaf. She sat throughout the lesson doing nothing – perhaps this was how she spent most of her lessons – and I felt deeply sad for her. Inclusion was clearly doing her no favours, and if it was to, she at least needed an LSA to help her.

A game of throwing began, and I asked one boy whose chosen missile was a pair of scissors to leave the room. I confronted him outside the classroom. He looked beyond me, mumbled, 'I don't give a fuck if I get in trouble,' and then walked out of the building.

By the end of the day, I determined that I had been mistreated in this school by students and staff alike, and sought out the Head of English.

'How did today go?' she asked as I walked into her classroom.

'To be honest, it was terrible,' I said.

'Oh,' she seemed taken aback. 'Why?'

'If you want the truth,' I said, allowing myself to become self-righteous, 'I'm disgusted by what I had to put up with today. In that last lesson alone, one of your teachers tricked me into taking her lesson, which I shouldn't have been teaching, and left nothing but a paltry printout of a PowerPoint which gave no indication what I was actually supposed to teach.'

'Well, I'm sure that…'

'And on top of that,' I interrupted her, too fired up now to allow her to continue, 'she failed to mention that there were two students in that class with severe learning difficulties – one with Tourette's, the other so deaf she couldn't understand a thing she was meant to do. Not that I had been left any work to give her.'

'Perhaps we could just…'

'I'd like you to know that I will be informing my agency of how this school treats its supply teachers, and I will also be putting in a request never to have to work here again.'

A silence. I had surprised myself with my outburst, but felt justified. She thought for a few seconds, and then spoke.

'Do you want a job?'

* * * * *

I returned to Pascoe grateful the next day – the last day before study leave for my Year 11 boys. The day had all the familiar rituals: the shirt-signings, the thousand photographs, the traditional terrorist fire alarm, the final assembly with cabaret-style acts and sketches, the strict Head of Year gleefully making a fool of himself while dancing to Right Said Fred, the congregation at the end of the day in front of the school, so many young adults crying, as if suddenly realising that now they have to go *out there*, the handshakes and good-lucks, first names used.

With the disappearance of Year 11, most of my afternoons freed up, and I was often out of school early, sunning myself in the local park with a book. The weather was improving all the time, and I took to walking to and from school each day along the canal which stretched down and through the town. I felt a long way from those frozen nights on the outskirts of northern cities, wondered if it could ever have been that cold. Summer was in blossom, and teaching suddenly did not seem so bad after all. Each night, I slept like a kitten.

Pascoe was quieter, its corridors wider and its students smaller. Soon, the Year 10s went on their two-week work experience placements, and it was like being in a primary school. Teachers love this time of year; it is a time for catching up, a time *of* time. Books and essays can be marked as thoroughly as the students deserve, homework can be set with meaning, lessons are better-resourced and far more dynamic, during lunch times one can enjoy lunch.

Within a week, the Year 11s began sporadically to reappear. They had about them a distinct air of nervousness, and crumpled leaves of scrawled-over A4 passed between them in the playgrounds. The Year 9s, too, were acting in the same fashion. They asked more questions than usual. Some gave up their lunch breaks to visit teachers and check over things. Assemblies were cancelled because the hall was filled with tables and desks. Large, ominous boxes appeared in reception to be carried off to various departments. Everyone grew jittery and displaced, students and staff alike. The exam season had begun.

I spoke to an ex-colleague from Nottingham on the phone that week. Within minutes, our conversation turned to the looming exams.

'The SATs are here again.'

'I wonder what will go wrong this year,' I said. Nobody liked the SATs.

'I don't mind them so much,' she said. 'I mark them. The extra cash pays for my summer holiday.'

I had never volunteered to be an exam marker. It is true that the pay is good, but the extra workload had always seemed to me to outweigh the monetary benefit. I told her as much.

'I suppose I do spend those weeks doing nothing but work, and even then I only just manage to get the papers back on time. But I don't take them as seriously as I used to. Last year, it was just a case of tick-and-flick, and I'll be doing the same this year, too.'

I was slightly appalled by this. 'Maybe that's why the SATs get sent back so often,' I snapped. 'If you lot gave them a little more consideration and marked them properly, maybe that would help?'

She laughed. 'The first year I did it, I paid them so much attention I was working 80-hour weeks. Thousands of papers were sent back that year. I did the same next year, and exactly the same happened again. So now I don't pay them the same attention. When you've got 250 papers in a pile on your desk, and you know that half will be sent back to be re-marked no matter *how* much time you put in, you learn not to care. It's not the markers that are at fault, it's the papers. You know how flawed they are. And I'm sure you know how worthless they are, too.'

I had to agree. SATs (one source says the acronym stands for 'Standard Assessment Tasks', another 'Statutory Assessment Tests', and yet another 'Standard Attainment Tests') were introduced into mainstream English education in 1991. After various union-led boycotts, they became standard across the country within a few years, with all students taking their first set of SATs in primary school, and others at the end of Year 9. A constant source of controversy, not one year passed without a large number of them being sent back for re-marking after they failed to reflect the true attainment levels of thousands of students.

'Anyway,' she continued. 'They'll probably be abolished soon.'

Though she was only joking, she was right. None of us expected it, but that year was to be the last of the Year 9 SATs. The news came suddenly at the start of the next academic year, and teachers nationwide breathed a sigh of relief.

The main contention surrounding the SATs was that they were so purposeless. Officially, they were supposed to be an indication of progress, and a means to tell the teacher where each student was in their learning. Promoted as an objective system of external testing which bypassed any unnecessary internal assessment to present all involved in a child's education – teachers, parents, LEAs – with a factualised account of where that child stood in terms of nationalised averages, they gave an uncomplicated calibration of numbers from one to eight. If your child scored a Level 4 in his Key Stage 2 SATs at the end of Year 6, he had reached the national target; if your child scored a Level 5 in her Key Stage 3 SATs, she had done the same. Based upon those results, your child would be put into the class which befitted their academic ability.

However, the SATs did nothing of the sort. Since the government-encouraged policy of inclusion (that all children, regardless of their learning needs, should be schooled together) has been put into place over the last decade, the majority of secondary schools tend to group their Key Stage 3 students into mixed ability classes, thus rendering any kind of setting meaningless. Likewise, though most GCSE students are put into sets for the core subjects (English, maths and science) at the beginning of Year 10, rarely were the SATs results relied upon for the setting. Time defeated such an opportunity. The results for the maths and science SATs were released between the beginning and the middle of July – at best, just three weeks before the end of the academic year. The results for the English SATs were released even later, often right in the middle of the summer holidays. To create the groupings of an entire year of students during such a time-frame was a ludicrous idea and, thus, was often ignored. Discussions for who should be set where in the core subject departments begin shortly after the Easter holidays, and concrete class-lists are usually demanded by SMTs in early July, before any of the results have even been gathered, let alone released.

Perhaps the initial reasoning behind the SATs was viable, but since their implementation was not, teachers began to see them as something else – first, as one more addition to the lunch-box of bureaucracy the government has over-packed for us; and second, as a means to create little more than a bank of statistics for the national league tables.

The league tables, initially implemented by the Tories, kept on by Labour, and then continued by the current Conservative-Liberal Democrat government, were first published in 1991 (the same year as the introduction of the SATs). Disturbingly similar to a sports league or the inter-store sales tables compiled by supermarket chains, the league tables have landed schools in an arena where befuddling statistics of 'Contextual Value-Added' and 'Limits of Confidence Intervals' attempt to address notions such as intake or poverty, but only really succeed in calibrating schools into a cold and one-dimensional list, where success and failure are reduced to numbers and letters.

The emotionless clarity of the league tables has never been popular with teachers. Pitching schools into a nationwide competition feels wrong. It is, of course, important for parents to know about their local schools, but numerical reductionism does not provide an adequate appraisal of a school's strengths and weaknesses. I would suggest instead looking to the school's most recent OFSTED reports.

(Despite what you may have heard, many teachers, myself included, see OFSTED as an important and valuable part of the educational system. Schools, and especially their Senior Management Teams, *must* be inspected on a regular basis, though OFSTED's findings can sometimes be diluted by the fact that they give notice of their visits, and therefore do not always see a school working as it regularly does.) Schools cannot be summarised by figures and percentiles, the very depth of everything a school can and cannot do for your child can only be described with words, not numbers.

This weird bureaucracy – one which defines success by a bank of statistics – is a legacy of the results-obsessed Labour government, though there is no indication that David Cameron and his colleagues will make any changes to it in the foreseeable future. This is a shame, for such bureaucratic indifference is a trial for teachers, especially those working in schools whose intake cannot compete with other more affluent areas. To compare an inner-city Sheffield school with Pascoe on the basis of exam-results alone is unjust.

This is not to say that all exams should be dropped. Qualifications of all kinds usually require some sort of summative exam, whether through undergraduate degrees, training at work, or in life itself – the driving test, for example. Education is no different: GCSEs are a vital component of English schooling which have, in different guises, been around for decades, and retain their importance by signifying to employers how successfully their potential employees can apply themselves to a task. But it does not follow from this premise that we should only teach children to the test. School is so much more than that. In basing our conclusions of a school's performance on exam results, we forget the other wonderful things schools and teachers do for our children. We forget encouraging the love of a subject. We forget reading a book just for pleasure. We forget teaching a child how or why to question, or developing the autonomy of voice, forget scaffolding a craft just for the enjoyment of the craft alone, forget delving into intricacies or idiosyncrasies, opinion and stylistics, reasoning and independent decisions, and forget even allowing them to make a decision.

Yet perhaps there is now some hope.

After the SATs were abolished, it was expected that they would be rebranded and reintroduced under a different, more user-friendly guise. When the coalition government ousted Labour in 2010, teachers nationwide held their breath to see if new Year 9 exams would be introduced within Michael Gove's long list of educational reforms. At the time of writing, still nothing has happened. There has been no new initiative, nor no excuse for the old one. This seems to be official recognition that there was a problem in the first place; perhaps our ministers are hoping that, if they continue with such a strategy, all will conveniently disappear. Today's teachers are more than happy to lend a hand to such window-dressing. It means, after all, that perhaps we can start assessing the academic abilities of our Year 9 students ourselves – a job we are trained to do – rather than relying upon external bodies.

Perhaps it also means something far more optimistic. The words you have just read about the SATs are mine, but they echo the thoughts of thousands of teachers throughout the country. And perhaps, we like to tell ourselves, the SATs were abolished because of these thoughts. Perhaps we were actually listened to.

Today, most schools still administer exams at the end of Year 9, some even using the government-prescribed APP (Assessing Pupil Progress) tests. These are then assessed internally by the teachers themselves, and are done so in enough time to be useful for GCSE groupings. Freed from the bureaucratic constraints of the externally-assessed SATs and, for the first time in nearly 20 years, officially allowed to publicise their own professional judgements of their students' academic progress, many teachers feel very positive about what is happening today. We all hope that such a system, as temporary as it may be, will remain. And, for the first time in a long while, there is a chance that it might. If it does, then we will have moved forward. If it does, then I, uncharacteristically but sincerely, will applaud.

LIVERPOOL

I LEFT THE WEST COUNTRY reluctantly, but the end of my journey was in sight. With only six weeks of the school year and two places to visit left, I reloaded the van and headed back up north.

I had no desire to return to work. The prospect of plunging back into the tides of challenging schools was uninviting, particularly in Liverpool. I thumbed back through those lists I had made almost a year ago, remembering how high Liverpool had come on most, and sighed. I needed one day before beginning, a day to at least explore the city and get some sense of it.

I drove into the city through its outskirts, packed with 'projects' and 'regeneration centres', miles upon miles of uninhabited, boarded-up, possibly condemned buildings which wore the graffitied St David's Star of 'GAS OFF, ELEC OFF'. Parking up, I found myself in the horrible centre, that pedestrianised grid of shiny surfaces, chain-outlets and characterless anonymity, all focused around the rising leviathan, the mother of all malls, Liverpool One; or the Radio City needle which pierces the clouds and dominates the skyline with a complete lack of belonging.

But such horrors were peanuts. I soon learnt that Liverpool had far too much to glory in to allow these graceless anomalies to bring down the tone. I adored the Cultural Quarter around St George's Hall with its formidable buildings, its Wellington's Column – as dramatic as Nelson's – its museums and libraries and water-features: a concrete example of neoclassical grandiosity, and of money. I delighted in the

Cavern Quarter, that tiny Venetian system of narrow, interlocked streets, the sense of how seedy and delicious the city centre may once have been. And I fell so deeply for the 'lambananas' – strange half-sheep-half-fruit public works of art which dot the city, exemplifying the playful side of Liverpool – that I took to noting down the name of each one I passed in my journal: 'SuperlamBananatree', 'Ba Ba Braille Sheep', 'Superlambgranada', 'Ewes Water Wisely'.

I ended the day down at the docks. The Albert Dock has been almost entirely regenerated over the past few years and now constitutes, perhaps even above Beatlemania, one of Liverpool's biggest draws for tourism. It is the focal point of all ten miles of docks on this stretch of the Mersey. For over two centuries, 100,000 people were able to derive employment from this area, and Liverpool became one of the largest ports in the world for shipping in goods and shipping out emigrants.

I took an expensive pint in a dockside pub, and then allowed myself one final hour to walk east towards the less regenerated, but far more striking, section of the immediate Merseyside. It was there that I found the Big Three: The Port of Liverpool Building, the Cunard Building and the Royal Liver Building. These audacious monuments were staggering, three immense and immoveable structures which smacked of power, wealth and self-righteousness. They had the attitude of Rome about them, perhaps intentionally, a borrowing from that ancient civilisation's ability to capture the notion of Empire in the bricks of a wall. For the millions who entered Liverpool by sea over the recent centuries, these three buildings must have been their very first sight of England. Imagine the impression they made. Those voyagers must have believed the whole country to be peopled by giants.

The good day came to its end, and I returned to the van, driving it out of Liverpool and towards a lay-by in the countryside south of the city. Invigorated by my day, I summoned the will to call Emma.

'Charlie!' she said. 'Long time! I'd almost forgotten about you! Still down with the sheep-shaggers?'

'No, not quite. I'm in Liverpool.'

'Liverpool… Liverpool…' I heard the clicking sounds of fingernails on a keyboard. 'Just having a look at the area. Only take a minute. So, how are you? How was Devon?'

I explained it had been Somerset, gave her a quick rundown, and asked how she had been.

'God, it *has* been a long time since I've spoken to you, hasn't it?'

'March. Just before I went to London.'

'Yeah,' she said. 'Lot's changed since then. Actually, I've got some rather big news.'

I left the possibilities racing through my mind unsaid. 'Go on.'

'I'm leaving. Had enough of it – English weather, English schools, English *people*. Been doing this job too long. I'm going to Virgin. Start in two weeks. I'm going to be an air hostess!'

'That's great news, Emma,' I said, and I meant it. 'It sounds like a good move.'

'Oh, I intend to make the most of it. See the world, explore new cultures, snort cocaine off a naked pilot's back, all that sort of thing.'

I laughed. 'I'm sure you'll fit right in.'

'Here we are,' she said, her voice businesslike again. 'I've got a school which needs someone immediately. You're in luck actually – they want an English specialist.'

'What's it like?'

'Do you want the truth?'

'Yes.'

'I can lie if you like.'

'No, I'll take the truth, please.'

'I'm really very good at lying.'

'That won't be necessary, thanks.'

'OK.' I heard her inhale. 'The position's been open for five weeks. We've sent in three people and the longest any of them stayed was two days.'

It was all she needed to say. I took down the address, agreed to start the next day, and then we said goodbye. As it happened, that was the last time I spoke to her: by the time I arrived in Middlesbrough at the end of my journey, she had already left for her new career. It saddened me a little. In a weird and purely telephonic way, Emma had been with me throughout my entire journey. Yet it came as no surprise that she was leaving – what did she say? *English weather, English schools.* She was, it seemed, conforming to the pattern perpetuating itself throughout England's educational system.

It was soon dark outside the van. I wanted to drink, to douse my nerves in some numbing alcohol, but I knew I would regret it in the morning. Instead, I ate a lot of carbohydrates and then crawled into bed to read. After a few pages, I put the book down. Nothing was going in. All I could think of was the morning.

* * * * *

Landstrom Technology College. Key Stages 3 and 4. 1,100 pupils, 350 of whom have special educational needs (far higher than the 17% national average). Within the English department, four permanent members of staff and, at any given time, between one and five supply teachers. Recently inspected by OFSTED, and now in Special Measures. For the next two weeks, my place of work.

I was put in charge of three classes, two of them like so many I had taught that year: rough but manageable. It was the third which took up more of my time than any other, and which became my focus for those two weeks.

The teacher I was covering for had taken on an abnormal post in this school. As the Special Educational Needs Co-ordinator (SENCO) for her previous school, she had been offered a position at Landstrom which combined everyday teaching with her specialist skills. For 14 hours a week, she taught a class of five Year 7 students whose emotional and behavioural difficulties were so severe that they worked on a different timetable to the rest of the Year 7 cohort. These five children had been excluded from their primary schools, and so this system had been laid out for them in an attempt to integrate them back into mainstream education. Following the timetable, I was to take them for two hours each morning, and all day Thursday. During this time, they were given extra sessions on the three core subjects of English, maths and science, whilst also following a special curriculum designed by their teacher to encourage personal and social learning. Outside of these lessons, they followed a normal timetable, though the fact that they missed all their morning lessons meant that they were often out of synch with the other students and the schemes of work they were following.

I wondered at the efficacy of such a system, but knew from past schools I had worked in – where this kind of thing often happens – that it was implemented for the purposes of inclusion rather than academia. What they learnt intellectually was perhaps secondary, it was more important that these children were put back into a society of their peers, rather than excluding them from it on a permanent basis. It was hoped that, after Year 7, after they had learnt how to appropriately interact with others, they would be placed back on full timetables.

Though I was to be officially in charge of this class, they were in fact run – and run very well, under the circumstances – by the LSA, Carla, who assisted me for each of my lessons with them. I was more there to support her than vice versa, and I felt some shame at the fact that I was paid far more than she. I would like to say we team-taught, but even that would claim too much. Carla planned all the lessons, collected the books, pens and worksheets, and set all the rules. I slunk from student to student, offering help – which was ignored. Carla ordered me about in much the same way as she did the kids, though with added contempt.

'How long are you here for?' she asked one morning.

'Just two weeks, I'm afraid.'

She snorted derisively. 'No change there. One week in November I had five different teachers with me. One for each day.'

'Do you often have to work alone?'

'You're the first teacher I've had in here for two weeks.' A pause. And then, 'Bloody waste of time.'

'So why do they need to keep bringing in teachers? If you can do it on your own?'

'It's against the law. I'm not qualified.'

'If that's the case, then how have you been able to carry on without a teacher for the last two weeks?'

She didn't seem to like that question. 'What else can we do when no teacher will work here? The kids still have to go to school. And I've done much more for them than any of the supply teachers who have come and gone.'

That last sentence was a clear and direct accusation, and so I deferred. It was in my best interests to. Without Carla, with just me and those five kids for 12 hours a week, there would have been chaos. But she had them well under her thumb, and had learned how to keep them calm. For most of them, I suppose she was the only stable thing in their lives.

I soon learnt, under Carla's directives, that my role with this class was to work with each child on a one-to-one basis or to lead a small group, never more than three. The five students were hard work, but

I found myself liking them. Prone as they were to bouts of wild-eyed hyperactivity, to moments of irrational rage, and to the careering peaks and troughs of emotional distress, they would always succeed in calming themselves down, and always apologise afterwards.

I started each morning with Alan, a slim, quiet boy who had been permanently excluded from his primary school for threatening his Design Technology teacher with a hammer. He could often go a whole day without saying a word to anyone, and the other students disliked him because he refused to join in with their mischief. Instead, he would sit alone, silently completing the task at hand or doodling images of murders and executions in his notebook. Beneath the posturing, I think the other students secretly feared him: he was the kind of boy one could imagine bringing a gun into school and emotionlessly squeezing the trigger. At first, he scared me, too. But after a few days, we seemed to find some common ground. He was always the first to arrive each day, sometimes before the teachers; the caretaker would often unlock the front doors in the morning and find him waiting patiently outside in the rain. I did not know or talk to any of the other teachers at Landstrom, so I would often drink a morning coffee in the classroom, and we took to playing chess together before lessons began. He played with the same poise he presented in everything, glowering over the board like a grandmaster. He was good at the game, too. If I made an interesting move, he would study it silently, and then intone, 'I like that,' as if the challenge was worthy of him.

We had sparse, spare conversations: quick exchanges, punctuated by long intervals of contemplation.

'Why are you always here so early, Alan?'

'I like it here. And I hate it at home.'

Silence.

'Why don't you sit in the staff room like all the other teachers?'

'I prefer to start the day this way.'

Silence.

'Why are you here?'

'At Landstrom?'

'Yes.'

'It's a job. Why are you here?'

Silence.

Then: 'There's less to worry about.'

As a result of our chess games, Alan became receptive to me. He liked me to set him challenges – answer these three questions in less than 15 minutes, complete that page by break-time – though he disliked me looking at what he had produced. Sometimes he would let me sit with him and help, but more often than not he would blank me, engrossed in his Dante-esque doodlings of urban hell. It was only while playing chess that he ever opened up. Looking back, I should not have answered his question *Why don't you sit in the staffroom* in the way I had. I should have told him the truth, that I liked our morning chess sessions, and that I liked his company.

Carla began the mornings with reading. The class were halfway through a novel aimed at low-ability children when I arrived, and I would spend this time with Saeed, who had moved to England 18 months before from Bangladesh. Though Saeed had picked up spoken English with relative ease and was already affecting a passable Liverpudlian accent, he still found the written language difficult, and I would have to underline each word in the book with my finger as we passed through it.

After reading came maths. I spent this time with Gloriya, who had eczema-ridden hands and giggled whenever I sat near her, and who often had to be removed from the room after rushing over to one of the boys and rubbing herself against their legs or screaming wordlessly into their faces.

This was usually followed by some science worksheets with Alex, the oldest in the class, who liked to bully Saeed and on whom an eye had to be kept at all times.

Following this, the students would go to their normal lessons, but on a Thursday I would spend the afternoon with them attempting to lead team-building exercises while Carla marked the day's work and planned for the next morning. These team-building exercises consisted of a game of Monopoly, or creating a dream-mansion out of Lego, or playing The Weakest Link on the interactive whiteboard. Invariably, Alan would opt out after 20 minutes and Saeed and Darius would begin a sequence of one-upmanship based on whose home country was best, ending in sulks, tantrums and the occasional scuffle.

I finished my first week at Landstrom. It had not been difficult. I was looking forward to returning on Monday, thanks to Carla. She had created this calming atmosphere, and it was her presence which maintained it. It was during the following week that I realised this, when she took a day off ill, and I was left alone with the class.

*****

Halfway through my Thursday morning game of chess with Alan, the Head appeared in the classroom to let me know I would be working alone for the day. She handed me a pack of lesson plans, emailed in by Carla, detailing exactly what I needed to do, thanked me, and then left. Gloriya arrived, giggling when I said hello and sitting at the back of the room. Saeed turned up, soon followed by Darius, and the two began an elaborate game of cards.

Once Alan won our chess match, I decided to make a start, standing up and turning to face everyone. I realised I had never spoken to them all as a class before. 'Right, I…'

'Where's Miss?' Darius interrupted.

'She's ill, Darius. I'll be teaching you today.'

Their disappointment was palpable.

'Has anyone seen Alex this morning?' I said. The question was rhetorical – Alex was late most days – but I wanted to create a semblance of formality.

'I saw him down the park on the way in,' Darius said, meaning he would arrive at some point, that he was in the area.

'OK, well I suppose we'll see him when he gets here. As for us, it's reading time. Put the cards away and get your books. Come on.'

They grudgingly obliged. With Carla absent, I could already sense the difference in the atmosphere. Saeed swore when he dropped his book and did not apologise. Gloriya was giggling far more than usual. Darius seemed to be getting louder with every word he spoke. Alan had not packed the chess board away as he usually did, but had set it up for another game and now sat toying with one of the knights. Something was bubbling.

We read with frequent interruptions from Darius but no serious incidents. I set them a page of maths tasks which asked them to solve some basic sums. Gloriya jumped up and made to run for Saeed, but I intercepted in time, blocking her charge with outspread arms whilst making sure there was no physical contact, and then verbally encouraging her back to her seat.

Break-time came and a sandwich was thrown across the room, splatting messily against the window. Darius jumped on to a table and began singing a Michael Jackson song, grabbing his crotch at the end of each line. I raced from one to the other, doing my best to calm them, but I could see they were getting worked up and ready to burst. I decided to ignore the lesson set for the next hour and use Carla's Plan B for such times: computer-work on a design project of their choice. Allowing them to use the internet (and turning the occasional blind eye to what they were researching) often succeeded in re-focusing them and, as with Carla, it worked for me, too. They began to settle.

After 20 minutes, the tension had dissipated. Each student faced his or her monitor in silence, and all were working hard on their projects. The door suddenly swung open, and I turned to see Alex arrive.

'Sorry I'm late,' he mumbled as he blustered through the door and then stopped to look around. 'Hey, where's Miss?'

'Mrs Morgan is ill today, Alex. Could you come over here, please?'

He hesitated, as if unsure whether to follow my request, and then walked sullenly over to my desk. Alex had been moved down a year in his primary school and so was a year older than the rest. Adding to that, his puberty had hit significantly early, and already his voice had broken and a dark fuzz was beginning to appear on his upper lip. He had the air of a bully about him – manifested whenever he was around Saeed – and evidently liked to think of himself as a gangster, affecting both a walk and a use of slang which, since they were rather new to him, gave him the appearance of an awkward actor. Nevertheless, he had always been polite with me and shown interest in his work.

'Why are you late, Alex?' I asked him matter-of-factly. There was no point being brusque or authoritative with him. He responded best when spoken to like an adult.

'Sorry, sir. I missed my bus.' He smiled, sheepish and innocent.

I knew it was a lie, and he knew I knew it was a lie, but it was unimportant. With Alex, lying was the least of my worries. It was more important to keep him engaged and accessed when he was there. To have confronted him would only have sent him storming out. He had apologised and managed to remain non-confrontational. That was achievement enough: he had been excluded from his primary school for hospitalising another boy during a playground fight. I did not press the matter of his lateness, instead explaining what we were doing. His face lit up at the prospect.

'How's your project coming along?'

'It's gonna be *so* good. I'm doing it about super-bikes. Gonna race when I'm older.'

He went to hang his coat up on the hooks by the door, looking eager to begin. I felt relieved at his receptiveness. His late presence could have created a disturbance, but the other students had barely noticed him arrive. He walked along the line of them to reach his own computer at the end, ignoring Gloriya and Alan as he passed them and then calling out Darius' name as he came to him. Without turning from the screen, Darius extended his arm behind his head and clasped the hand Alex offered.

'All right, Darius.'

'Mate.'

They unhooked and Alex moved on, passing Saeed. I watched.

'All right, fuckwit,' Alex said, flattening his palm and slapping Saeed hard across the back of the head.

'Alex!' I shouted. 'That was…'

I was interrupted by Saeed launching himself to his feet, kicking his chair back in the process and facing Alex. He was shouting something in his first language and Alex was grinning. I stood up to move over to them, and then froze. In Saeed's left hand was a small knife. He began waving it in front of Alex's face. Alex stopped grinning, backed away two steps. Saeed was still shouting. Gloriya gave a quick scream. Darius stared up at Saeed's back. Alan, I noticed, was looking at me.

Saeed stopped shouting. The hand which held the knife was steady. I began to step forward, cautious and unsure what I was going to say or do. Alex had his hands on the chair behind him and was leaning back into it. Slowly, Saeed raised his right hand, extended the forefinger, and lightly placed it on the tip of the blade. He gave a slight pull, and the knife bent, twanging back into place when released. It was plastic.

Saeed suddenly started to laugh, a keen so high-pitched and ringing it scratched at my ear-drums. I leapt forward and grabbed the toy knife from his fingers, putting myself between him and Alex to thwart what I imagined was going to be the next stage of this episode. But when I looked at Alex, I could see he was laughing as well. In fact, they all were, even Alan. I felt like the room was spinning.

'Get out,' I said to Saeed. 'Now.'

He did, though he laughed all the way. Darius was now on his feet hugging his knees in a weird hysteria. Gloriya had started up something halfway between a laugh and a shriek. Alan had calmed and was back at his work. I looked around at Alex as I left the room behind Saeed. He was stood beside a table, slapping it with both hands and hooting. 'Fuck me!' he hollered. 'Fuck *me*!'

Carla came back the next day and I told her about the incident. 'Was it all just some elaborate practical joke?' I asked breathlessly. 'Were they just winding me up?'

'I doubt it. That level of preparation isn't really their forte.'

'So why… I mean… how could they all just laugh about it?'

'I don't know. What were they like after you took Saeed to the office?'

'I didn't go back to the classroom. Joyce went instead and took them for the rest of the day. I had to write a very detailed incident report. I mean, I know *now* it was only a plastic knife, but I didn't then, and I'm not sure Alex did either. There was a moment – actually, more than a moment – when I genuinely thought one of my students was going to shank another.'

'Eh?' Carla said.

'Sorry, I mean stab. I genuinely thought a kid in my class was going to stab another. But that's bad enough, right? Saeed *could* have had a knife. That knife *could* have been real. So how the hell do you just laugh that sort of thing off?'

Carla took a mouthful of coffee and then shrugged her shoulders. 'Different world,' she finally said, and I was offered that as my only justification. I never found out what that episode had been about. It was not mentioned in class that day, my last. The only indications that it had ever even happened were the absence of Saeed – he had been temporarily excluded – and the occasional knowing smirks from the students. Alan did not talk to me that day, though perhaps that was because I had missed our chess game that morning.

* * * * *

I took a few days off to enjoy the heat wave which hit the country at the end of June. England is beautiful in the summer, and I wanted to witness it free from work and knife-threats. I drove north out of Liverpool and pulled into a coastal Cumbrian lay-by for three days. They were rare times, filled with an intentional nothingness. Morning drifted in through the van's open windows at sunrise and settled over the oil and petrol stink which I had learned to ignore months before. After breakfast I read novels for hours, and stuck to my plan of having no plans. I enjoyed the van, and sat with my feet, sockless, hanging out the open slide door. I took long, solitary walks, and then watched longer films on my laptop. I spent hours lost in reflection, considering this singular year which was nearly at its conclusion. Protracted and weird it had been, but – I realised with some happiness – it was still a novelty. This van was still a novelty. Never had a home maintained its charm for so long, and I have had a few. I took pride in its compact nature. Everything I owned was there with me. Over the last year, together we had packed up and left every day, and arrived and settled every day. The van had given me shelter, comfort, a means to store and cook my food, and the carefully-utilised electrical energy of its leisure battery. A daily ritual consisted of boiling the kettle, pouring it

217

into the sink, mixing in some cold water procured three days before from a service-station tap, and then having a long wash. I watched myself shave in a tiny plastic mirror fixed to the wall with blu-tack.

Even as an itinerant, I had been a member of communities. Strange and distanced communities, but communities nonetheless. On the road, I took part in a tribal handshake every day – the VW Wave. When passing, T25 drivers wave at each other. Bays and Splittys do the same. There are rules: a T25 cannot wave to a Bay or Splitty unless they wave first. And no one waves to the T4s.

Off the road, on the lay-bys, I was part of another fraternity. Motorhomes rarely stay on lay-bys, but when they do they gravitate to those which the lorry-drivers favour, for to pack seems natural to the human condition, and there is always safety in numbers. Sometimes I talked with the truckers, balanced on the kerb with a cup of tea, or stood at the counter to a burger stand. Mostly, though, people hid themselves away behind their cab curtains: then, a nod would suffice, but even that might be overdoing it. The sole courtesy demanded was that each leave enough space for the others around to pull out on to the road. It was a basic but important etiquette.

I realised I had been very alone for most of the year. It had suited me, and the van. We had all that we needed. A cupboard full of books and writing paper. Another filled with dried pasta, tinned tuna, soup and beans and chopped tomatoes. Teabags, condensed milk, desiccated garlic, cooking oil and the odd bag of sweets or thick bar of chocolate. I kept sausages and cheese in the fridge, but it did not work so I had to eat them hastily, before they went off. I filled it with pre-chilled beer, which helped but made me urinate like a diabetic. Wine was better, or whiskey. I had been drunk a lot.

One cupboard was given over solely for the storage of four five-litre water bottles which I refilled whenever I could. I had soon learned how difficult fresh drinking water is to come by, and how much water

I used each day – not just for drinking, but for cooking and washing also. The itinerant needs his tricks to maintain such a supply, and I found mine: school drinking fountains and service station taps. If a campsite was nearby, and if I had stayed there, I would park up the road and walk on to the site with my empty bottles bouncing off my legs, filling up under the cover of darkness.

I found myself one day sitting staring out over shimmering water at the distant Isle of Man, a book on my lap and toast-crusts left for the sparrows on the ground beside me. Over the last year, I had led a life which had been, in its unconventional way, something quite beautiful. As I looked at the silhouette of the island beyond, I understood that I was going to miss this.

*****

I drove back to Liverpool and spent some uneventful days at Dewa Arts College. It was there that I met Louise – a Modern Foreign Languages teacher – one afternoon in the staff room, when she came and sat next to me and introduced herself. She had just started that September after taking a year off. The year before that – undergone in Nottingham – had been her induction year, her first in the profession. I assumed she had taken the year out to travel, but she soon corrected me.

'Not quite,' she laughed, a little nervously. 'No, I had to take a year off because I… well, I kind of had a bit of a nervous breakdown.'

There was an awkward silence. I considered changing the subject. But Louise, sensing my discomfort, said: 'It's all right. I'm much better now. I can tell you about it, if you like.'

And so she did.

'I loved my PGCE year. I'd already taught for two years in Spain, TEFL, and I knew that teaching was for me. But I wasn't prepared at all for the NQT year. It was, without a doubt, the hardest year of my life, both professionally and personally. I actually started it in the last month before the summer holidays. I was really geared up about it: observing lessons, reading departmental handbooks and drinking tea with the other NQTs. When September came, I had the opportunity to introduce a Spanish course into Key Stage 3, and I dived straight into it, writing up a whole new scheme of work for the school. But, by October, I already wanted out. My passion for teaching had completely died, and I found myself doubting my abilities as a linguist, teacher and person.'

She took a sip of her tea.

'I was given more classes than I was supposed to have, including a Year 9 PSHE lesson… you know, showing hormonal 14-year-olds how to put condoms on bananas. The weekly hour I had with my NQT mentor was basically a two-sentence, 10-second chat because she was up to her eyes in her own work, and I was getting no support at all, despite the fact the kids were running rings around me. I had a Year 9 French group, for instance, with 34 in the class. My room didn't even have enough tables for them, let alone chairs. It was like teaching in a cinema: heads everywhere. I remember asking one boy to move seats, and he just looked at me and said, "Ah, stop talking bollocks miss, and fuck off." I spoke to his Head of Year and he said, "Yep, he can be a rascal, that one." Nothing happened to him.'

'That sounds familiar,' I said.

Louise smiled bleakly, obviously casting her mind back. 'I began drinking more than normal, especially at the weekend. It was the only relief from all the panicking, crying, flapping, panicking again, and then crying again. I started dosing myself up every morning on Covonia, paracetomol and various other drugs because I was mistaking these constant feelings of anxiety for a physical illness. One morning I even threw up whilst standing in the school's car park. It was a mixture of drugs, feeling sick and being so wound up and nervous that I was a huge ball of anxiety. At this point, I remember seeing one of the Deputy Heads get out of her car, see me throw up a second time and just walk off into school. Every day I could feel myself getting worse. I actually used to hope on the way in that I would be involved in a crash so that I could take a few months off. I began taking days off here and there with colds, flu, stomach bugs, ear and throat infections. My body was suffering. In eight months, I had lost a stone and a half. I couldn't sleep, barely ate, and I was so miserable and angry that my friends were all drifting away. I started to get panic attacks. In the end, I went to a doctor and told him everything. He gave me a prescription for an antidepressant, and made it pretty clear that I was on the verge of something terrible. A week later, I handed in my notice.'

'It must have been a really tough time,' I said. 'What did you do?'

'I moved up to Liverpool and got a job in a call centre, answering phones to aggressive adults, which was far easier than teaching. I started having counselling. I weaned myself off the antidepressants and cut down on the drinking. I really needed that year to just re-group and get myself together. I applied for this job last Easter and got it, thinking that I would have one last stab at something I've wanted to do since I was 14. So far it's good, this seems to be a nice school, and I'm starting to love it again. But I'm under no illusions. If I ever start down that road again, I'm out of this for good.'

(Most of the above is taken from an email Louise sent me, at my request, a few weeks after our conversation. We have remained in touch and she is still teaching.)

Louise's story will be familiar to any teacher. Stress is a major factor, and the illnesses it can cause are rife in the profession. In one school, a colleague of mine took six months off with stress, and he was only 30 years old. Another was in school for no more than two weeks of the entire year – she was clinically depressed – and yet another reduced her hours to part-time after only two years due to concerns over her mental health. I remember a history teacher who took eight months off, a science teacher who took five, a geography teacher who appeared for one half of one day during an entire year, and a maths teacher who had not been seen for seven terms – all off with stress. The phenomenon is no longer a phenomenon, it is disturbingly commonplace. Of all the teachers I covered during my year through England, perhaps a fifth of them were absent due to a stress-related illness.

Every teacher can recount the same story. We all know at least one person who is 'taking a bit of time off' now, and countless others who have in the past. Teachers of all ages are involved – even those right at the beginning of their careers, the PGCE students, with 20% of all trainees failing to qualify or refusing to continue into their NQT year. Numerous surveys undertaken by teacher unions and independent research groups have revealed that over half of all teachers believe that it will be stress and its effects which eventually lead them to quit the profession. A recent report into occupational stress found that in six of the main professional vocations, one in five workers reported what is termed as 'high stress'. In teaching, it was two in five.

I am the first to admit that teachers love to moan about their job (indeed, this book might be seen by some as one long, protracted moan), and am not suggesting that teaching is the most stressful profession around. I have a soldier friend currently stationed in Afghanistan, another who works as a nurse in a London hospital, and yet another whose job is a prison guard. I have the highest admiration for these people, and understand that theirs is a far more terrifying and stressful job than mine could ever be. Perhaps yours is, too.

Maybe teachers get so stressed because, as a type, they are just more susceptible to it. It is a plausible theory, and one I would not discard. Nevertheless, the fact that stress is so prevalent in teaching is real, and should not be ignored – as it should not be ignored for soldiers, nurses, prison guards, police officers and others. Stress in all professions, in *life*, must be addressed, and this is my attempt to address it in teaching.

So why are so many teachers falling victim to stress? There are a score of answers, many of which are also the reasons why so many teachers are leaving: poor student behaviour, a lack of support, endless targets, an insurmountable workload, perhaps even, as I said, an innate susceptibility. But what is being done about it? Very little. As I'm sure is the case in most professions, stress – its causes and its effects – is largely ignored by the managers. And, as a result, some teachers are either leaving or taking long periods of absence. As attractive as a year off work might sound, those teachers who find themselves in such a situation have effectively ended their careers. Their schools cannot fire them for taking time off with their illness – for this is how it is regarded – but no other school would ever employ them again, and with the many redundancies which are taking place throughout Britain's schools as the coalition government makes massive cuts to the public sector, these teachers will be the first to go.

It is a sad fact that this has become the state of affairs in many of Britain's schools and for many of Britain's teachers. One viable way of combating the increase in resignations and extended periods of absence would be to put in place a system of support which attempts to counter, pre-empt or assuage the symptoms of stress. Some schools are beginning to realise this and are setting up group therapy sessions and buddy-systems for their staff, or just advertising the phone numbers of union-based helplines on the staff room wall.

Sadly, such pre-emptive tactics are uncommon. I only have to think back to my own PGCE year when, amongst all the lectures and seminars I attended, one single hour was devoted to how to deal with stress. Generally, the system seems to support ignorance over recognition, leaving many teachers stuck in a quagmire, a definitively *British* restraint, which tells us to maintain that all-important stiff upper lip, and fight on regardless. Teachers are not encouraged to admit if they are struggling, and instead it is implied that any weakness is just that, a *weakness*. So we keep it to ourselves, pretend it will all be better tomorrow. And, in this, teachers have themselves to blame as much as the Senior Management Teams and governors who ignore them.

MIDDLESBROUGH

ONE OF MY CLOSEST FRIENDS comes from Middlesbrough. When I told him I was going to live and work in the town for a month, he coughed twice, and then changed the subject.

Reputations do not come much worse than Middlesbrough's. It has the country's poorest postcode, TS15, where nearly half of the household annual incomes are less than £10,000; the TV property programme *Location, Location, Location* named it as 'The Worst Place To Live In The UK'; my friend's father, a doctor in the area, told me that Middlesbrough sees more broken jaws on a Saturday night than any city in the country.

It seemed fitting that this was where my long and fluctuating journey would end. It had been a rough yet bizarrely enjoyable year, a year of challenge, surprise and dichotomy. I had experienced things I never wanted to do, see or hear again, but was glad I had endured. These travels around England's most challenging schools had taken me up and down the country in odd zigzags, and they had matched the conflicting emotions of each day. They ended here.

I left Liverpool on the Saturday morning, making my slow way north-east. With only three weeks of the school year left, I made myself available for work immediately: the end of the academic year is a dead zone amongst supply teachers, and work at that time is scarce and fought over. Fortunately, my phone rang early on the Monday morning.

'Good morning, Mr Carroll,' came the male voice from the other end of the line. 'Are you available to work today?'

'Yeah,' I muttered, still hazy from sleep. I looked at the digital clock blu-tacked to the wall next to the sink. It was 5.45am.

'I'm glad to hear it, Mr Carroll. I have a single day on offer at Baldry Arts College. Are you interested?'

'Of course... yeah, of course,' I mumbled, pulling my head up from the pillow and opening the curtains to be inundated with bright sunlight which made me squint. 'You must be Emma's replacement. What's your name?'

'I'm Peter, Mr Carroll. I will be your new liaison.'

'Great,' I said, sitting up in bed. 'Fantastic. How was your weekend?'

'I don't see that that's any of your business, Mr Carroll. Would you like Baldry or not?'

'I would, I would,' I said. 'It's just... it's just very early.'

'The early bird gets the worm, Mr Carroll. I'll put you down for Baldry, then.'

I suddenly hated Peter. He was clearly humourless, devoid of personality, and had an unfortunate penchant for clichés. I looked at the clock again. At least he was efficient.

'Yeah, thanks, Peter.'

'Good. The usual stand-in is ill, and they requested someone tough, so I called you first. Emma told me a lot about you.'

'What did she say?' I asked.

'That you're as cool as a cucumber.'

'I doubt she used those words. But she probably told you about me moving up and down the country each month. The fact is, what I'm trying to do is…'

'I don't see that that's any of *my* business, Mr Carroll. I've put you down for Baldry. Thank you. Goodbye.'

Peter hung up, and I realised I missed Emma. At least I only had to communicate with his emotionless personality for the next three weeks. Then, it would all be over. I brewed some tea, sipped at a mug of it until the clock struck 7, and set off for Baldry Arts College.

I arrived at 7.30am. There were only a few other cars in the car park, and I pulled in next to an old blue Golf. The school day did not start for another hour, so I moved into the back of the van, opened the window, boiled another kettle, and read my book.

I was engrossed in it when the shrill beeping of an alarm clock ripped through my consciousness. I looked out towards the source of the sound, my eye caught by movement in the car next to me. I was amazed I had not seen him before, for there in the car next to me was a teenage boy stretched out across the front seats, a bottle of milk next to his head and the still-beeping alarm clock on the dashboard. He opened his eyes, yawned, reached out to turn off the alarm, took a swig of milk, and then sat upright. I noticed he was wearing a school uniform. Casually, opening the car door, he picked up his meagre belongings, stepped out and walked around to the front of the car, pulling a rusty BMX out from under a nearby bush, and then cycling away.

As the day passed, I was surprised that Peter had used the word 'tough'. This seemed a pleasant enough school, and throughout the day nothing remarkable occurred. I walked towards the final period, where I was to cover a music lesson, thinking along the way that, when Peter called tomorrow, I would give Baldry Arts College a glowing review. A young LSA called Jenny met me at the door and unlocked it for me. With her was her charge, a 12-year-old boy called Lewis.

'Awesome! A supply teacher!' Lewis shouted when he spotted me. 'I'm gonna be dead naughty for you!'

'No you're not, Lewis,' Jenny laughed, ushering him in. The rest of the class soon followed. 'Don't worry about Lewis,' she said. 'He'll probably be a bit manic – he's got severe ADHD – but if there's any problems I'll take him out.'

'Thanks,' I said, and we walked in.

The lesson progressed without difficulty. I walked around helping individuals with the work that had been set, and after 10 minutes I noticed Jenny had left Lewis and was working with a girl called Thandie, offering to write for her because her arm was in a plaster cast.

As the lesson drew to a close, I was congratulating myself on a day free of stress, when I heard a loud and sharp, 'Oh!'

It was Jenny.

She stood up quickly, knocking her chair over, and, with her hand over her mouth, she ran out of the classroom. I followed her, but she had disappeared by the time I reached the door. I came back in and looked over at Thandie, who seemed confused, and then at Lewis, who seemed to be searching for his book under the table. His cheeks, I noticed, were flushed. With no idea what had just happened, I continued the lesson, and then dismissed the kids as the bell sounded.

I was clearing the floor of the few paper aeroplanes which had managed to sail across the room without me noticing when Jenny walked back in.

'I'm sorry about that,' she said. 'I thought I should probably come back and explain.'

'What happened? Are you all right?'

'Yes, I'm fine, I'm fine. It's just sometimes... I've been working with Lewis for the past year. And just when I think I've got to know him, he pulls something out of the bag which knocks me off my feet.'

'What did he do? I thought he was behaving really well.'

She looked away from me, and seemed to be weighing up whether or not she should tell me. Then she broke into an impulsive, slightly disbelieving giggle.

'Sorry,' she said. 'Sorry, I shouldn't laugh. It's actually quite horrible.' She took a deep breath, walked to one of the tables and perched on the edge. 'Lewis was getting on with his work so I left him to it. I try and do that every now and then, give him a bit of independence, and I knew that Thandie needed a hand.' She giggled again. 'Sorry. Bad joke. I always make sure that, when I do leave him, I'm still positioned so I can see him and check if he's starting to get hyper. I'd written out a few sentences for Thandie, looked over at Lewis and he...'

She broke off, not giggling this time, but perhaps trying to stop herself.

'What was he doing?' I asked.

'Wanking,' she said. 'Right there, right in front of me, he had his flies open, his hand under the table and wrapped around... himself... and then he saw me looking at him. So he took his other hand, picked up his book, placed it over... himself... and carried on.' She paused. 'He stared at me while he was doing it.'

There was silence for a few moments. Jenny eventually broke it.

'Bollocks to this,' she said. 'I need a new job.'

* * * * *

I called Peter the following morning.

'No work today, Mr Carroll,' he said. 'The phones are as dead as a dodo.'

I wondered who had had the misfortune to be Peter's English teacher.

'Just so I know,' he continued. 'Do you only want to work in Middlesbrough over the next few weeks?'

'Why, is something available elsewhere?'

'Not today, but if you're willing to take on schools throughout Teesside, it will widen your chances of getting anything.'

I agreed, and put the phone down. With the day now free, I decided to spend it seeing my new catchment area, and set out to explore Teesside.

Middlesbrough forms the rough centre of the four towns which run along the Tees Valley, the others being Hartlepool, Stockton-on-Tees and Darlington. This is a forgotten part of England: an area unmentioned by guidebooks and avoided by tourists, an industrial civilisation dropped in the middle of nowhere. Is this Yorkshire? Cleveland? Tyne-and-Wear? No. It is Teesside, barely even a real county, just something made up for the sake of a name.

I started in Darlington, driving up and along the valley through Stockton-on-Tees, and ending in Hartlepool. I did not stop once. Nothing caught my eye. As soon as I entered each town, all I wanted to do was leave. And so I did, again and again until I reached Hartlepool, where I stopped only because I could go no further. I parked up on the coast alongside the most depressing stretch of beach imaginable to miserably eat some lunch. I felt an overwhelming surge of sadness as I looked out over my bowl of cold pasta at the grey seascape. The sand did its best to achieve a golden sheen, but never improved on an oaky brown. The beach was dominated at one end by the large, smoking power station and chemical plant, and at the other by a bleak, crane-filled harbour. In between, the horizon was filled with incoming and outgoing oil tankers, and the beach-side promenade swarmed with JCBs. The water is notoriously dangerous, polluted with petrochemicals, and the waves gave off a strange aroma of aftershave. Local surfers use this stretch of coast warily.

I returned to my lay-by on the cusp of the North Yorkshire Moors that evening, depressed with my day of exploration. The towns were even more characterless than Sheffield, and the prospect of spending the final weeks of my journey working in them filled me with a kind of anticlimactic boredom.

But I should not have been so quick to judge. Peter called the next morning with the news that he had booked me into three different schools, one for each remaining day of the week, and they turned out to be three of the strangest days not just of the year, but of my career. The first was the Ian Thomas Centre: a Pupil Referral Unit.

'I thought you might like this one,' Peter explained.

'Why?'

'Because it's pretty nasty. So nasty, in fact, that they're offering time and a half.'

'I'm on it,' I said, reaching for my suit and cursing my need for these challenging schools, and my greater need for money.

I arrived at the Ian Thomas Centre over an hour later. It was composed of whitewashed rows of long, single-storey corridors, like tenement blocks which had fallen over. The entrance doors were locked, and I had to hold a button down on the wall-mounted intercom and repeat my name four times before finally being buzzed in. The Deputy Headteacher, Mr Holden – a short, stout man with a pony tail which deposited trails of dandruff over his sagging shoulders – came to greet me at reception, shaking my hand and placing in my other a pack of lesson resources for the day, a map of the Centre, a list of extension phone numbers for the 20 members of staff and their classrooms, and a strange plastic spatula with a small metal disc at its head.

'What's this?' I asked.

'Your key,' he replied, motioning at an 11-year-old who charged past us and slammed dramatically into the closed doors I had just walked through, grabbing the handles and pulling at them so that they rattled and clunked, but remained closed. 'Josh!' Mr Holden shouted. 'The school day has started, and you're going the wrong way. Your classroom's over there.'

'Fuck off!' Josh shouted back. 'I'm going home!' He continued to pull at the doors, which stood fast.

Mr Holden took a walkie-talkie from his belt and murmured something into it that I could not hear. Only seconds later, two men – dressed in suits identical to Mr Holden's – appeared and took Josh by each hand. Josh smiled and chattered at them as they led him off down the corridor.

'Come on, let me show you around the Centre,' Mr Holden said to me. 'I'll show you how your key works.'

We set off down the corridor. It was demarcated by four sets of strong double doors which chopped the hallway into small, impermeable chunks. Every door had a round slot beneath the handle, and if I placed my key into it, it would magnetise the mechanism into action. As we passed between and along each of the thin corridors, I began to realise that every door was locked, including those to the classrooms and at the entrances and exits of each building.

'All the teachers have a key,' Mr Holden explained on our tour. 'But, obviously, none of the students do. Until we got the system installed last year, our biggest problem was that students wouldn't stay in their classrooms. They'd just barge into each other's and cause havoc, or get up and leave the premises. These days they can't. It's done wonders for the Centre as a whole, though it does tend to make the kids feel somewhat caged in their classrooms. And I suppose you can't really blame them for that.'

I was not sure I liked the subtext of what he was telling me: students who could not leave were a boon for the Centre as a whole, but I wondered how this impacted on their behaviour inside the classroom. 'How have the teachers been finding it?' I asked.

He laughed. 'Don't get me wrong, it's not made things easy for them, but it has for us.'

'Who?'

'The Senior Management Team.'

We came to my classroom for the day and he opened the door for me, ushering me in and then walking in behind and shutting it.

'It was actually one single incident that made the Head decide to get these locks,' he said, perching on the edge of a table and lowering his voice to a conspiratorial whisper. 'We got OFSTEDed at the beginning of last year. You ever been OFSTEDed?'

'Of course,' I said. 'Who hasn't?'

'So you know the drill. We cleaned up as best we could, told all the staff to wear suits, got all the books marked and up to date, put wall displays over the graffiti, made sure all the really bad kids thought they had the day off so they wouldn't come in, that kind of thing. We got all the kids into their classrooms by the time the inspectors showed up so that we could take them down the lovely quiet corridors to the Head's office where we all had a big meeting. Five minutes in, there's a banging at the door, and we all turn around to see a girl called Maria burst in and start shouting, "Ah, yah fuckin' fucks with your fuckin' suits and fuckin' rich cars, I 'ate the fuckin' lot o' yous!" I got up to take her back to the classroom she had escaped from, but she sidestepped me and started running around the room shouting at the inspectors – fuckin' this and fuckin' that. Eventually, I managed to grab her and pull her outside and...' He began to chuckle at this point. '...and all I remember is hearing the Head saying to the inspectors: "Please, it's best if we just ignore her."'

Mr Holden dissolved into a fit of laughter, broken from it only when a sharp knock came at the door.

He stood up and opened it. 'Ah! Hello, Maria! We've just been talking about you!'

Maria shrugged and sat down at the back of the room, ignoring me as Mr Holden introduced me to her. After explaining that she was the first of the four I was to have that day, he silently mouthed a word I could not quite comprehend, and then left.

'He said "Ritalin",' Maria said, without looking at me. 'It's all right. I've had me pills.'

She stood up and pulled a Michael Morpurgo novel from the bookshelf, and then sat down to read it in silence.

My three other students for the day filtered in over the next hour: Amy, who was just as quiet and unresponsive as Maria, and two boys, who insisted I ignore what my register said they were called and instead refer to them as Mocs and Phase (though they spelt them, I noticed later when they labelled their work, Mocs and Faaz). Mocs was the most talkative of the quartet, frequently bouncing over to my desk and repeating: 'Doctor... I... err... Doctor, Doctor, I have... you know... Doctor...,' while the rest remained mostly quiet throughout the day, interspersing the work I gave them with attempts to fall asleep with their heads on the desk.

Maria and Amy occasionally broke into conversation.

'I 'ate Victoria Beckham. The plastic cow.'

'Me too. But I like that Katie Price. 'Cos she's like real, int she?'

'Mate, Katie Price... fuckin' love her. 'Cos she had a tit job. But then she got it reduced.'

'I want a tit job. Me mum says she'll buy me one if I get three GCSEs.'

'You fuckin' need one.'

'I know. Me tits are shit. But, see, I've got good legs, innit. Me mum says you can't have it all.'

'So why's she gettin' you a tit job?'

'Of course she fuckin' int. How the fuck could she afford it? She's just sayin' it so I pass. I will, though. Not the tit job. Pass. I will pass.'

I wanted to interrupt them. Mocs and Faaz were starting to get too interested in what was being said. But I liked Amy's conclusion, and liked it all the more because, once she had made her proclamation, she picked up her pen and continued with her work until lunchtime.

The lunch break was only 30 minutes long. A free and nutritious meal was provided for everyone, students and staff alike. I took my class into the canteen, letting them take their seats and then choosing my own. The rest of the staff sauntered in after them, taking a free table which was evidently always theirs, and which I had had the misfortune not to choose. Mr Holden, perhaps sensing my self-imposed ostracism, came and sat with me.

'It's quiet, isn't it,' he said over a slurp of carrot and coriander soup.

I looked around at everyone, and realised that it was.

'This is the only time when we can put them all together. No-one kicks off in here. They know that, if they do, they won't get lunch for the rest of the week.' He dunked his bread roll into his soup and noisily sucked the juices over his beard. 'That's always been the most effective punishment we've ever had here. If they mess around, they won't get fed. For a lot of them, this is the only regular meal they'll get each day.'

'Are you allowed to do that?' I asked.

'We are because the food is free. Students are always welcome to bring their own lunch, or they can buy from the canteen if they've been denied free lunches. But that's hardly an option for this lot – even if their parents did give them lunch money, they'd spend it on other things.'

Mr Holden was not speaking quietly. With the silence in this room as kids shovelled and chomped, I knew his words could be heard clearly by all. But no-one corrected or confronted him with self-righteous disagreement. 'Mind you,' he said, just as loudly, 'they've then got an hour outside. We all have to go out, too. That's when things usually kick off. How have you found it so far?'

'Actually, really good,' I replied. 'They've been well-behaved all day. I've enjoyed it.'

'Just wait. The nicotine cravings haven't kicked in yet.'

We all filtered out to the playground together. Instantly, Mocs and Faaz disappeared behind one of the buildings, and Mr Holden motioned me to follow him after them. Sure enough, they were already trying to light the chipped Marlboro Lights hanging from their lips.

'Come on, lads, hand them over,' Mr Holden said.

They both did, though Mocs protested, 'But Doctor... err... Doctor... I have... you know... Doctor...'

I spent the next hour out there with the staff, our only job the frequent chasing of students who attempted to slip away for a sneaky fag. Jordan, who had seen me arrive that morning and had a love of VWs to match my own, sat with me for a while and we talked about our favourite vans. I was lovingly detailing my own when suddenly a scream interrupted all of us. I realised that Maria and Amy had managed to disappear unnoticed, and followed the rest of the staff as they sprinted around the corner.

It took me a few moments to comprehend what I saw. Amy was knelt on the floor with her head angled in an unnatural position, left cheek facing up. Maria stood above and leaning over her. Inexplicably, Maria seemed to have her finger in Amy's ear. Amy was crying and softly bleating, 'Please, Maria... don't...'

I looked closer. Maria did not have her finger in Amy's ear – in fact, it was curled through the loop of Amy's earring and tugging away so that the lobe stretched away from the face.

'Christ, Maria,' Mr Holden said. 'What are you doing?'

'This bitch wouldn't give me a cigarette,' Maria snarled.

'I said I'd go twos with you!' Amy wept, and then stopped as Maria applied more pressure.

'Maria,' Mr Holden said, edging towards her. 'Let go of her. You know what will happen if we have to get the police involved again.'

Maria stared at him for a few seconds, and then removed her

finger. Amy dropped to the ground and cried. Maria began to walk towards us, and then stopped. She had fixed her gaze on me.

'What?' she said. 'What are you looking at?'

'You've behaved so well today, Maria,' I said, keeping my voice soothing and calm. 'I just think it's a shame you had to go and do that.'

That was a mistake. She suddenly screamed, 'You don't fuckin' know me!' Then she ran towards one of the plastic chairs which sat around the benches, picked it up and hurled it at me. It missed, smacking brutally off the wall behind me.

'You'd better not be here tomorrow!' she shouted, turning on her heel and marching off. One of the teachers went to follow her, but Mr Holden told him to leave her and let her go home. He turned around to me.

'Maybe it's a good thing you're not coming back tomorrow,' he said. 'She can really hold a grudge, that one.'

He laughed and then charged off to pursue Mocs and Faaz, who had disappeared again. I turned around to see the chair Maria had thrown at me – in pieces on the ground – and gave a small, internal thanks to Peter for booking me elsewhere for the following day.

Thursday was spent at Nicholls Heath School, and when I returned to my lay-by I immediately poured a glass of wine and opened out the bed, settling down to make a few quick notes on the day in my journal.

This journal had been a form of catharsis for me: the ability to spew out the events of a stressful day on to paper was my way of moving on from whatever I had just endured. I never found it easy – the act of writing itself involved reliving unpleasant experiences – but I always felt better for it afterwards. This time, however, I found myself deeply involved in my scribblings, and realised more than once that I was laughing out loud as I documented the happenings of the day.

I started with a Year 7 English class. They were wonderful, polite and hardworking, whilst also exuberant and full of life. Media work had been set, and they were to create their own original newspaper front pages. I spent the first five minutes talking through what should appear in their work.

'Let's say you write the main story on the front page,' I said. 'In order that the reader knows who wrote that article, you insert a thing called a "by-line" at the top. So what should your by-line say?'

Dave, a shy lad at the back, meekly raised his hand.

'Yes,' I said, pointing to him.

'By Dave,' he said.

'Yes,' I agreed, thinking – obviously – he had got the point that the writer's name should appear, and not wanting to damage his confidence by asking him to expand.

Twenty minutes later, as I walked around the room, I checked the students' work. Each one had written on his or her article, 'By Dave'.

I had to stop Period 2 for five minutes when Wilfred raised his hand, beckoned me over, and whispered to me: 'Sir, I've got 5p stuck in my ear.' How it had happened was not explained.

After break-time, a benign group of Year 10s came into their science lesson and diligently settled down to their coursework. I was unfamiliar with the topic, and they seemed not to need any help, so I sat at the front and let them get on with it. With nothing to do myself, I soon grew bored, and so reached into my bag for my journal. A large group sat directly before me, and the candour of their conversation suggested that they had forgotten my presence. Their randomly criss-crossing chit-chat was an interesting insight into students' perception of teachers, and I surreptitiously noted it down as they talked.

Boy 1: Do you have him for maths?

Girl 1: Yeah, he's all right.

Boy 1: Does he always go on about water?

Girl 1: Was anyone in maths that time when Julie was touching Mrs Adams' bum?

Girl 2: When was that?

Girl 1: Remember, she kept prodding it with a ruler.

Boy 1: That substitute teacher – she was a right cow – she used to lean over and put her boobs on the desk.

Boy 2: I quite liked her.

Boy 3: Who had Mr James?

Boy 4: I remember when Freddie kicked the ball against the wall and it hit Mr James in the face.

Girl 3: He had a right squeaky voice, like a mouse (makes squeaking noises).

Boy 2: I had that Miss Fox once or twice. She brought us scones.

Boy 1: Don't you think Mr Michaels is weird? I'm sure he buffs his head. I've never seen a shinier head.

Boy 3: Shiny-head!

Boy 2: And he only knows two things – the rules of rugby, and where pies should go.

Girl 1: That's not very nice.

Boy 3: Shiny-head!

Girl 2: Miss Markle is dead nasty, though.

Boy 1: I quite fancy her, actually.

(There is an awkward ten-second silence from the group. Eventually, they begin talking again, though no-one talks to Boy 1. He, realising his wrong, lowers his head and works quietly.)

The last lesson of the day was even easier. When PGCE students are sent into schools for training, they will often take over a selection of classes within their subject and teach them a module or unit as if the class were their own. The PGCE student will have to plan all the lessons, mark all the work done over that time, and attempt to deal – though with support – with any behavioural issues which may arise in their lessons. It is something of a baptism of fire for the young teacher, a drop in the deep end, but it is necessary. This is what, after all, they will be doing for the rest of their careers, whether they last three years or 30. For my final lesson – another English cover – I already knew that a PGCE student would be leading the class. I was only needed to sit at the back of the room and be the legal requirement, the present qualified teacher.

Sadly, the PGCE student was late, and I had to bring this Year 11 class in myself. They were a small group, a lower set I presumed, and they paid little attention to me as I asked them to take their seats, find their books and pens, and wait for Miss Crowther, the PGCE student. They finally sat down, but after five minutes Miss Crowther had still not arrived.

I was about to make up some work for them to do when Kwame burst through the door. Over six feet tall and with hands twice the size of my own, he sauntered over to a seat at the front of the class, sat down, stared at me, and said, 'Who are you?'

'I'm Mr Carroll,' I replied, noticing that the rest of the class had fallen silent.

'Where's Miss Crowther?'

'On her way, I hope.'

'Me too,' he said, folding his arms, leaning back in his chair, and continuing to stare at me.

After the lesson, Miss Crowther would tell me about Kwame, describing him as a hulking menace of a boy who had left his African home-country at the age of nine after experiencing and seeing things no-one should ever have to. He had joined Nicholls Heath School at the same time as the rest of his year-group, and his original shyness had led some teachers to conclude that he was autistic. However, by the time he reached Year 11, he had turned into a towering thug. Miss Crowther had once seen him throw a table across her classroom, his stomach-muscles rippling beneath his shirt. Another teacher had caught him one day with a double-edged razor blade, intently shaving the skin, layer by layer, off the palm of his hand.

Kwame found it difficult to make friends at Nicholls, mostly because he had a habit of stealing food from his peers. It took a few years before anyone brought this to the attention of the teachers and, when the victims were questioned, some said they had not pursued it because they were scared of him, while most revealed that they had kept quiet because they knew Kwame was not fed at home. The food he stole was his food for the day: one boy admitted he secretly made and then brought in jam sandwiches whenever he could, so that he could give them to Kwame in the morning.

Ten minutes passed, and Miss Crowther had still not arrived. No work had been left, so I wrote a task on to the board: *Describe your favourite place*. I tried to explain that this was the kind of question they might be asked in their English exam, but few heard me, and even fewer made an attempt at it. Kwame had never taken his eyes off me, and I was beginning to find his silent inquisition unnerving.

Suddenly, she appeared through the door: young and pretty, and wearing a short skirt with high boots. In one hand she had a mug of tea, in the other a plate of buttered toast. I noticed that, for the first time since he arrived, Kwame looked away from me and fixed his gaze on Miss Crowther. The glimpse of a smile played across his lips, and there was a perceptible longing in his eyes as they followed her movement across the front of the classroom.

'Phwooarr, look at miss!' he suddenly exclaimed, rising up from his seat and pointing at her with a limp hand. His eyes had widened further and his mouth had opened, while the hand he had pointed with found its way to his head to run itself through his short hair. 'She's got toast!'

My first week in Teesside came to its end with Rowe School. With over 2,000 students it was almost twice the size of the average secondary school and I was given a day of general cover – some English, some maths, some geography. As I flitted from department to department, I felt my anonymity acutely. Between lessons, students moved in gigantic migratory herds, and teachers on duty worked in small packs, flanking them and then guiding them on to wherever they were supposed to go next. I edged along the periphery, feeling like I was on safari.

My first lesson was English, on the top floor of the huge main block. The class were Year 7s and, as the tiniest in this massive arena of teenagers, they were suitably humble. All, that is, except for Tia Cadgwith, who – while the rest worked on their posters for the latest production of Romeo and Juliet – patrolled the classroom, loudly refusing to do any work. I was tired, and had no time for her.

'Tia,' I said. 'This is unacceptable. Either stay in your seat, or I will have to send you out.'

'You can't make me do anything!' Tia shouted at me. 'I can do what I want!'

'Fair enough,' I said, rising from my seat. 'Then you can go. To be honest, I think I'll be doing everyone here a favour. They're all trying to work, but you're not letting them. You're just being selfish. So I think we would all appreciate it if you left. Go and wait for me outside. I'll get someone to take you away when I'm ready.'

Tia flounced out with her chin high. Perhaps she had wanted to be sent out, perhaps I should have spent more time working her around, but I was in a particularly utilitarian mood, and was feeling sorry for the 31 others who were genuinely trying to work. I sat back down as the door slammed shut behind Tia. I would deal with her in a minute or two. For now, she could wait for me.

Thirty seconds passed, and Sean raised his hand. 'I'm sorry, sir,' he said. 'I don't get what I'm supposed to be doing.'

I walked over to help him.

'I just don't know how to start it…' Sean was saying, when the door swung open and smacked loudly against the wall. A large girl stood in the opening, her hands on her hips and her face red. She raised one hand and pointed a stiff finger at me.

'Did you just call my sister a selfish little bitch?' she shouted.

'I beg your pardon?'

'My sister's just come to me and dragged me out of my class. She was in tears. She said some supply teacher just called her a selfish little bitch. Well?'

She had not moved forward, but remained standing in the same spot from which she had made the original accusation. Behind her, Tia appeared. She was smiling. Her sister began to rant again. 'My dad's a lawyer. He's gonna sue you. How dare you talk to my little sister in that way?'

Fighting anger with further anger is the wrong course of action when working with teenagers, often escalating confrontation rather than alleviating it. It has never been a strategy of mine, and nor is it for most experienced teachers – generally because it is not effective. But perhaps I had not slept well that night, for, within 10 minutes of being at Rowe, I was sick of it already.

'Get out of my classroom now!' I bellowed at the girl, noticing Sean wince at the sudden volume above him. 'Get out right now! How dare you come in here and accuse me of using such insulting language?'

I was marching towards her, covering the room in long and rapid strides. She backed out of the doorway as she saw me coming, stepping on Tia's foot and stumbling back on to her. I swept through the doorway and felt some satisfaction at the crash the door made as its hinges snapped it shut behind me.

'Do you understand how serious what you've just said is?' My cry was that of a thousand teachers who had been wrongly accused of a misdemeanour, whose professionalism had been stripped from them at the hands of a whimsical teenager, who had lost careers and integrities through casually-invoked and wholly-invented stories of children with a grudge. 'Have you ever heard of witnesses? Do you want to get excluded?'

My barrage of rhetorical questions was interrupted by the English teacher in the room next to mine who poked his head out of the door. He took in this strange tripartite gathered in the corridor, and stepped out to join us. 'Daisy,' he said, approaching the elder sister. 'Why aren't you in my lesson? The register says you're absent today.'

'I'm sorry, sir,' Daisy said, her sudden meekness startling me somewhat. 'I only just got in.'

'So what's going on?' the teacher asked.

Daisy turned to look at Tia, reproach in her eyes. 'I don't really know. What is going on, Tia? Did this man say what you said he said?'

Tia stared at the floor and said nothing. The teacher turned to Daisy.

'I think it's time you went into the lesson, don't you, Daisy?' Daisy began to walk towards the classroom. 'Haven't you got anything to say to sir first?'

'Sorry,' Daisy mumbled, and then disappeared from view.

'Tia,' the teacher continued, 'go and stand outside my office now. I'll see you in a minute.'

Tia humbly walked away and around the corner. The teacher turned to me.

'What's your name, mate?'

'Charlie.' We shook hands.

'Don't worry about Tia. I know all about her. I'm the Head of her year. Let me guess – she played up and then refused to admit she had done anything.'

'Something like that,' I said.

'Yeah, she does that. Daisy's just as bad. I don't know why they're like it. Compared to a lot of others here, those two have got it easy. Good home life, really supportive parents. But they've just got this whole thing in their heads – you can't do this, you can't do that. I don't know where it comes from.'

'Maybe I shouldn't have blown up like that at them.'

'I don't know, mate, it seemed to work. Impressive set of lungs on you!'

We both laughed, and I thanked him for taking over and sorting it all out.

'No worries, mate,' he said. 'I'm Marcus. Mr Bauer. If there's any other problems with any kids today, let me know.'

'Thanks, Marcus,' I said. 'I really appreciate it.' He raised both thumbs, grinned, and then turned to walk back to his classroom.

My next lesson was a Year 11 maths cover, a good five minute walk away to the far end of the school. The lesson progressed well, albeit for the pugnacious young man who burst into the room twice, each time screaming, 'Who wants some reggae-reggae sauce?' and then darting out again. On his third time, I was ready for him, stopping him at the door and casually explaining that I was good friends with Mr Bauer. I never saw him again.

Break time followed, and I went to the staff room for a cup of tea. Marcus arrived after ten minutes and brought his coffee over to sit next to me.

'Thanks again for your help this morning,' I said.

'Don't mention it. It was nothing.'

We chatted amiably for a few minutes until he drained his coffee and stood up. 'Sorry, Charlie, I've got to go,' he said. 'There's a lad waiting in my office. He's only just got in. Got kicked off the bus and had to walk two miles.'

'Why was he kicked off?'

'Showing off to his mates. He picked up another lad by his head.'

Marcus vanished and I made my way to the geography cover I had for Period 3. Laura Hobbs proved riotous throughout the first half of the lesson, sitting with her friend Meena and shouting acidic abuse across the classroom at anyone, including me, who dared look their way. After she told me my breath stank and I should brush my teeth, I was ready to send her out when a small and apprehensive girl entered the classroom.

'Hello,' I said, leaving Laura Hobbs and Meena and walking over to her. 'Why are you late?'

'Dentist appointment,' she said quietly. Between the slight movements of her lips I could make out the gleam of a thick brace.

'What's your name?' I asked. 'I'll need to mark you down on the register.'

'Laura Hobbs,' she whispered, and then slunk over to an empty seat on her own. A loud guffaw enveloped the classroom.

'Ah-ha-ha!' Meena was shouting. '*Busted*! See ya later, Anita!'

Anita/Laura Hobbs stood up and calmly walked towards the door, kicked it open with her foot, and left.

The bell eventually went for lunch, and I followed the coursing students out the door. I sat for a while in the staff room hoping Marcus would turn up, but he never did, so after 20 minutes I left and made my way to where my next lesson was to be. Deep inside the plastic wallet of lesson plans I had collected for the day was a key.

The receptionist for the school had explained that this would open my room for Period 4, which was inside a freestanding hut at the top of the sports field. The hut was one of three dotted randomly about the school which comprised the history department, and was kept locked outside of lesson-times because a teacher's laptop had been stolen one breaktime a few months ago.

To get to the hut from the staff room, I had to walk along the thin concrete lane which separated the fenced-off tennis courts from the science block. Packs of students crowded the pathway, immoveable and deaf to the entreaties of the supply teacher endeavouring to pass through them all. So I was somewhat surprised when one circle of girls heeded my pleas and cleared the way for me before I even had to repeat them. It was, of course, nothing to do with me. The girls had scattered because they were innately tuned into what I was not: the plummeting arc of a booted football. It bounced heavily off my head, sending me reeling. A chorus of breaking male voices cheered from the tennis courts, and I heard above it all the exclamation: 'Ten points!'

The pack of girls had regrouped further down the pathway, and the chicken-wire fence which separated me from the football team was being penetrated by fingers and patches of cheeks.

'Nice header, sir!'

'Sweet!'

'Oi, throw it back?'

The ball had come to a rest at my feet. I thought for the second time that day how sick I was of all this, and picked up the ball. 'You can have it back at the end of the day,' I called back to them, and walked off towards the hut, the football in my hands, the sound of booing so loud behind me that I felt I had just died on stage.

I entered the hut and locked myself in. Within seconds, the door began to shake and rattle in its lock as it was pulled heftily from outside. The shouts began with a frightening immediacy.

'Give us back the ball!'

'That's my ball!'

'Fucking cunt!'

And then it stopped. The noise decreased back to the tolerable clamour of the generic playground, and seeped in through the small, metal-reinforced windows. I pulled my book from my bag and sat at the desk to read. Suddenly, a loud and resounding thump interrupted me. It was followed by another just as loud, and then another after it. The thumps increased, and the intervals between them decreased, until I found myself in a cage of loud and violent noise. I walked to the small window and looked out. The figure of one of the boys from the tennis courts charged past with a large branch, smacking the side of the hut as he did so. Another followed suit, and then another, and then another. The next saw me at the window and stopped.

'Give me my fucking ball!' he screamed, punctuating the end of his cry with a muscular swing at the window. 'It's *my* fucking ball!'

I backed from the window. The volume and persistency of the thumping increased. I tiptoed to the door, feeling like I was in some bizarre horror film, and crouched down so that I could see them but they could not see me. I counted 11 boys, all revolving around the hut in a weirdly tribal *Lord of the Flies* dance, smacking the walls of the hut with long and knobbly sticks, screaming for the return of their football. I backstepped to my desk, noticing with some concern that my hands were shaking. With each pound on the walls of my prison, my heartbeat rose and my adrenaline surged. I looked towards the fire exit at the back of the room and briefly considered flight from it. Its shakes with each beat kept me seated.

And then everything stopped. First the jeering of the crowds outside which had now, for me, taken on the proportions of a Roman matinee at the Coliseum, and then the incessant tribal beat which bore its way from the walls of the hut to the white heat of my panic.

I walked back to the door to see Marcus standing outside, 11 boys surrounding him, looking as humble as kittens. An amnesty of sticks lay on the ground beside them, and, as I unlocked and opened the door, I noticed that most of them were adjusting their ties back into the traditional position. I came out on to the concrete and Marcus turned to look at me.

'Haven't you got something to say to him, boys?'

'We're sorry, sir,' one said. 'Now can we have our ball back, please?'

I looked at the 11 of them, at all their hopeful faces. They had atoned, were looking sufficiently apologetic. I looked over at Marcus, who nodded at me.

'No,' I said, walking back into the hut and locking the door behind me.

* * * * *

I drove straight back to my lay-by after school and pulled out the bed, falling on to it and drifting off into exhausted sleep without even removing my suit. I woke a few hours later, shivering. It was cold for July – perhaps because I was so far north. I stepped outside to urinate, looking up at the heavy, inert clouds, and feeling the Baltic winds as they whipped my tie over my shoulder and smacked against the side of the van. It did not get dark until half past ten, and I knew from the past week that it would start getting light again at three. My sleep had been fitful that week, and I was so tired that, after undressing and eating a bowl of soup in bed, I fell back into unconsciousness with ease.

The next morning, with the weekend before me, I decided to explore. I had never been to this part of the north-east before, it had only ever served as a dull gate to pass through on the way to Newcastle or Edinburgh, and so I ventured out into the North Yorkshire Moors, a wide and empty land of bleak heaths, mossy sinks and abandoned abbeys. I pushed out to the coast, to Whitby, where the bustling crowds filled the pavements and forced me to walk on the roads; and then on to the prettier, quieter Robin Hood's Bay, an arresting stretch of sand and cliff wedged between two headlands, where I spent the night, perched at the top of a campsite which overlooked the entire vista. I took long walks along the beach, took short whiskies in the pubs, and tried my hardest to prompt anyone into conversation. The best response I garnered was from the owner of my campsite who, on discovering I was from Cornwall, asked if I would like to help him shear his sheep. I felt the stereotype, saw that it was in fact double-edged, and returned to the van to drink some cold beers bought from the village's Post Office.

      I returned to Middlesbrough on the Monday to find no work available. Tuesday was the same, as was Wednesday. I visited the town. After the wild heaths of the moors to the south or the marshy, green flatlands of Sedgefield to the west, the first sight of Middlesbrough on the horizon is repulsive. Packed with grotesque towers and factories and warehouses and cranes and various other aberrations, its grim ugliness surpassed everywhere I had visited that year. I drove towards the Transporter Bridge, a local landmark, and soon became lost in a never-ending network of industrial estates, road closures and half-built workshops: one huge and looping builder's yard. When by chance I stumbled upon the famous bridge, it was closed.

I drove into town. Oddly, the centre of Middlesbrough itself is clean, handsome and much smaller than you might imagine. There is a fine town hall built in the late nineteenth century, backed by an airy square which is flattened with minimalism. On this square sits *Mima*: a glassy collection of galleries and 'event spaces'. It is a beautifully-kept building, an homage itself to modern art, but I got the feeling that it went largely unused. I arrived at 11 o'clock in the morning and had to ask for the art galleries to be unlocked. As I walked from work to work, members of staff lurked within my peripheral vision, desperate perhaps for a question or comment to respond to, to break this over-hanging silence.

On the Wednesday evening, I returned to my lay-by and called Peter.

'There's nothing, Mr Carroll,' he told me. 'And I doubt there will be until September. Most schools are closing for the summer holidays this time next week. Work at this time of year is... er...'

'Not to be sneezed at?' I offered.

'*Exactly*, Mr Carroll, exactly.'

I ate some supper and crawled into bed, drifting off to sleep before it grew dark.

At midnight, I was awoken with a start, a deep and repetitive bass-line boomeranging itself around the inside of my skull. Suddenly alert, I realised a car had stopped directly beside the van. Over the loud house-music screaming from the car's speakers, I heard a door open, followed by the jolting sound of someone banging on my windscreen. I froze.

'Oi, you fucking pikey!' a young and male voice shouted.

I remained still.

'Come out here! I'm gonna fucking smash you!'

I looked towards the front. There was a clear path to the driver's seat. As quietly as I could, I picked up my keys from where they rested next to the sink and sat up in bed. The banging started again. Gently peeling the duvet off me, I sat up, and, trying to make as little noise as possible, crept to the end of the bed. I eased on to my feet and took the few steps to the front, trying to identify the correct key with my fingers so that I could start the engine straight up, pull open the front curtains, and drive off in a matter of seconds.

And then, just as I was slipping into the driver's seat, I heard a door shut and the car rev off and out of the lay-by. High above the engine and the still-playing house-music, a quickly fading voice was clear: '*Pikey!*'

I sat in the driver's seat for the next hour: wide awake, too paranoid to even open the curtains and see if I really was alone again. Finally, I wrestled myself out of my paralysis and drove off to find a different lay-by on another road. I eventually found one, and settled back into bed, but sleep was an impossibility, the sound of each passing car a wrench on my frazzled nerves.

I knew the next morning that it was time to leave. To finish. I drove the van south, stopping for a night in the Peak District at a favourite lay-by. Lining the northern edge of this lay-by is a long, low wall, beyond which a smooth and deep valley plummets for over a hundred feet. The steep hills behind the valley dip down through levels of field and crevassed wall and winding path, culminating at the base in a model-like row of tiny houses with their own communal lagoon, nestling just beneath the single rail-track which cuts through it all. The summer had transformed the valley into a solid gash of bright cliff-faces and deep green slopes, the sky was cloudless and the sun fierce. I took a novel, a sarong and my trusty bottle of single malt down on to one of the smooth precipices, and lay happily amongst the fearless sheep. At the base of the valley, a young family were enjoying a noisy picnic on the bank of the calm river, their laughs and trills ricocheting up the rises of the hills to resound as an unintelligible burble in my ears. I suddenly felt very lonely. And very tired. I wanted to go home.

CONCLUSION

In May 2010, the 13-year Labour government came to an end. Back in 1997, I was too young to vote, but if I could I would have voted with the majority. Like so many others, I still remember one of Tony Blair's earliest and most famous speeches when campaigning in 1996: 'Ask me my three main priorities for government, and I tell you: education, education, education'.

That sound-bite alone would have won me over.

Throughout Labour's reign, six ministers held the role of Secretary of State for Education (though the title, conforming to New Labour's penchant for rebranding, took three different incarnations: Secretary of State for Education and Employment; Secretary of State for Education and Skills; and Secretary of State for Children, Schools and Families).

The most memorable of these ministers were David Blunkett (the first), Charles Clarke, and Ed Balls (the last), and, between them, they changed England's educational system significantly.

Some of those changes were very positive. Over a thousand new schools were built, and many others renovated. Per pupil funding rose by 48% (working out, on average, at an extra £1,450 per year per child since 1996). Teachers themselves also saw a rise in their pay by 18%; and 172,000 extra Learning Support Assistants were employed across the country. All schools were encouraged to upgrade and expand their Information Technology facilities with increased funding.

But many teachers, and even more students, suffered from the new system.

Exclusion levels were forcibly reduced, meaning a large number of children who could not cope with mainstream education were forced to remain within it. Class sizes were not reduced – in fact, seemed to grow – and perhaps the reason the official figures stated classes were smaller than ever was because more Learning Support Assistants had been employed, rather than more qualified teachers.

New schools were built, but many smaller, local schools were closed (particularly at the primary level – since 1984, over two and a half thousand primary schools have closed across England) or amalgamated into these new schools.

National Testing soared to make England's children the most tested in the world, meaning that for most of their educated lives they were taught to the test.

Teachers slowly lost more and more of their rights and powers to teach and protect children effectively, and instead were handed a bureaucratic minefield of paperwork, targets and a rigorously implemented National Curriculum.

The year I travelled England and its toughest schools, the year of this book, came at the tail-end of Labour's time in power. What I saw, and what you have read, is the consequence of Blair's drive for education, education, education. And, if you do not believe me, I urge you to visit your local secondary school yourself, and draw your own conclusions. I doubt they will differ much from mine.

Though I did not vote for David Cameron, I will be very interested to see the changes he and his new Secretary of State for Education, Michael Gove, make to England's schooling system. Already, there appear to be many, though the Tory-Lib-Dem coalition government are not flooding the system with money as Labour did (perhaps this is because there is none left).

Indeed, a pay-freeze has already been enforced across the entire public sector, and it is not difficult to imagine that all those monetary perks introduced over the last decade to encourage postgraduates into teaching – including a grant-maintained training year, a propitious starting wage followed by guaranteed pay-rises for the first five years, a Golden Hello and even a repayment scheme of Student Loans for those who teach shortage subjects – will be gone in the next few years.

For me, this is not such a problem. Money is not the answer. It never was. No teacher does the job for its financial benefits. Coaxing postgraduates on to PGCE courses with the lure of a get-rich-quick scheme is approaching the problem from entirely the wrong angle. Teachers teach for much more abstract reasons – be it a love of children, an appreciation of academia, or a deep and passionate interest in their subject. And it is these reasons which the new government must nurture if they truly want to keep teachers in the profession.

So what is my answer? For it is the easiest thing to poke holes in a system, but far harder to provide any solutions. I have criticised the system, but what use is that when devoid of application? Cynicism is just snide talk, the belligerent outburst of the pub-philosopher. To propose an alternative system which encourages teachers to stay rather than just highlighting the myriad reasons why they are fleeing would be much more constructive.

I can say only this. Michael Gove, and whomever will inevitably follow him, must start from the ground-level, from the front line, where education really happens (or, as is sadly the case, does not). The mere acknowledgement of all the issues I have highlighted throughout this book would be a start, and then the systematic alleviation of each would affect a noticeable difference in teacher-turnover statistics and, as a result, in the education of Britain's children.

Give teachers more powers to stop their students fighting, and more support when they themselves are assaulted. Ensure that teachers can say what needs to be said about a student without fear of reprisals from parents, and encourage parents to take a more active role in the life of their children's school. Lift the embargo on exclusion and allow schools a greater independence on matters within their own environments. Reduce class sizes by stopping school closures and amalgamations and employing more teachers, and, if this is not possible, then continue to encourage more support staff into the profession with better pay. Allow schools to take a zero tolerance approach to bad behaviour so that teachers are better able to deal with it. Effect changes in the laws to protect us more against litigation. Lessen the gap between state and independent schools by raising the conditions of the former to meet the latter. Reduce the all-encompassing importance of the league tables and continue to encourage teacher-based assessment up to GCSE level. Include courses and sessions as part of directed INSET training times which will encourage teachers to develop better stress-management techniques. Give teachers more room to focus on teaching by reducing the unnecessary bureaucracy so prevalent in schools.

Some of these ideas are far more difficult to achieve than my simplistic wording gives them credit for (such as changing the liability laws, for instance), and some, I know, will never happen (such as raising the standards of state schools to meet those of the independent sector). But most are plausible, achievable, intuitive even. If at least some changes are not made on the front line, and made very soon, the professional exodus currently taking place will continue, and its consequences will be disastrous. Already, there is a vast rift between younger and older teachers in England and, as the young continue to leave and the old continue to retire, few will be left. Almost 50% of all England's Newly Qualified Teachers are leaving the profession within their first five years. I saw why, out there, on the edge of things.

Epilogue

I left Middlesbrough two months ago, taking a slow course down through the country to reach Cornwall. I visited my mother. A speeding fine had just been delivered for me – on the way down, through a Somerset village, I was snapped doing 32mph in a 30mph zone. I didn't know the van was capable of speeding.

For the last six weeks, I've been working behind the bar in a small village pub not far from the coast. The hours are short, the responsibility is zero, and I'm having the time of my life. I park the van in a local farmer's unused field, quietly watch the families of rabbits which dance about at dusk, and then loudly chase the buzzard that wakes me up at dawn. I cycle everywhere. My personal hygiene is slipping.

I think about the journey a lot. I walk outside to urinate at midnight in just a pair of shorts, and can't believe it was ever so cold that I had to sleep fully dressed under a mountain of duvets. I come home from work happy and energised, not on the verge of sickness. A customer threatened me the other day, but I stood up to him and he left. I remembered Ralph in West Yorkshire.

Most of the time, I stay very still, marvel in the novelty of it after a year of perpetual movement. Two days ago, I drove up to a cliff-top, St Agnes Beacon, and sat for five hours on a slim patch of grass hidden from the National Trust walkers with an uninterrupted view of the horizon. I tried to write, but instead found myself lost in swampy reflection. I remembered squealing Matthew, obstinate Rebecca Pinder, foul-mouthed Caroline and broken Louise. I remembered rain-lashed playgrounds, thrown equipment, corridor stand-offs, and a thick, blunt fist. But there was light with the dark, too – how about

Gilbert School in Birmingham? How about Linda from Coggan and Stuart from Anstee? How about the warmth of Pascoe, and the knock-out face-flushing cheer of thirty-two teenagers glad to see their old teacher again? The sun began to set over the calm sea.

Mostly, though, when I think about my year (I've started calling it 'my year'), it's not the work I think about, it's the travelling. I think about England, about that portion of a tiny island in the North Atlantic which kept me so enthralled and invigorated and amazed and staggered for so long. Sometimes I tell people about my year and they laugh. I laugh with them. It was a silly journey, a weird little self-indulgent foray, a 13,000 mile drive which, done at once, could have taken me from Land's End to John O'Groats and back again seven times. But teaching, working, coping aside, it was fun. So much fun. On the road, lost in the highs of the Moors, the lows of the Peaks, the chaos of London, even the disappointment of Sheffield, I loved every minute. Because I got to see something. Something few people do. I got to see my own country from a traveller's perspective. And, in doing so, I fell in love with England more than I have ever fallen in love with any of the countries I have ever travelled.

And more and more, when I remember my year, I remember England. I remember 'GOURANGA' stencilled in large letters on motorway flyovers; the prevalence of parks, commons, downs, heaths and greens; car boot sales and flea markets; lorries with 'Clean Me' finger-painted in the dirt on their rears; Avon ladies and lollipop men; a national penchant for tame and mainstream sitcoms; dogs, ears flapping, grinning moronically at the wind from the open windows of passing cars; WiFi access in chain pubs; snowless winters and warm, exciting springtimes; coastal waters as blue as the Pacific or as brown as the Mekong; the great finds on the bookshelves of high street charity shops; the warm fug of a village pub and the chaos of a city bar; Cadbury's chocolate by the tills; hedgerows and drystone walls;

pedestrians with matching scarves and gloves; mildewed public toilets; children in martial arts attire karate-kicking through fallen autumn leaves; persistent, gregarious colds and flus; having your own mug; apple trees and lane-side foxgloves; home delivery vans; fenced-off allotment patches in the middle of soaring cityscapes; curryhouses and kebab takeaways; middle-lane drivers; front page reports about reality television; pirate radio stations and illicit late-night beats; football in the afternoon, on TV screens and in back gardens; the suspended student village societies in their crumbling homes; red for stop, green for go, amber for uncertain stallings; BBC 1 and Channel 4; mobile phones with indie music ringtones; smokers huddled in pub doorways; 'Baby on Board' stickers; night-prowling cats; urban foxes; the rabbit in the headlights; posters for touring bands and stand-up comedians; sheer tower blocks and sheer valleys; cat's eyes; trams; MP3 players and street-evangelists; landfills; the chavs and the emos, the rockers and the ravers, the mods and the punks; gaudy garden decorations at Christmas; a pint of ale and a vodka and coke; trees which bend over a road; barges lazily ambling along canals; retail parks and timber-framed houses; a bric-a-brac sale in the local church; twenty languages on one street; bus-side adverts for Wiis and Stairlifts; the smell of freshly-cut grass in May; Bank Holidays and Folk Festivals; fragmented islands you could swim to; sirens; shops selling dream-catchers and sarongs; city buskers with fingerless gloves and crimson cheeks; spiders in the bathtub and gritty wallpaper; spice racks; walls of glass; cows at the side of the motorway and village bypasses; cloud cover so thick it's claustrophobic; country lanes; a nationwide love of music, art and the written word; a means to knowledge and growth on every street... to be found if you look for it.

Charlie Carroll, Reen Cross, Cornwall, October 2010

And a *huge* thanks to ...

all and everyone who supported me this year, who gave me a spare room or even just a couch to sleep on, who fed me much-needed, home-cooked meals to allow a grateful respite from van food, or who just joined me for a pint of ale in some English pub, providing the conversation and company that I otherwise would have lacked. Without you all, this book still probably would have been written, but it would have been a shit journey. Cheers.

To Olly Wyatt, for a Festival of cheap cans of Carlsberg on a kerbside; to Alistair Greaves for the last-minute Russell Howard gig; to Tim and Lara Reid – '*that song should be the Scottish National Anthem*'; to Ted Eglinton and Louise Himan, not forgetting little Honey and General Harvey the Dread-Stealing Cat; to Sarah Boak for the introduction to mussels; to Adie Smith ('*Cheese-hat! Cheese-hat!*') for chest-hair-burning frolics and face-planting frivolities; to Beth Hall for a whole house to play in just when it was getting cold; to Lisa Gray for a much-needed teacherly rant; to Debi Ferguson for some filthy dub reggae; to Shirley, John, Lisa, Jonno, Tammy, Jayden and Kiah, but most of all to Sylvia and Grandma, for not just giving me a spare room, but for giving me a home; to Ben Faulks for failing to appear at the gig, but for making up for it later with an immaculate beard-presentation; to Margaret, Andrew and Mel for peri peri chicken; to Lee, Carole, Leigh and Steph – I haven't had a weekend like that since I was 19; to Danny for the rugby; to Ruth Arnold for valuable emails – Writer/Campervan-Owners Unite!; to Mary and Jodi for the endless support, encouragement, and Christmas; to Dr Abi Sheldon for shelter during the rainiest month of the year; to the Holy Trinity of Dave Hartley, John Arnold and Marcus Fairhurst – check out www.onepercentscheme.org if you want to see just how cool these guys really are; to Anna Ray and Amy Robertson, ridiculously tanned, who stole my thunder and travelled Sri Lanka while I was just travelling flood-swept England... to Ex-Step Tom Frankland (you'll always be Thomas to me) and Supervisor of Naboo, Laura Frankland... to Jimmy D and Alistair of the Big Balls – fellow social smokers even when it stopped being sociable... to Rachel Creed for the Shoreditch party and giving me the chance to dress up like Jack Kerouac... to all of the CIL (Corns in London) Massive – Lewis Davies, Gav Jones, Gwen Scolding, Simon Johns, Carole McWilliams and Bronia Housman – for Betty Stoggs in alien territory... to Joe Clements, Caroline Silman and Jacob (and whoever the next will be – my vote lies with Rafael)... to Charlie Von Moll and Jasper Wenban-Smith for double barrels and double vodkas... to Dr Ruth Martin for living with the Queen... to Luke for managing to cycle halfway around the world and still remain entirely nonchalant about it... to Henry for making his mark... to Leon Moran for leaving the flood plains just as I was entering them... to Will Randall, Rory Stewart, Francis Gilbert and Frank Chalk, wise and kind writers all... to Debbie and Alistair for eggs a few minutes old... to Allie Hawkins for conversations on teachers past... to Aaron Letheren – Minimum Wage slap the Queen!... to Ian Carroll for taking to the road himself, and seeing that it is good... to all of the staff at Pascoe school – I wish I could name you one by one, but it doesn't matter, you know who you are, and you know you all collectively make it by far the best school in the country... to Barrie, Neyni and Keryn... to all the staff and locals at the White House Inn... to Ben Job and all the prophets of doom for late-night jam sessions... to Richard King for towing the van out of a rain-soaked field... to Adrian for the loan of a bicycle to tackle Perran hills... to Volkswerke for MOTs, starter motors and a multitude of second-hand gearboxes... to Uncle Ern for pretty much the same, though far cheaper... to Katie and Ian and the kids

– we appreciated your presence even if it did cost you seven hundred quid… to my agent Steph Ebdon and my publisher Dan Collins for taking the risk… to Radiohead, Manu Chao, Joe Driscoll, Gideon Conn, Esteban and all at the Whistle Binkies and Tywarnhayle Open Mike Nights for punctuating my journey with bursts of brilliant live music… to Josh for graciously putting up with my haphazard visits and humouring me into believing that the music I listen to could still be considered cool… and, finally, to Michelle, for the kind of patience I've never known, the kind of welcome I'll never get tired of, and the kind of love I'll never deserve, no matter how hard I try.

Also from Monday Books

Not With A Bang But A Whimper / Theodore Dalrymple
(hbk, £14.99)

In a series of penetrating and beautifully-written essays, Theodore Dalrymple explains his belief that a liberal intelligentsia is destroying Britain. Dalrymple writes for *The Spectator*, *The Times*, *The Daily Telegraph*, *New Statesman*, *The Times Literary Supplement* and the *British Medical Journal*.

'Theodore Dalrymple's clarity of thought, precision of expression and constant, terrible disappointment give his dispatches from the frontline a tone and a quality entirely their own... their rarity makes you sit up and take notice'
- *Marcus Berkmann, The Spectator*

'Dalrymple is a modern master'
- *The Guardian*

'Dalrymple is the George Orwell of our times... he is a writer of genius'
- *Dennis Dutton*

From all good bookshops, online from
www.mondaybooks.com or via 01455 221752.

***Wasting Police Time* / PC David Copperfield** (ppbk, £7.99)

The fascinating, hilarious and best-selling inside story of the madness of modern policing. A serving officer - writing deep under cover - reveals everything the government wants hushed up about life on the beat.

Perverting The Course Of Justice / Inspector Gadget
(ppbk, £7.99)

A senior serving policeman picks up where PC Copperfield left off and reveals how far the insanity extends – children arrested for stealing sweets from each other while serious criminals go about their business unmolested.

'Exposes the reality of life at the sharp end'
– *The Daily Telegraph*

'No wonder they call us Plods... A frustrated inspector speaks out on the madness of modern policing'
– *The Daily Mail*

'Staggering... exposes the bloated bureaucracy that is crushing Britain' – *The Daily Express*

'You must buy this book... it is a fascinating insight'
– *Kelvin MacKenzie, The Sun*

In April 2010, Inspector Gadget was named one of the country's 'best 40 bloggers' by *The Times*.

**From all good bookshops, online from
www.mondaybooks.com or via 01455 221752.**

A Paramedic's Diary / Stuart Gray

(ppbk, £7.99)

STUART GRAY is a paramedic dealing with the worst life can throw at him. *A Paramedic's Diary* is his gripping, blow-by-blow account of a year on the streets – 12 rollercoaster months of enormous highs and tragic lows. One day he'll save a young mother's life as she gives birth, the next he might watch a young girl die on the tarmac in front of him after a hit-and-run. A gripping, entertaining and often amusing read by a talented new writer.

As heard on BBC Radio 4's Saturday Live and BBC Radio 5 Live's Donal McIntyre Show and Simon Mayo

In April 2010, Stuart Gray was named one of the country's 'best 40 bloggers' by *The Times*

From all good bookshops, online from www.mondaybooks.com or via 01455 221752.

So That's Why They Call It Great Britain / Steve Pope
(ppbk, £7.99)

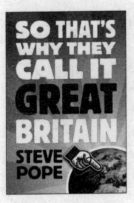

From the steam engine to the jet engine to the engine of the world wide web, to vaccination and penicillin, to Viagra, chocolate bars, the flushing loo, the G&T, ibruprofen and the telephone... this is the truly astonishing story of one tiny country and its gifts to the world.